A BROAD
ABROAD IN IRAN

An Expat's Misadventures in the Land of Male Dominance

A Blind Person Who Sees Is Better Than A
Seeing Person Who Is Blind

IRANIAN PROVERB

WHAT REVIEWERS HAD TO SAY:

"It's the best manuscript that has come across my desk in months."

**Mike Foley, Writer's Review, Editor
and Creative Writing Instructor,
CSU Riverside Campus www.WritersReview.com**

What a terrific book! This personal account of one family's experiences during the last days of the Shah's reign is a fascinating tale - a glimpse into not just the family's education about a very different culture, but also of an important time in recent history from the family's front-row seat. With just the right amount of humor amid the building tensions of those last days, the tale that unfolds is riveting, right down to the drama-filled conclusion. —

**Margie McArthur,
author of Wisdom of the Elements, Faery Healing –
The Lore and the Legacy. www.faeryhealing.com**

"While reading Dodie Cross' memoir, A Broad Abroad in Iran, I felt the author's anxiety in trying to leave the country. She, along with the other passengers, sat in an overcrowded jetliner with no air conditioning, her terror building with each moment's delay to become airborne, terrified the Islamic police would board and demand they return for interrogation. One powerful sentence beautifully expressed

the mood aboard the plane: 'We are all breathing each other's fear.' With an opening page that dramatic, the rest of the story is a page-turner."
Brenda Hill, Editor and Author of: With Full Mallice, Ten Times Guilty, and Beyond the Quilt. www.brendahill.com

"A year before the fall of the Shah of Iran and full-blown anarchy, a California housewife, her husband, and three children relocate to that country for a new job. A Broad Abroad in Iran is the latest in the "A Broad Abroad" series, and with it, Dodie Cross delivers a fast, funny, and often scary read. We don't usually experience geopolitics from the standpoint of a loving family trying to make the best of a year in the midst of looming turmoil. Through it all I kept wondering how Dodie kept it together - and then I'd burst out laughing (cleaning vegetables in the washing machine?) Just a fascinating story! This is one book you'll want to recommend to family and friends."

Lynne Spreen, author of Dakota Blues
www.anyshinything.com

"I've never been to Iran, and I'm not sure I want to go there. However, the last time a book kept me holding my sides because they hurt so much from laughter, was Dodie Cross' A Broad Abroad in Thailand. This lady is just naturally funny, no matter how dire her circumstances, and at times they were very dire. If you have never visited Iran and would like a treat (and a treatment) this is the every-season book for every man, woman and others of the species. As an expat in this dusty, wind-blown land, Dodie finds sand in her hair, between her teeth, and other various crevices—and hilarity in most things she undertakes. Buy it!!!!!!!!"

Raymond Strait,
Author, Biographer and Book Reviewer

A BROAD
ABROAD IN IRAN

An Expat's Misadventures in the Land of Male Dominance

DODIE CROSS

Published by: CrossRoads Publications, 2012

Printed in the United States of America

Cover Design by: Joseph W. Shine

Illustrations by Ernie Towler

Library of Congress Cataloging:

To order additional copies of this book go to:

www.Amazon.com or www.abroad-abroad.com

ISBN: 0985040904

ISBN 13: 9780985040901

Library of Congress Control Number: 2012914830

CrossRoads Publishing, Palm Desert, CA

This book is dedicated to my three children;

none of whom I'm sure will have the time to read it.

And also to my nine grandchildren,

who may someday have the time..

IT FELT LOVE

HOW DID THE ROSE

EVER OPEN ITS HEART

AND GIVE TO THIS WORLD

ALL ITS BEAUTY?

IT FELT THE ENCOURAGEMENT OF LIGHT

AGAINST ITS BEING,

OTHERWISE WE ALL REMAIN

TOO FRIGHTENED.

FROM "THE GIFT"

...HAFEZ

ACKNOWLEDGEMENTS

I would like to thank all those who helped me along the tortuous trip to complete this book. First off I'd like to thank my long-time friend, Linda Brown, (AKA Beettee),who made copies of the one letter I sent her every month, then mailed them off to friends and family for me. If not for her, I doubt I could have written a letter to everyone.

Next on my list of thanks would be to my thoughtful friends who saved my letters, then gave them back to me, which gave me the fodder for this book—all eighteen months of it—some thirty years later. Next I'd like to thank the host of people who edited, and edited...and edited: My sister, Margie McArthur, a fine writer and ferocious editor, for lending her keen eyes to my first draft, which was pathetic. Also thanks to Kathryn Jordan and Dolores Carruthers, both fine authors and editors for going over my manuscript with a fine-toothed comb, giving me red marks where needed, and "atta-girl" where deserved.

My last editor, about the tenth draft I think, was Mike Foley, Instructor of Creative Writing at UC Riverside, and owner of http://www.writers-review.com. Mike was instrumental in convincing me to carry on with my vision of this book when I wanted to give up. Thank you again, Mike.

I'd also like to thank my friends who've rudely nudged me forward to complete this by continually asking: "Aren't you done with that book yet?"

And, last but not least, I'd like to thank Joe Shine, my publisher and long-time friend (the 5th grade, would you believe?). How he put up with all my changes is a miracle, or PFM as he calls it. Thanks for the beautiful front and back cover; I should sell a million!

CONTENTS

Note To Reader. . . . .*xvii*

Prologue . . . . *xix*

1   Farewell to Life as I new it. *1*

2   Six months on Auto Pilot *9*

3   Packing, Farsi & History Lessons. *21*

4   The Last Week. *35*

5   Up, Up, and Away *43*

6   Culture Shock *49*

7   New Home & New Friends *63*

8   The Incredible Esfahan Bazaar *73*

9   Grocery Shopping & Food Prep. *81*

10   Acclimating & School Days. *95*

11   Schmoozing Iranian Style. *103*

12   Dorothy Hamill & the Accomplice *109*

13   Trips, Gypsies & Opium *129*

14   Cheating Death *147*

15   A Stoning *157*

16   Shah and I go to USA *163*

17   Back Home to Plea Bargain. *179*

18   Home in the Country. *187*

19   Bounced Checks & Murder. 197

20   Now-Ruz & Field Trips. 209

21   Ole' to Toro 217

22   Martial Law Comes to Esfahan 231

23   "Go Home". 245

24   "It'll Blow Over". 251

Epilogue. 259

Life Changes 265

NOTE TO READER

In light of the turmoil that is happening around the world, I would like to say this: I respect all expression of God, and other people's beliefs, no matter how they experience their deity, their saints or their martyrs. I wonder what a great world it would be if all people did the same.

Memory is a notoriously biased and sentimental editor. I have tried to hold close to the facts, as memoirists must do, but as more than thirty years have passed since the revolution, I would not have been able to recall it all without the help of some wonderful friends. I'd faithfully kept a journal while living in Iran, and once a month I'd pull from it to write a letter home about my life in this faraway land. I'd then mail the letter to a very helpful friend who'd offered to make the necessary copies and mail the letters out to my friends and family. This saved me from writing the same thing to thirty different people, which I doubt would have happened.

Thankfully, when some of my friends heard that I wanted to write a book about my time in Iran, and that my journal was mysteriously missing from my shipment, they offered those same letters to me that they had saved. This was a huge help as it gave me dates and times, *and* events that I would not have remembered more than thirty years later.

I've taken a bit of creative license with my dialogue, but did try to stay as close to reality as possible. Some names and identities were changed for privacy reasons, and I have placed an asterisk (*) behind the name the first time it appears.

PROLOGUE

IRAN 1978 – THE ESCAPE

Our plane sits on the tarmac, engines whining. The main cabin door leading to the jet-way is closed, but the plane hasn't moved. We've been held here for over three hours. I'm afraid if we don't become airborne soon we'll be permanently grounded, grabbed by the Islamic revolutionary police and hauled into a holding room for interrogation: *Who were we? What crimes had we committed against Islam? Were we CIA, the evil spies of the hated American government?*

My eyes burn from fatigue and fear. A trickle of perspiration slides down my spine, as the plane becomes a sauna. Over two hundred people crammed in with no air coming through the vents. We're all breathing each other's fear. From somewhere on the plane children whine. Adults sit quietly as though silence makes them invisible.

My three children are fast asleep in the seats next to us. My husband takes my hand, squeezes it. "We'll be airborne soon," he says. "Try to close your eyes and picture Thailand, we'll be there before you know it."

I wish I had his control. My thoughts are filled with terror. My heart's beating double-time and I feel light-headed. Can I be having a heart attack? Please, God, not now.

It was 1978. We were leaving Esfahan, Iran, a country whose population, it seemed, had deteriorated to a state of radicalism and terror.

We'd gone to Esfahan for my husband's employer—to build refineries for the Shah of Iran—and had been living there for close to a year when rumors of unrest in the country began to circulate. But as rumors are part and parcel of the expatriate community, we didn't pay them much attention. Most American expats felt safe; our country would never leave us in harm's way—*would they?* But after a while the rumors carried more weight because of where they came from—Iranians. They told of *SAVAK* raids and the killing of protestors in other towns around the country. SAVAK, the Shah's secret intelligence service, were supposedly doing the dirty work, along with the military. According to rumors they were everywhere, and responsible for atrocious acts perpetrated at the behest of the Shah.

Along with these anti-Shah rumors, we also heard from pro-Shah Iranians: the Shah was a noble man. He wanted only to bring his people out of the dark ages and give them a better life. To that end he'd sent graduate students out to the remote villages to teach the illiterates how to read and write—in their own language. His father, Mohammed Reza Shah, had also wanted to change his country's archaic ways. In 1936, while in power, he tried to outlaw the *chador*—a black robe that women wore to cover themselves—but some of the older women stubbornly defied him, refusing to abandon their Islamic customs. The real culprits, they said, were the Tudeh, (The Iranian Communist Party) who wanted the Shah out, and who were spurred along by the mullahs—the Islamic clerics.

Yet, these stories and many more left us in a conundrum. We had no way to decipher the truth as the State-owned television and radio stations offered only government-controlled news. As the months passed we heard more ominous stories: the Shah was hated by his people, or: it wouldn't be long before he'd be pulled from his Peacock throne, or: do not discuss politics *or* the Shah in public. And, scariest of all—Americans would be targeted.

None of it made sense to the expat community. The Shah had the backing of the U.S. Government, didn't he? Surely our country wouldn't support a despot. We'd heard the Shah had an army of over half a million men and loyal generals, as well as his infamous Imperial Guards who'd vowed to protect him to the death. I'd heard it all, but wondered deep inside my otherwise optimistic heart, could the rumors become a reality?

Then the *mullahs* began to appear in great numbers. They came from rural areas, and most were said to be illiterate, educated only in the *Koran*—the Islamic Holy Book. They were raggedly poor, but revered by their flocks. Most dressed in dark robes, rags wrapped around their heads, and long scruffy beards. Before any of the serious rumors started, I might see one or two in the city in a weeks' time. But soon it seemed the streets were awash with them. They began to gather on corners, at the bazaar, glaring with penetrating eyes that made me feel paranoid and vulnerable in my westernized skin and clothes.

Then the tanks appeared, along with the armed soldiers.

I don't remember at what point things began to change. One day I was enjoying life as an expat in this extreme, exciting, polluted city, and the next thing I knew, *mullahs* were behind every bush and minaret, tanks and soldiers appeared and we were under Martial Law.

Things had definitely changed, although most of us had no idea what—or why. We'd naively thought everyone liked Americans. Now we weren't so sure. What would happen to us if the Shah were dethroned?

Would we be able to leave the country?

Alive?

Exhausted by my jumbled thoughts, I leaned back against the headrest and closed my eyes. I tried to come to terms with how our grand adventure had turned into these horrifying circumstances...

✲ ✲ ✲

1976 – California

1

Farewell To Life As I Knew It

How'd you like to live overseas for a couple years?" My husband, Earl, had called from work. "Just think about it," he said, "we'll talk when I get home."

I daydreamed after his call, visualizing great opulence. I pictured myself reclining on a white Adirondack chaise, surrounded by pristine white sands and tepid turquoise water alive with exotic multi-colored fish, while a pool-boy served me Mai Tais and tended to my every whim. Then I woke up.

Stop! I told myself. You can't go anywhere until the kids are out of school. Just relax until you hear his plans. But it was difficult. I've always had a vivid imagination, even dreaming in color, and in chapters. My dreams have a strong beginning, then arc, and then plateau out with a great ending. Too bad my life never worked out that way.

"It's a great chance for us to see the world *and* make big money," Earl said as we talked in the kitchen that night.

I couldn't think of anything to say, except "Where?"

"In the Middle East. In Iran."

My jaw dropped. "Where?"

"Listen, before you panic. The company just won a contract to build refineries for the Shah of Iran, and it's a huge promotion for me."

"But…" I had no idea who the Shah was or why he wanted my husband to build him refineries.

"We have to talk about this, Dodie. I need to give the office an answer if I'm going to take the job." He dug out our old Atlas and pointed to Iran on the map. I was sure I'd learned about this faraway country in grade school geography, but that was a few centuries back. As he rattled on about the great opportunity to live and travel overseas, I half-listened and continued on with my dinner preparations. As he left the kitchen, he added, "The job's scheduled to start sometime around the first of the year, so if I'm going to take it, we need to discuss it and make a decision pretty soon."

Over dinner other topics took precedence: the kids' school news, who hated who and why; the old-lady teacher who spit when she talked; the cat who dragged its kill onto our front steps, and Denny, my ten-year-old son, offering up every disgusting detail of the bloody corpse while shoveling food into his mouth; the constant telephone calls from giggling girls hoping to talk to my two older boys, Chris, sixteen, or Jim, seventeen, while Lauri, my soon to be twelve-year-old, looked disgusted with it all. Normal stuff.

I didn't put much thought into my husband's plans. After all it was still just an offer. Besides, it didn't seem possible that I'd leave my home, family, and friends to move to some remote country halfway around the world.

In bed that night, Earl brought the subject up again. But after I'd cleaned up the kitchen, helped with homework, packed school lunches and got my wild-child son into bed, I was too tired to think. "Let's talk about it tomorrow." I wasn't too keen with the idea of disrupting my life or the kids' lives, *especially* in the Middle East. *The Caribbean...maybe.*

The next night at dinner, Earl chose to bypass me and went right for the kids: "So, what does everyone think about going overseas in January?"

I stopped mid-bite. "You *are* talking about a long way off, right? You don't mean *this* January?" My two youngest were still in school, and Jim, our oldest, would graduate from high school in June.

"Yes," he said. "The first of the year, I told you that."

"But what about the kids' school?"

"That's a huge bonus," my husband said, "the company pays for the kids' schooling while we're there. It's a private school with American teachers. Anyway, I think they'd learn more from traveling the world than sitting in a classroom here in the States."

"Cool dad," Denny said, "You mean we'd travel the world *instead* of going to school?"

"No, son, but you'd have a better chance to see the world if I worked overseas."

I looked at my two oldest and wondered what they were thinking. Earl was their stepfather. We'd married when the boys were three and five years old, two years after their father died in a car accident. As they got older, behavior problems arose, mostly teen rebellious stuff, but Earl felt it was to demean his authority, and he reacted with a lot of yelling and harsh discipline. Jim had experimented with pot for a short time when he was a sophomore in high school, but Chris had other problems. He was ditching school on a regular basis, so I took him out of school and enrolled him in a home study program for his GED. But soon I learned that he was stealing, and also hanging with some drug dealers. We'd been to counseling with both of them, but nothing seemed to change with Chris.

Jim had a part-time job after school and tried to distance himself from Chris as much as possible, but when Chris got hell for something, so did Jim. It was not a "Norman Rockwell" scene at our home.

"Don't look at me," Chris said mid-bite, "I ain't leavin'. You guys can go, I'll stay with a buddy." He looked at Jim for validation.

"Yeah, me too," Jim said, without looking up.

The boys picked up their dinner plates and headed for the kitchen. "That's not going to happen," I hollered after them. "We'll discuss this later." No reply.

This conversation had gone in the wrong direction. Because of the tension between Jim and Earl, I really didn't blame Jim. But, Chris was my problem son, and that had to be dealt with before any trip could be planned.

"I guess I thought overseas jobs were for people who had no ties," I said, steering the conversation away from the boys. "Aren't those jobs just for wanderlust, hippie-types who travel from job to job?"

"Where'd you get that idea?"

"Well, I mean our WASPish lifestyle is far from the way those people live."

"They might be free-spirited, yes, but they're professionals. Also, the salary would be much more than they could get in the States because of the tax break and hardship pay."

That got my attention. "Hardship pay? What kind of hardship? We can't go traipsing off to a country with hardships. Does that mean it's dangerous?"

"Of course not. The company wouldn't send us some place that's unsafe."

I would remember that statement for years to come.

"It's just that the living conditions aren't as comfortable as what we're used to."

So much for sunning myself on exotic, white sandy beaches.

For the next few nights we went back and forth on the issue. I wrote up a list of pros and cons, with the pros side empty while the cons side went to two pages. I deliberately kept Jim and Chris out of the equation until I could deal with that problem.

4

I had a stack of reasons why we shouldn't go to some place on the other side of the globe. I began with my mother: she needed me. I couldn't leave her alone while I flew off to God-knows-where. She counted on me for many things. Because of her financial problems, we paid her bills, and I'd made a point to take her out to lunch at least twice a week. She looked forward to our time together. How could I leave her?

"Look, I can see your worry," Earl said, "but I'll make enough money to pay your mother's bills and her rent. You could even fly home a couple times just to see her."

He won that one.

When I presented other items on my cons list, Earl's answers were always spot-on. He'd thought of every worry I might bring up—and was ready with a solution. "What about the house? We just can't walk away from it."

"Lease it out for two years. No problem."

"What about the kids?"

"Lauri and Denny could enroll in school over there mid-term. Jim could stay with your sister, and fly over after graduation if he wanted to."

"What about Chris?"

"I think you know the answer to that. If he isn't able to follow rules at home, we know it would be more of the same in Iran. The company made it very clear when they described the job offer, and told me where it was: No drugs! If the employee or anyone in his family is caught with drugs, they would be imprisoned, and the rest of the family would be sent back to the States.

He was right. Chris could not go. But there was no way I would go and leave him unsupervised. Chris had wanted to be an emancipated minor since he was very young, but of course I would never agree to that. "I can take care of myself," was his mantra, however his choices were not good. I couldn't leave him with any of my friends, and my family was not up to it.

Earl wanted this job with a passion, and he wanted his family there with him. "I'll talk to my brother and his wife," Earl said. "Maybe Chris can live with them while we're gone. Don't worry, I'll work it out."

Earl called his brother, Cliff, that night and they talked for over an hour. The feeling was that Cliff could put Chris to work on his job, which would give Chris something to do during the day, and he could continue with his home study at night. He told Earl he'd talk it over with his wife and let us know. I sincerely hoped that Cliff would welcome my son into his home; otherwise, the job was a no-go.

"Something else I just heard from one of the guys who worked overseas for the company," Earl said at dinner the next night. "Every three months I'll get a week of R&R. We could fly to Spain, see the Flamenco dancers, and maybe even see a bull fight, or, we could fly to Switzerland or Austria and go skiing."

"Cool, Dad, do they rent skis there or do we take ours?"

"I'm sure we can rent them, Denny. I was told the Shah built a world-class ski resort in the mountains above Tehran." Now he had everyone's attention. "Jim, are you up to coming over after graduation? I might be able to use you as a local hire, and you'd make a better salary than you could here."

Jim looked surprised. The last person he wanted to spend time around was his stepfather. "Maybe," he said. "Not sure. I'll think about it."

Earl looked rebuffed, then turned to Chris. "Chris, I know you don't want to go with us, and I don't think you should. The country has rules about drugs, and if you're caught with anything like that, you'd go to prison and we'd be sent home. I'm sorry, but I can't take that chance."

Chris opened his mouth to say something, then thought better of it. Earl continued, "I talked to Uncle Cliff about you staying with him and working on his job. He says he has no problem as long as you follow his rules and no pot on the jobsite. Do you think you could do that?"

Chris looked shocked. "Sure," he said after gaining some composure. "It's better than goin' to Iran, and Cliff and I are cool."

Earl looked relieved, but I wasn't. What if he did smoke pot on the job? If Cliff threw him out, where would he go? I needed some sort of reassurance that my son wouldn't be homeless. That night I called Cliff. He felt that he and Chris had a close enough relationship, and that Chris respected him enough to follow his rules. "Earl's too hard on your boys," he said, "and I think that's why they defy him. I won't throw him out. Don't worry about that."

The next night at dinner, Earl turned to Lauri and Denny: "How about it, guys? Are we up to the trip?" He needed an answer from all of us. Time would soon run out on the job offer.

I grappled for something to slow down these crazy plans. This wasn't just a "trip," it was a two-year commitment, but the kids were already in on the deal. "Dad, do they have ice skating rinks there?" my daughter asked excitedly. Her life revolved around ice skating lessons. She'd given notice that she would be an Olympic skater one day—and she had the Dorothy Hamill Wedge haircut to prove it.

"I'm sure they do, honey."

He had the four of us. I swallowed my concerns as I saw the excitement in my two little one's eyes. He was the glue that held us together. We knew we'd follow him anywhere—or risk coming unglued. I told Earl we would join him after Jim's graduation; I was not going to miss that. I was sure I could talk Jim into coming with us by the time June rolled around.

Chris would be looked after and he seemed glad to stay with his uncle. I now felt it all might work. My heart ached at the prospect of leaving Chris behind, but I knew he wouldn't—and shouldn't—come with us. The thought of him in an Iranian prison terrified me.

I spent another few days tossing around all the information, and slowly my husband's enthusiasm began to rub off on me. The thought of living abroad for two years didn't seem that bad. It might be kind of exciting. When I said the word "abroad" it did sound rather exotic.

1977 – California

2

Six Months On Autopilot

The airport shuttle's engine idled forebodingly in our driveway. I wanted to tell the driver to take off. Pick up someone else. I wasn't ready to have my husband leave. We embraced, kissed, and then he was gone, backpack over his shoulder and dragging a bulging duffle bag loaded down with foul weather gear.

A pang of loneliness hit me as I walked back into the house. The kids had said their tearful goodbyes the night before, and were still asleep. The house was too quiet. I could almost feel the second-hand moving on the Grandfather clock two rooms away. I sat down with a heavy heart to record this sad day in my journal:

1/6/77: Earl left this morning for Esfahan, Iran. Supposed to join him in June after Jim graduates. Still not sure why he's so determined to

9

work overseas, we have a great life, friends, family, beautiful home, he's
happy with his job. Maybe it's his problems with the boys, or maybe it's
male menopause that caused this wanderlust in him.

I watched the coffee pot while it brewed, and pondered what would be in store for us in my Gypsy husband's plans. As I began to write the list of what had to be done before leaving, I wondered how I could get it all accomplished by then. Four kids to deal with, school, homework, dentists and orthodontists, sports, and most importantly, medical visits, inoculations, and passports. And of course, empty the house and find a renter. My mind reeled.

How many passports would I need? Jim had no plans after graduation. He still hadn't made a decision about going to Iran with us, but then he didn't want to stay here without us, either. He said he'd try to find a buddy to room with. I asked him to consider the military; a chance to learn a career *and* have the government pay for his college. He said he'd think about it. Lauri and Denny had no clue where Iran was or what might be in store for them, but they were excited by their father's enthusiasm, and were ready to pack.

I made more notes. Thoughts tumbled around in my head like bingo balls in a drum— with the next thought dropping before I had a chance to address the previous one. Iran? I needed to get used to the idea of living in a foreign country, half a world away from friends and family.

I ended the page in my diary:
Can't think about it now, have to fix breakfast, will think about it later.

When the radio-alarm went off at 5:30 the following morning, the pain hit me like an electric shock. He wasn't there. We'd been separated before by his work, but only in short spurts. He'd gone to work on the Alaskan pipeline, and every three weeks we got together. We joined him in Anchorage, then caught a flight to Hawaii for a week. He was able to fly home a couple times during that employment, so we never were apart more than three weeks at a time. This was going to be a long six months.

As the days passed, I developed a rhythm. I had a job to do. With Earl gone I now had to be mother, father, guardian, disciplinarian, chauffer, chief cook, welterweight fight referee, and all round genius. I went about my normal daytime schedule, but I had an ache in my gut— like a heavy meal you can't digest. I was half-tuned to my tasks, not quite in the present, going on autopilot. I put off bedtime until my eyes could stay open no longer. I'd grab a book to read in bed, trying to avoid the empty space next to me.

We'd always gone to bed at the same time, habit more than anything. Now the room seemed ghost-like. I rolled over onto his side, inhaled the after-shave scent on his pillow and felt the old familiar urge to cuddle. I would not wash his pillowcase. The scent brought back many memories: After a shower and shave, he'd dab some Lagerfeld on his face and neck and strut into the bedroom, sans undies. Heavy breathing, he called it: "Are you up for some heavy breathing tonight, Babe?" A slow dance of lovers; a routine that melded us together. It always worked when I inhaled his Lagerfeld.

Hours became days and days became weeks. I had so much to accomplish each day that little time was left to worry about what might be ahead of me. The nights crawled. After the kids were in bed, a foreboding seemed to encircle my thoughts: what if we uprooted our family and the job didn't work out? What if one of us became ill while Earl was gone? Could he fly home? Would the company fire him if he had to leave Iran? What if he got sick while there? Did they have good doctors and hospitals in Iran? Then I realized I was what-iffing myself to death again and reached for my paper and pencil on the nightstand and made more notes.

I needed to talk to my husband. I needed to hear his voice. Two weeks had passed since he'd left and still no phone call. He'd told me about the unreliable phone system in Esfahan, and he'd also told me he'd be working odd hours, and chances of getting to a phone after work might be hard. Every time the phone rang we'd all leap for it, certain it would be him.

Our front door had a mail slot that creaked as the carrier pushed the mail through. I constantly listened for that noise. Every few minutes I'd rush to the door and expect to see mail on the floor, only to find bills or sale papers. Then one day I spotted some odd-sized envelopes mixed in with the sale papers. Three letters! My heartbeat quickened. I grabbed the envelopes and ran to the kitchen table. None were postmarked with a date, and all three looked as though they'd been through a Class IV hurricane. Water spots smeared the envelope fronts, and dirty fingerprint smudges were front and back. Two had been torn open and resealed with what looked like gum. I didn't care. I was ecstatic. I put them on the table and tortured myself, staring at my husband's handwriting until I had to open one. Without a date I had no idea which one to open first. Eeeny-meeny-miney-moe! I grabbed one and tore it open.

The letter was filled with exciting news, which covered everything from the job to the people, to the city, to the country. His letter rambled on about work: his job entailed overseeing the piping, concrete, millwright work and anything else they might throw at him. His main job was the cooling tower, without which the refinery could not operate. His crew had grown to forty-two Iranians, using German blueprints with an Armenian supervisor, Koreans running power supply, and an Okie over it all (that would be Earl). How's that for International Labor Relations?

He wrote about the Iranian men who worked for him: hard workers, willing to do anything to please him. He said his limited Farsi, arm waving, and a lot of four-letter words seemed to be getting the job done, with an occasional *achtung* thrown in.

He said the tower was the second largest in the world, the first being in Germany. Some of the complications, he said, were the breakdowns and replacements. The parts had to come down from the Mediterranean Sea and then up the Persian Gulf, overland some 600 kilometers, which a few years ago was just a camel trail. The trip took eight to nine months.

At this time, he wrote, ninety percent of the personnel on the job were Iranians, some 7000 in all, who before this job came straight from the villages, remote even from their city cousins. They were thrown into this situation, given tools and taught to do this kind of work, which was completely alien to them. All they had ever handled were shovels and antiquated tools for their farming.

The other two letters were more of the same with stories of the people and how the *Kamikaze* style of driving overwhelmed him. He also sounded enchanted with it: "The country is beautiful but dirty," was one of his more visual passages.

Long hours at work left little time to rest, he said, but also helped to keep loneliness at bay. The men worked six days a week, Saturday through Thursday, from six in the morning until six at night. Friday was Iran's Islamic holy day and the Muslim-owned stores shut down, including the mail and phone service. He wrote about all the sightseeing he'd been doing on his days off, his job and the people he'd met. He'd not found a place for us to live yet, but company housing was giving him leads to check out. He counted off the days until we arrived. He missed us. He'd enclosed a money order, which I found in the last letter I opened.

1/23/77: Earl called at 8 this morning, evening his time, from a friend's phone. So good to hear his voice. Wants us to leave the day after Jim's graduation. Tells me it's hard to describe the place, lots of gold stores, I will love it. He gives me lists of things to do: rent house, find place to store car, rent P.O. Box in Texas for permanent address, change bank information, open an account for company to deposit his pay. More for my list. My heart sinks like a rock dropped down a well when he hangs up.

Earl's call left me frustrated. The phone connection was beyond dreadful. We had to repeat each sentence several times, then the line would go dead. I had to wait for him to call back. The roller coaster of emotions wore thin. I was ecstatic to hear his voice, then dejected when the call ended. I did feel some relief; he was well and loved his job. I told him I couldn't possibly come before July. I'd hoped that would give me time to get everything done. He accepted this, but I could hear the disappointment in his voice.

I wondered. What would I find in that far off country? What would I need to take that I couldn't find there? Would there be restrictions on what we could bring? Was Iran a third-world country or contemporary? I would need answers and of course make other lists. Earl said the company would call me for a dependent orientation meeting, so I'd have to wait until then to get answers to my packing questions.

One Saturday while the kids were off at their friends, I thought it prudent to find out where we were headed. Time to visit the library, check out a few books and spend the weekend getting acquainted with my future home. I approached the research desk and told the clerk I'd be moving to Esfahan, Iran, and would like to check out a book about the country.

"The library has a vast assortment of material on Iran," she said, "follow me."

She proceeded to pull various history books from the shelves, stacking them onto my outstretched arms. I wasn't sure I wanted to pour through all those huge tomes. I found a desk and opened a massive tome, and then another, and then another, but they only covered Persian history. I was mainly interested in the "here and now." I approached her desk again and explained that I was most interested in what the living conditions were *now,* like the shopping and local attractions of Esfahan. "Really," she said, in a tone that showed displeasure. "I would think you'd want to understand the culture and its people before you visit a country."

Read, learn and better yourself her frown said. I've always liked to make nice with people. I couldn't leave and have her think I was illiterate, so I ended up with four history books and one book—hopefully—with current facts about life in Iran—*in this century*.

Once home I got out my trusty tablet to make notes. Picturing *Ms. Prim's* face, I thought I'd start with Iran's history. I sat down and opened the book: Historically know as Persia, all sorts of marauders had invaded and occupied it since its birth: Arabs, Turks, Mongols, British, Russians, and Greeks to name a few. Amazing! However, as evidenced in the history books, the nation had thrived since 625 BC, which gave me small relief. Maybe they had finally worked out all that invasion stuff.

I read on: The Islamic conquest took place in the 8th Century, which was known as the Golden Age of Persia. The country had been a monarchy, ruled by a Shah or Emperor since 1501. After centuries of foreign occupation, Persia became an independent state in 1502, with Islam being the main religion. The next invaders to help themselves to the spoils of the rich oil fields were the Soviet Union and the British, who occupied Iran in 1941. Since the sitting Shah at the time, Reza Pahlavi, had no plans to share in the oil proceeds with the Ruskies or the Brits, he was forced by the British to abdicate in favor of his son, Mohammad Reza Shah Pahlavi, who now occupied the Peacock Throne. Since that time the sitting Shah had the backing of the U.S. and Great Britain. The country had been a monarchy since 1941. And... most importantly to me, the book confirmed that: "The Shah was loved by his people."

Next I opened the travel books. They offered a more picturesque side of the country. Esfahan had been the capital of Persia from 1598 to 1722, located 355 km from the new capital, Tehran, a city Earl had said was very cosmopolitan and we'd visit on his days off. He'd also told me Tehran had five-star restaurants, nightclubs with belly dancers, floorshows, and boutique shops with expensive imported clothes from Europe.

Now you're talking my kind of travel.

Also, I read, about a four-hour drive from Tehran was the Caspian Sea, the world's largest salt water lake, and the largest enclosed body of water on earth, which measured 750 km long from north to south. I visualized balmy days on those shores, kids swimming, Mom sun bathing, Dad snorkeling. I made a note to pack our bamboo sand blankets.

I also made notes on all the important statistics I'd read. You never knew who might ask and I so wanted to sound cosmopolitan. The travel books claimed that Esfahan, in the 17th Century, had the reputation of being one of the largest and most beautiful cities in the world. *That's not the description I'd gotten from my husband.* I did hope some of that beauty still stood, but the 17th Century was a long time gone.

Pictures of Esfahan and its beautiful squares, bridges and incredible architecture from the 3rd Century were striking. Gold-filigreed mosques and lavish palaces were in vivid colors and stunning. The description of the bazaar and its treasures got my attention. The article claimed that the great Esfahan bazaar had the longest roofed marketplace in the world, and was central to the Iranian social life. I could see that: Shop, meet friends, meet new friends, shop. I was ready. It listed Persian carpets of silk; gold and silver shops; fresh fruit from all over the country; imported clothes from Europe, jewelry, and much, much more.

Years later, I was amazed to read in the *Iran Chamber Society*, that "Archeologists could find proof of the existence of bazaars in different areas of the country; Kermanshah (9000 B.C.), Zagheh hills in Ghazvin(7000 B.C.), Sialk hills in Kashan(6000 B.C.), Hasanlu in Kerman (6000 B.C.), Tal Eblis in Kerman (5000 B.C.), Khabis in Kerman (4000 B.C.), "the burned city" in Sistan (3000 B.C.) and Shush (from 4000 B.C.)"

I guess bazaars are the businesses to be in if you're looking for a long-term job.

Esfahan in the 70s had a population of over one million, and Tehran over four million. The move now didn't seem so scary. I knew it would be a life-changing experience for all of us. How could it not be? History and treasures abounded in this place.

After I'd read my fill, I put the book down and closed my eyes. Hopefully, we'd be safe for the next two years.

How wrong I was!

One of the first things I had to do was visit the kids' orthodontist. We'd spent a gazillion on their braces and I didn't want to jeopardize their teeth or our money. I had no idea if there were any orthodontists in Esfahan. I grabbed my "To Do list."

The appointment didn't go well. Dr. Bernstein was aghast when I told him our plans. "Where did you say you were going?" he shouted over the noise of the saliva ejector while tightening my daughter's braces.

"Iran," I yelled back, "for two years."

Dr. Bernstein stopped and looked at me with disgust. He turned off the machine. "Fine!" he said, in a not too fine voice. "I'll take their braces off. I will not have those idiot Arabs touching my orthodontia!"

My mouth must have dropped open.

"What? You have a problem?"

I could imagine his little Jewish heart pumping wildly. "Um, well, I don't know about that, I believe they're Iranians, not Arabs."

"Same-same."

"I guess I don't understand," I said meekly. "Why you'd take off their braces, because..." I stopped myself. I didn't want him to unload on me about the whole Arab-Jewish history.

"What's to understand?"

I put on my "concerned-mother" face. "Can't they wear them while we're gone? I'd hate for them to lose two years' worth of straightening."

17

"No! They haven't been on that long. Come see me before you leave and I will remove their braces. When you return come see me and I will fit them again."

He was fired up now. His fingers moved at warp speed inside my daughter's mouth as he twisted her wires. Lauri's eyes held a pleading expression: *Say something nice, Mom.*

"Well, um…okay I guess that would work," I said to placate him, "but won't their teeth get crooked again if you take off their braces?"

He was quiet for a moment as he assessed his work. "Okay," he answered after an audible sigh, "I'll make temporary retainers for them to wear while they're gone. When you return, come right back to me. They won't lose that much time. I can fix them. But I won't fix anyone else's mistakes. You understand?"

Lauri turned to me again with a pleading look: *Say yes, Mom.*

"Okay, um, yes, that'll work. What about the charges? I've…"

"Forget it. No charge." He proceeded to mumble something more, but obviously not for my ears.

Next on my list was a property management company. Could they find a renter for our home and manage the property while we were gone? No problem, the agent said. But I was worried. The house was not a cookie-cutter house. It had been custom-built on a quarter-acre of land. We'd purchased the home from friends three years earlier, and I'd loved it the minute I saw it. Close to twenty-five hundred square feet, the floor plan included three bedrooms, two-and-a-half baths, a huge family room and living room. The kitchen was oversize with a built-in brick barbeque. The architecture was called "Ranch Style" and sported a large, tree-lined front yard. The back yard was enormous, lined with various plants and flowers, along with three huge avocado trees, a large swimming pool with two dressing rooms, and a covered patio with a built-in barbeque and a regulation pool table. At first I was concerned about the upkeep and size of the house, but it proved to fit us just fine. We could entertain family and friends, and the kids had a continuous backyard swim party. I was eager to see what the agent thought we could get for rent.

"This should be easy to rent," she assured me after inspecting the house and the grounds. "You should be able to get about fifteen hundred a month."

"What?" I couldn't believe I could get that much. "The mortgage is only …"

"But you'll need to pay for a gardener and pool service out of that," she interrupted. "You can't leave that to a renter. I've found in my business that renters tend not to take care of a home like an owner would, and you'll need to ask a good amount to insure you get a tenant who has the money to take care of it."

I was shocked. How could I ask that? Our mortgage payment was only five hundred a month. "Who would pay that much?"

She answered me as though I was feeble-minded. "My dear, if you don't get the right renters in here you could return to a nightmare. I've seen homes where the renters tore down everything but the studs."

Oh! Yes! Fifteen hundred a month sounded fair.

1977 – California

3

Packing, Farsi And History Lessons

Earl's letters now arrived every other week, and still looked like they'd been flotsam and jetsam in the Bermuda Triangle. They were short, he said, because he had little time to write, what with working so many hours, and sightseeing on days off.

How nice! Wish I had time to sightsee.

He kept me updated on all the expat tips he'd received: where to go for a good meal, happenings at the Clubhouse, where to go to see great belly-dancing floor shows.

He could have kept that info to himself.

The company Clubhouse sounded great: a large lounge, bar and dance floor, an outdoor movie once a week on a huge drive-in type screen, weekly dances for the teens and an outdoor snack shack for all sorts of munchies and drinks. Also, a tennis court and large, oversized pool.

2/14: Earl called to say Happy Valentine's Day, his voice cracked, he misses us. He said weather still cold, but warmer in a month or so. Bought a beautiful Esfahani carpet—camel and goat hair. Job going good. He found an apartment I'll love—we'll see about that, wish he'd waited for me to see it. Says it's nice, it's upstairs, with friends from job downstairs. I'll like her, name's Trudy and her daughter is Lauri's age. Place is in center of town, close to lots of shops, which cheered me up. Asked if I'd found a renter. I told him what the agent priced the house at, he says "Do it! If no one comes in a month, drop the rent a little." Another to-do I add to my list.

Earl's letters were filled with instructions for the family: Call the company for a list of inoculations we would need: yellow fever, malaria, tetanus. Pack plenty of warm clothes for the winter; daytime temps were in the 30s, and nights dropped to the 20s. He tried to raise our level of excitement in his letters: Tehran was near 5000 feet elevation and maybe we could go skiing at the Shah's resort. All the rich Iranians and Europeans skied there and it was much cheaper than our slopes at home. Then he dropped me down into abysmal reality: "Be sure to pack cool clothes, the weather can get up to 120 in the summer."

I'm unpacking!

3/3: Earl called, I wasn't home. Left a message that sounded so forlorn I cried. I wanted to tell him I would get things done, that I'd made progress on my lists, to ask him what to bring, what had he already bought for the apartment.

Between trying to keep the house neat for potential renters, filling boxes scattered helter-skelter around the house, doctor's office visits for medical records, school visits, ice skating lessons, basketball practice, my life was out of control. My emotions would flare up then fall flat.

I was a mess. Friends continued to call with the same questions: "How can you leave your home and go gallivanting off to some place no one's ever heard of? We all think you're nuts!"

But, maybe we weren't so nuts after all. How many people had the chance to travel on the company's dollar? We'd see sights we'd never have been able to afford, and I could call myself "A World Traveler." None of my close friends had ever travelled more than a five-hour drive to Las Vegas, which was their big adventure. I felt rather uppity as I daydreamed and filled more boxes.

Eat your hearts out, peasants!

A friend suggested I take a class in Iran's language. What a great idea; I'd learn something about the country and its language before we left. I located a school in Los Angeles that offered night classes in Farsi. I cajoled my daughter into going with me that first night. Denny wanted nothing to do with it. "I'll probably learn Farsi in school," he said.

Lauri only attended the first night. I had to agree with her—Farsi was not easy, and it sure wasn't fun. The instructor was a dour-looking woman whose age was indeterminate, possibly because of her clothes: a long dress with a high neckline, long sleeves that covered every inch of epidermis—other than her stern face—and all very dark and unadorned. A black flowered scarf covered her head and every follicle of hair, which she constantly tried to push back when a loose strand happened to creep onto her forehead. Her shoes were the black sensible type my grandmother used to wear. She was all business, no smiles, and had a bland affect as she tried to teach us her difficult language.

When words were mispronounced, she puckered up her face and frowned. I worked hard to keep that frown from forming. She took us through the Farsi words asking us to pronounce them as if we were Iranian.

The "ch" and "k" pronounced in the English language have the sound of: "chuh or "khuh," whereas the "ch" and "k" sound in Farsi has a "khugggh" sound, vibrating somewhere between the soft palate and the epiglottis. I thought I pronounced the words quite well, but still got a few puckers from *Ms. Dour**. I attended two more nights, then gave up. I'd learn the important words when I got to Iran, such as "please" and "thank you," and more importantly, "store," "shops," "gold," and "bazaar."

I was busy during the week running errands, checking off items on my lists and adding new ones. However, weekends I had to chaperone, so not too much got done. The house was like Grand Central Station with wild-eyed kids and their friends racing in one door and out the other; continuous refrigerator raids, incessant phone calls, the pool echoing with shouts of "Marco Polo" or "I'm telling Mom." Everyone yelling and splashing, while my neighbors' two dogs barked and ran in circles at all the excitement.

And, then there was me and my handful of lists. I've always been a list maker. It's my Virgo-ness I guess. Either that or I'm really screwed up. Even before all this life-changing mess began, I'd always have a list somewhere: on my desk, on my refrigerator under a magnet, on the bedside table, on the bathroom mirror, as well as on the dashboard of my car. Most lists were two-sided, filled with doctor appointments, school appointments, special sales I must not miss, things I needed to pick up at the store and bills to pay. Whatever thought invaded my fertile brain I'd write down immediately. Then of course there was the list that traveled with me around the house in various pockets—to take on my errands—that I didn't find until I'd returned home from my errands. The longest list was the packing list: household items to be set aside for our company shipment, items that had to go into storage, and items that would go with us in our suitcases. And my last writing of the evening: my faithful journal by my bedside.

The chain of events I like to call "The Cross Crises" began one beautiful spring morning as the kids and I worked in the yard. Chris was off on his paper route; Jim was vacuuming the pool while I trimmed some shrubbery. Denny pulled weeds while Lauri swept the patio—a rare family event.

"Hey, Mom, when'd we get this crack in the pool?" Jim yelled.

"*What?*"

"There's a crack on the bottom, all the way across."

"Oh, no!" I ran to the edge of the pool. The crack ran from one side to the other. "How did this happen?"

"How should I know?" Jim drawled, "Why don't you ask your precious baby boy? He probably threw your bowling ball down the diving board just to see how hard it'd hit."

"No way," Denny hollered from the flowerbed "I'm sure it was you and your fat dorky friends doing cannon-balls. Mom, you should see them when you're not home. They even jump off the dressing room roof so they'll get a bigger splash."

Oh, God! Here we go again. "Stop!" I yelled. "Denny get busy. Jim, if I hear you jumped off that roof again, you're eighty-sixed from the pool."

Sibling rivalry! Would it ever end? I normally tried to believe my children, but...

I made a mental note: *Check bowling bag for signs of water.*

Storming back into the house, I could still hear them bad-mouthing each other. I slammed and locked the door. I then called the rental agent. She sounded like she might stroke-out right there on the phone. "Well...oh, my...how did you let this happen? You must get the crack fixed immediately before I bring over any prospective renters. We can't have them see that!"

I wanted to suggest she move in and take my place, and I'd go sit at her desk and file my nails. Instead I said: "I'll call someone."

The pool repairman arrived with a price.

"*How much?*"

"Look lady, that's a huge job. We have to drain the pool, fix the crack, plaster it, then wait until the plaster seals before we can fill it again. You're talkin' at least a coupla weeks' work. My men make union wages and I..."

Yeah, yeah, yeah. Just fix the damn pool.

After closer inspection, the repairman felt the problem could be the rebar under the plaster. "This might cost ya more, lady, cuz rebar ain't cheap, and my men are union workers..."

Help me Lord.

The next crisis arose when someone put a hose through our mail slot, flooding our den, which then lifted some of the wood flooring and sent me over the edge. "Why would someone do this?" I wailed.

"Relax, Mom," Chris said. "It was probably Darcy. She's mad at me 'cuz I phoned her girlfriend."

"*Relax?*" This is going to cost a fortune. It's going to destroy the wood floor, and how will I get all this water up and..."

"Mom! Calm down. Call the fire department. They have hoses that'll suck up all this water."

"Right! Like you'd know that," I cried. "You get down right now and start mopping up. I'll call for help." I phoned our neighbor who told me the fire department had suction hoses. Okay, I knew that. Thanks.

Orange County's finest arrived with water-sucking equipment and got to work, while I sat at the table and tried to read the morning paper. I had to take a breather. I wanted to kill someone. The only thing that held me back was I really didn't think I'd look good in prison-orange.

I thought I detected looks of judgment going on with the water-suckers, like: What kind of mother lets this happen? She needs to get control of her kids. I wanted to ask them to move in, enjoy the pool and its problems, the uncontrollable kids, and I'd go to the firehouse and play poker and watch sports on TV.

The next disaster involved a leaking hose in the dishwasher. One morning as I walked into the kitchen eager for my first sip of fresh-brewed coffee, I skidded halfway across the floor. I became an expert at calling for help. The next call was to my homeowners insurance. The agent asked how old the dishwasher was. Who cares? I'm old and I still work. They also wanted to know how old the flooring was. What is it with insurance companies? They take your money right out of your wallet, offer to cover everything but the garbage, but when it's time to pay a claim, they have a million reasons why they shouldn't cover it. I didn't need this! Earl had been gone a little over two months and the house seemed to collapse under my feet. I searched the phone book for a help line for the Temporarily Insane.

The call finally came from Earl's company for orientation, mandatory for all expat dependents. I'd hoped to learn more about the country from the meeting, as well as needing answers to some Where, Why, What and How questions on my list. Bob*, the relocation guy, went over the handouts he'd given us. First listed was the dress code. In capital, bold letters, it read: WHAT WE MUST NOT WEAR: shorts, short dresses, halter tops, tank tops, or any item of apparel that might reveal too much of our body. But we *were* allowed to have our neck, face, hands and feet hang out. *Well, thank you very much, Bob.*

Wait a minute! What kind of a place are we going to that we have to cover up? No mention was made about this in the books I'd read. I mean at forty, I didn't plan on running around town in a Fredrick's of Hollywood's teddy, but come on! I did read that some of the Muslim women still preferred to wear the *chador*—a black robe that covered the head and body—but many wore westernized clothes. Surely we could wear a sleeveless blouse in 120-degree heat. My hand shot up. "Why the cover up? We're not Muslims."

Bob's face resembled an overripe persimmon. "Well, yes, ah, in a foreign country we always ask our employees to dress accordingly. Uh, that is, if you're in an area where the Iranian women are in western dress, then you should have no problem. But, please be careful, we don't want to offend our host country."

I didn't like this sort of walk-on-egg-shells dress code.

"But the good news is you can wear anything you want in your own home."

Well, thanks again, Bob.

Ms. *Dour's* image—our Farsi instructor—flashed before my eyes. I raised my hand. "Do we have to cover our heads when we go out in public?" I'd already decided if his answer was in the affirmative, I was unpacking.

"No! You don't have to cover your heads, but keep covered as best you can."

I could see he was a little perturbed at my questions, so I forged ahead. "Do you mean we have to wear long pants and long-sleeved blouses?"

A few giggles could be heard from the other wives, but no questions were broached. I gave them the eyebrow-raise. *Come on ladies, speak up. I don't want to be the only one bitching here.*

"No, I mean, ah, just don't reveal too much. Be sensible."

Really! I'd already packed our swim suits, sun lotion and beach towels. What would we do? Lie out in our backyard with the sprinklers on? I needed to have a "Come to Jesus meeting" with my husband.

After Bob finished his presentation, we began to gather our paperwork to leave. "Oh ladies," he said, "I've one more item to discuss that was not on the hand-outs, but which we should *not* forget."

Please, no more!

He picked up a sheet from his desk and began to read: "When in mixed company please do not talk about, or get into a discussion about, the Shah, politics of the country, or politics of America." He cleared his throat and looked rather apologetic. "In fact, ladies, maybe it would be best to just omit any discussion on those issues anywhere, even in your own home."

3/15: Earl called. I told him about orientation and he laughed, said not to worry. Not all Muslims wear the chador, and westerners dress like they want. I feel better. What about swim suits? The company pool, he says. What about the Caspian Sea? Probably not to swim in, he says. What about politics? No problem. He asks if we're getting things done (meaning me) to leave. I tell him life goes on as usual; kids in plays, sports, and constant fights.

Jim and Chris were at each other's throats constantly. Their fighting escalated until I thought they'd kill each other. I knew the absence of a father figure in the home had a lot to do with it, but I was an expert at smacking a wooden spoon across a tight, Levi-covered butt. That didn't stop the bugging, but at least it slowed down a little. One morning while I prepared breakfast, I heard loud, angry voices coming from the backyard. Denny looked up from his bowl of cereal, "Don't worry, Mom," Denny said, laconically, "it's just *them* fighting again."

I ran outside to find the boys actually trading blows. "Stop!" I yelled, to deaf ears. I tried to wedge between them, pushing each away from the other. And BAM! I had no idea where the fist came from, but I took a right hook to the nose and went down. I thought, well now that should stop them, but then heard: "Look what you did to mom," and the fighting started again. I kicked at both sets of legs until I got their attention. "STOP IT!" I screamed. "Help me up, you little shits, right now!"

They continued punching while I scrambled out from between their legs and ran to find something to stop them. I grabbed the garden hose and turned the sprayer to high, aiming it right in their faces, which finally stopped them. My God, I thought, I'm raising dogs.

I sent them to school and then went in the bathroom to have myself a good cry. When I saw my face in the mirror I cried even harder. Then I reached for a tissue to blow my dripping nose. OHMYGOD! I looked like Kermit the Frog. The skin around my eye orbits had puffed up like a blowfish. The doctor at the emergency room said the cartilage had been cracked, and when I blew my nose, air had escaped into the eye orbits, causing the Froggy look. Now I was furious. The boys were put on lockdown for a week. I would rather have sent them away for a week, but then again, someone might have reported me.

4/25:When Earl called tonight he was philosophical. "Never get between two men fighting." Well, thank you, I think I learned that lesson. He told me to put them on the phone. I lied and said they were asleep. I can't do this long-distance parenting. Why wasn't I a nun?

My lists began to shrink. The kids' school records finally arrived in the mail, and the next day I was able to pick up all their medical records from the doctor. Boxes were beginning to fill up, which showed progress. Dates were made for inoculations and passport pictures were taken and mailed in with our applications. The clerk assured me we'd have them in six weeks.

Things were moving along.

As the old idiom goes, "Cheer up, things could be worse!" Well, I did cheer up and things did get worse.

April 4th: Bad night. Jim fell asleep at the wheel of his hopped-up Camaro on way home from party, ran into the back of his buddy's van, igniting gas tank. Nobody hurt. Van and car totaled. Police at my door at 1 a.m. is this your kid? I want to say I've never seen him before. When Earl calls I tell him about it. He's furious at Jim for his drinking (of course Earl never drank at age 17), rants at me about thoughtless kids with no responsibility. Why do I always get hell for what the kids do? Can't I control my kids?

The Easter holiday was upon us. I wasn't going to stay home and mope, worry about kid problems, personal injury lawsuits, car insurance premiums skyrocketing, or rental problems. I picked up my mother and we all set off to Los Angeles to see my favorite, bohemian aunt and uncle. They lived in a sprawling home in the Elysian Park area of Los Angeles. In its heyday of the 40s, the house played host to artists and intellectuals of all sorts. As a kid I remember being overwhelmed by it all: bespectacled men dressed in brown corduroy jackets with patches on their sleeves, sucking on pipes or cigarettes in long porcelain holders. They looked so important as they sipped fine sherry in a smoke-filled room. I imagined they would have great conversations and debates about the world and its meaning. My mother thought they just liked the sound of their own voices.

I'd not seen my aunt and uncle in years, and expected to find them aged with liver spots and thinning hair. But, quite the contrary. I found them as vital and energized as I'd remembered them, albeit somewhat grayer. My aunt, who'd been an acclaimed artist and trained in Paris, used to hand-paint Easter eggs with incredible miniature drawings. They were spectacular and we all clamored for them as she passed them out to her guests.

When we arrived at their home, people were milling about the yards and in the house. My two youngest were amazed at the surroundings. They discovered the Koi fishpond and the stream behind the house, while Chris and Jim zeroed in on a couple long-legged, short-skirted girls. Before they could make their macho moves I thought it best to tell them those girls might be some long-lost cousins. "No way," Jim said, "they're way too cute to be our relatives."

The day brought back many fun memories. Before we left, I hugged my aunt and uncle, not knowing if they'd even be alive when I returned. I hated to leave their warm, friendly home and return to my cold, near-empty house. The day had helped us get through an otherwise sad holiday without Earl. I would now try to focus only on the day we'd all be together again as a family.

My living room had disappeared, hidden behind three piano-sized boxes that were overflowing with things we couldn't live without. I had to take four tennis rackets, which took up way too much room, however some things were important to me. Also, my sewing machine was a must-go, a sort of feel-good must-go. On top of all that, Earl's letters said to throw in some dressy clothes as there would be a few company banquets to attend. I only had one pair of dressy shoes, which I seldom wore, and they were way too tight, so new shoes would be added to my lists. Why couldn't they just plan a barbeque or swim party? I still looked pretty good in a swimsuit—if I wore my wonder-under tummy tightener and my Lift-em-up-Joe bra.

> *5 / 2: Earl called today, our 14th anniversary. He didn't forget. His calls come more often now since he has a phone in the apartment. Static is still terrible, disconnected at least 3 times each call. Met more people, everyone wants to meet "Big Red," his name for me. Weather warming up, he says, nights great at Clubhouse watching 100-year-old movies. Getting a lot done. Starting to look forward to this trip.*

In his next letter, Earl had enclosed some photos he'd taken on rides into the country on his days off. The kids each grabbed one and I took what was left. I felt my stomach tighten as I looked at them: such a desolate landscape. Sand. Lots of sand! No trees, and more sand. Mud huts in the background with donkeys, goats or sheep lying about. Shabby-clothed men either stood in the periphery or were next to Earl with an arm draped around his shoulder. The men looked ancient, showing huge, toothless smiles as if this was the best day in their lives. This was so typical of my husband. He'd never met a stranger. Even though he couldn't speak any language other than English—and that was sometimes subject to interpretation—he never let such a minor thing stop him from jawing away at someone who had no idea what he was saying. He'd normally raise his voice at that time, assured that what couldn't be translated, could easily be heard. Smiles as he sat on a river bank with what looked like a picnic lunch; smiles as he stood on sand dunes and waved at the camera; smiles as he stood in front of a mud hut and shook hands with an ancient man dressed as a shepherd; smiles as two of them sat atop a very skinny donkey, while the donkey's owner offered a toothless grin.

"Look, how cool, Mom," Denny said, "Dad's on a camel!"

"Look at this one Mom. Dad's buying some stuff at the bazaar," Lauri shrieked, "I hope it's for our house."

That night I looked at all the pictures again. And cried. Okay, grow up! We'll all be together soon, sans the old men.

5 / 15th: Earl called last night. Misses us terribly. Put the house up for sale at the end of the month if no renter, he says. Keep it clean for prospective renters my agent says. Impossible with four kids. I clean, turn around, it's a pigsty. I yell a lot. Kid's too busy with homework and having fun to help. Denny wonders why I clean all the time, it just gets dirty again. I like his thinking. Our agent doesn't.

Finally things seemed to come together. Everything, that is, except the house; it hadn't rented yet, and Earl was pushing me to sell it. I kept stalling in the hopes some huge corporation would find my house a great place to put up their visitors. I loved my home. I wasn't *in* love with it, but it was a great place for the kids and entertaining.

May 20th: Earl calls to tell Jim he can use him on jobsite as a local hire. He needs to know before someone else fills that spot. Jim is interested, the money's good, but I worry. They don't get along. Earl's too hard on Jim. Maybe they can get closer on the jobsite. Job's going well, likes the men who work for him. Got a promotion, more money. Feels good about our move. Jim seems intrigued about the prospect of making good money, but not too thrilled to be working for his dad. I'm on the fence. List growing smaller, things falling into place. I pray for a renter.

Lauri and Denny were excited about the move. They wanted to be with their father, and I guess that trumped sadness for the friends they'd leave behind. I checked their boxes and saw they were not going to close. Little bulges were sprouting out around the side seams, and they still had more to pack. "Mom, we need these," they would say in unison as I held up a battered Monopoly box that was shoved in against immovable objects such as brass baseball trophies and team pictures. "We'll be gone a long time! We need to make sure we have enough to do for two years," Denny wailed, exuding pain.

I began to move things around in the box, hoping I could make everything fit. Mixed helter-skelter between Denny's clothes I found his skate board, scrapbooks, comic books, baseball cards, chalk, records, eight-track player and tapes, a baseball and glove, volleyball and net, books and miscellaneous junk. Also, jeans with holes in the knees as if we were destitute. Lauri's boxes were a bit more orderly. Hers contained photo albums, records, tapes and ice skates, along with the costumes she performed in. But how could I fault my kids? I was busy packing personal things as well: family albums, pictures, tennis rackets, shoes, and cute little tennis outfits, and favorite pillows. I'd hoped Earl wouldn't ask how many boxes we were shipping. Anytime the topic came up about our shipment I'd change the subject. There are some things a man doesn't need to know, and most things a man wouldn't understand. It's a woman's DNA that pushes her to such lengths. She's compelled to nest wherever she touches down. All things that bring comfort must be included. But, if he did ask, I could always pull the "poor me" card like my young son: "I'm leaving behind so many friends and family, at least I should be able to take along things that will make me happy."

I wasn't ashamed to use that card. I'd used it many times over the course of my life. What woman hasn't? If they say they haven't, they're either lying or never been married.

1977 – California

4

The Last Week

How could it be June already? What happened to the months after January? My agent, *Ms. I Know the Market,* had showed up occasionally with a prospective renter. But for one reason or another, it never panned out. She said some clients wanted a smaller house, or some said the rent was too high. Again I reminded her that we were on a time constraint, and should lower the rent. No! She insisted she knew the market, and I should stick to the original price. She had a problem returning my calls, and I felt she wasn't aggressively marketing my house. But again, maybe she didn't return my calls because she'd had it with all my house catastrophes, and was off to greener pastures with clients who were childless.

I wasn't ready to give up on a renter, so I would try once more before I made the decision to sell. Possibly a new agent might have some names of renters in his files. I fired her and called another agency. Did he have anyone on a waiting list for an outstanding home? And could they move in, like, in a couple of weeks? And move out in two years?

The new agent, *Mr. Get-The-Sale* rushed right over. As I walked him around the house he seemed surprised I'd even considered renting. "Why would you rent out such a beautiful home? Chances are when you return in two years the house could be a mess and you'd have to spend thousands to repair it."

I'd heard this line from my last agent. "But if the rent was high enough," I paraphrased *Ms. Market* here, "they'd take care of it, wouldn't they? And, besides, not everyone trashes a house they rent."

"That's not the point. You're taking a huge gamble you'll get the right person in here, and you say you're on a tight schedule. My best advice to you would be to sell." I told him I only had a few weeks before I had to leave the country. He laughed. "You don't have to be present to sell your house. There's the mail service and Faxes that can take care of anything that needs to be signed."

It was now my turn to laugh.

"What's funny?" he said, looking wounded. "I've done this many times."

"Sorry," I said. "It's just that the mail from Iran takes forever, and I don't know if they have Faxes where we're going. Also, the phone service is abysmal. It's full of static and the calls drop right in the middle of a conversation."

"Believe me, if there's a will…"

As he rambled on, my thoughts took flight. For the first time the reality of being homeless hit me in the gut. "If we sold the house we'd have no home to return to."

"You'll be gone two years, right? You've got eighteen months to buy another home to avoid taxes."

What was with this guy? We'd be gone twenty-four months, not eighteen. We couldn't fly home to buy a house. We knew nothing about a tax time limit on purchasing another home. I could feel my spastic colon going spastic. I didn't like this high-pressure sales gig he used on me. He'd just as soon get the sale and not worry about what happened to us in eighteen months.

"Look, I can take care of all this. I can arrange to purchase a small rental condo for you, then you can resell it when you get back and are ready to buy a new home." I stared at him, unable to comprehend all the plans he'd laid out. "You won't want to come back to this neighborhood, anyway," he added, as he looked up and down the wide street. "Already there are houses up for sale on this street and they're being purchased by minorities. You could return and find the whole neighborhood's a ghetto."

I asked him how that could happen in two years? This was a great neighborhood. And, yes, we did have what he referred to as minorities on this block, but we preferred to call them neighbors. In fact right next door, and they were wonderful people who kept their property up better than most of the neighbor's yards, including ours.

He looked at me with sympathy oozing from every pore. "Very easy, my dear. I've seen this too many times. People are in a hurry to sell so they lower the price and you get low income people buying, and the next thing you know there goes the neighborhood."

That didn't bode well with me, but then again, nothing did. I didn't have time to think clearly about my future. All I knew was I couldn't imagine we'd ever find such a perfect house again. However, the thought of leaving my home empty terrified me, and sent me whirling with negative thoughts: what if someone broke in and vandalized it? What if some homeless people found a nice comfortable pad here? What if the house reeked of garbage and B.O. when we returned? What if there were rat feces and human waste, and... *Okay, enough!*

The broker put up the For Sale sign the next day, and three days later he called with an offer.

The next day the house sold.

I cried, then packed up the rest of my life.

The company called and gave me a date they'd pick up our boxes for shipping. They would pick up the furniture for storage the day after we left. I had myself a good pity-party and then put my fears away for another day. We'd be leaving in less than a month and so much still had to be done. Jim's graduation preparations were taking precedence over packing: senior pictures, invitations to be ordered, and pictures to send to relatives in those invitations. Denny stood by the table while I addressed envelopes. "How much money do you think Jim'll get, Mom?"

"Honey, it isn't about the money. We're just letting our relatives and friends know about his graduation. Some will come, some are too far away so they usually just send a card."

"Yeah, that's what I mean. Shouldn't they put money in the card if they can't come? You do it when you get someone's graduation card."

I didn't know he'd watched me do that. *I'd raised such a thoughtful child.*

Then last minute runs to the school for cap and gown, forms to fill out to make sure everything they were supposed to do at school had been done. *Shouldn't that have been done weeks before?*

6/12: Jim graduated last night, got cash from family members, with Denny counting. Boys took off after presents were opened. Cliff will be legal guardian for Chris while we're gone, put him to work as a carpenter, good money. He needs a gentler man in his life. My heart hurts to leave him behind, but thoughts of drug problems in a foreign country terrify me. Last minute things getting done. Proud of myself.

By the third week in June the place was downright depressing; it was no longer a home, just a house. The normal homey ambience had now turned cold and uninviting. All knick-knacks were either packed or given away; throw rugs were packed or tossed; family photos no longer smiled out from gilded frames placed around the house. It was bleak.

The passports finally arrived, way too close to our departure date to suit me. I looked at the pictures then considered sending them back with a note: *Not Ours!* Why do they make you look so stern when they take your picture? I looked like Ma Barker and the kids looked like my gang.

Next on my list was a visit to the orthodontist. The kids were seated in dental chairs as they tried hard to suppress their smiles. Dr. Bernstein walked in, nodded to me and with a stern look, began to extract Lauri's braces. I heard him say, "So you're still going through with this foolish move?"

Was he speaking to Lauri or me?

She gave me the pleading look again: *Mom, be nice.*

"Well…yes. We don't have much choice. You see my husband's job…"

"No more said," he snapped, "just make sure they wear their retainers every day."

I wanted to salute and say "Aye-Aye Sir."

Lauri and Denny were ecstatic to have their braces removed, while I pictured their teeth moving a millimeter every second.

Can't do anything about that now. Don't want him to stop mid-extraction. I'll worry about it later.

On our drive home from Lauri's last ice skating lesson, she proposed an idea to me: "Put this on your last minute list, Mom. I need to get my wedge trimmed before we leave, and I think you should get a wedge too. We might not find someone over there that can cut my style." The Hamill Wedge was the rave in the States after Dorothy won the Olympics. The ads boasted: *This haircut can take ten years off your face!* I could live with that, but what about the rest of my body?

I'd thought about the Wedge before, but somehow couldn't picture my face and Dorothy's in the same frame. "I thought the Hamill Wedge was just for young girls."

"No way," said my daughter, innocently, "my instructor has the same cut and she's old."

Thanks!

I've always felt great after a good cut and style, sort of revitalized. It was time to cheer up. I had the cut, and loved it, but the ten years the ad promised would be gone—hung on.

6/21: Earl called to congratulate Jim and ask if he's coming. Jim says yes. The thought of good money trumps problems with Dad. I tell him I put the house up for sale and it sold. Good, he says, we'll worry about a place to come home to next year. We leave July 9th. When we return we'll be homeless. Can't think about that now. Must concentrate on my adventure.

It was now show time. For three weeks the kids and I had taken inventory. Did we pack everything on our lists? After the movers had trucked the last box to the van, I had a sudden pain in my chest and finally realized this was for real. I curled up on the sofa and pulled Lauri and Denny down next to me, trying to build excitement for our trip—for them *and* for me. "Just think, we'll be with Dad in less than a week, and then we'll have all the boxes to unpack. It'll be like opening Christmas presents."

I should have been used to all of this. I'd moved many times in my life, and this, I told myself, was just another adventure. After all, what was a house other than brick, mortar, and a few pieces of lumber? I could always make a new home, which would be where my husband and children were, no matter the geography. *Just as long as we're together* was my mantra. The kids had no idea where we were going, but they were excited. Oh to be young again with such trust. Chris and I had made peace with our decision, and he was happy to be going to his uncle's. The thought of learning a trade and making money was a great motivation for him.

Once the boxes were gone and most of the furniture had been taken to storage, our footsteps echoed throughout the house. To avoid this emptiness, I did a lot of visiting with friends and relatives, went to movies and out to dinner with the kids. My friends threw a going-away party for me two days before we left. They roasted me for being crazy enough to leave, then wished us God-Speed. Gene, a long-time friend, offered up his normal cryptic thoughts: "Knowing Dodie, she'll probably start a revolution over there."

Chris moved over to his uncle's house the night before we were to leave, amid hugs and tears. He felt emancipated and full of himself. I had to remind him that he was still under his uncle's rules, which were no different than ours. "No problem, Mom, I know his rules. See you in two years." We hugged goodbye and I finally felt that I was doing the right thing. He'd be in good hands, learn a career and have a more understanding male figure in his life. Maybe things would turn around for him while we were gone. I prayed it would be so.

On our last night, Lauri and Denny spent with friends, and Jim and I went to the movies. I let him pick the movie: wrong thing to do! *Airport 77,* told the story about a 747 jetliner loaded down with priceless art, sabotaged in mid-air, and things went downhill from there. The plane began to lose altitude over the North Atlantic and landed on its belly in the ocean. It took most of the two-hour movie for the plane to sink to the bottom of the ocean, while the passengers shrieked and gurgled. My son chuckled nervously, elbowing me to show he wasn't scared.

He laughed.

I ran to the bathroom with diarrhea.

I wrote in my journal before I retired that night:

7/8: Tomorrow we leave for Iran. Lauri and Denny excited to go but sad to leave friends. Chris stays with Uncle Cliff; at nearly 17 he wants no part of the trip, I've come to terms with this. Jim going but with reservations. Will miss everyone, but so excited to see Earl and have a home again, even if it's so far away. I pray all goes well.

1977 – California

5

Up, Up And Away

I stared out the back window of the van until the house was out of sight. It now belonged to someone else. With mixed feelings I said a silent goodbye—to my home, the neighborhood, and life as I knew it. I would look ahead now, not back.

A friend had rented a ten-passenger van to drive us to the airport. The van bulged at the seams with the four of us, and enough luggage for a ten-year stay. *Be prepared* was my motto. Other friends were waiting at the airport cocktail lounge where they pushed drinks toward me until my teeth stopped chattering. I'm not a happy flyer, nor a drinker, so the first drink had me loose-tongued and ready to hit the wild blue yonder. The second found me crying and refusing to leave the country. I hate to fly. It's not natural. If God had meant humans to fly he'd have given us wing flaps. I couldn't get rid of those terrifying scenes from the movie the night before; visions of the 747 jet sinking into the deep, black depths of the ocean occupied every inch of my body, as evidenced by the gurgling and cramping in my lower intestines.

I've never really cared for the taste of alcohol. I'll have a glass of wine at a social gathering if someone hands me one, but I normally end up holding the glass until it's as warm as a Petri dish. I watch people toss drinks down one after another and it amazes me. Why can some people drink until they fall on their keister, while the smile never leaves their face? I get thick-tongued—and diarrhea.

After a couple dashes to the restroom, my friends insisted I have one more drink; it'll help you sleep on the plane, they said. The third round found me happy again as I tried to focus through a blurry fog of Freddy Fudpuckers, ready to take on the world. "Don't cry for me, my friends. I'm off on a wondrous trip around the world," I slurred. "You'll all be jealous when I return with Persian carpets of silk, enough gold trinkets to decorate Times Square, and other treasures from the Middle East."

As we waited for my flight to be called, I began to sober up at the thought of what was ahead of me: Nine hours to Copenhagen with two children and one teenager. My fear of flying had been somewhat reduced while I tossed the drinks down, but now fear began to well up again in my gut. I had to stop this shaking.

My two little ones were engrossed in the TV across from the bar, and Jim had an eye out for the giggling girls who sat nearby. I was grateful they couldn't see their mother crying, laughing, and crying again. Then I heard the boarding call. I immediately sobered up. Oh, no, not yet! I wasn't ready to leave my friends. I wanted to pull them onto the plane with me. Better yet, hide in their van and go home with them. My kids would understand—someday.

We hugged our goodbyes, one by one. When I got to my long-time friend, Gene, he hugged me longer than most and whispered in my ear: "Don't be afraid, Dodie. Remember, if it's not your time, it's not your time."

I held him tight. "Thanks for that, Gene," I whined, "I hadn't thought of it that way."

"But," he added, "It could be the pilot's time."

The plane was packed. "Please take your seats as fast as possible so other passengers can get by." I noticed the seats were squeezed so tight together everyone had a pinched look on their face. If I'd been five pounds heavier I would've hung over into the aisle. The space between my knees and the seat in front of me was nonexistent. This would be a loooong trip. Why wasn't I born rich? I'd noticed the first-class passengers stretched out in rapturous smiles as we filed by. I glared at them. Next life, I told myself.

After everyone had settled in, the cabin was darkened and the movie began. My three were in dreamland and how I envied them. I was bone tired after all the preparation for the trip, and miserable from the alcohol I'd imbibed: sleep had left the building. I'd had one drink too many, and for me that would be one drink. My stomach was painful and distended from the altitude, as well as the alcohol. I decided to take a walk, dispel some wind, and check out the other passengers.

Most of them were already asleep, and that amazed me. Suspended in a metal sphere 35,000 feet above the ground, which at any moment could plummet to earth, I wondered how anyone could sleep. Crashes happened all the time and televised in all their gory details. Didn't anyone read the papers? Where was my Freddy Fudpucker when I needed one? I would have loved to be in that state as well, but I told myself I had to stay awake to help the captain. I was convinced he couldn't fly the plane without my unremitting vigilance. I finally settled down and watched the movie for a while, then dozed off and on over the next few hours. When awake I tried to picture my new home in Esfahan, the friends I'd meet, the trips we'd take to Austria and Spain. Next I tried to visualize all the exotic treasures I'd bring back to the States. Then stopped short: Where would I put them? I had no home. I would not think about this now. I closed my eyes…

When I felt the plane descending, I looked out the window to a most lovely sight. Red roofs and flowers filled the landscape as we set down in Copenhagen. My heart swelled at the beauty. Why couldn't my husband get a job offer here?

I was dog-tired, but the kids had slept through most of the flight. What we had here were two wide-awake kids, one ready-to-party teenager, along with one droopy-eyed mother. A company employee met us at the airport, helped collect our luggage and herded us to his van. We were to spend the night in Copenhagen, then fly to Iran in the morning.

The drive to the hotel was spectacular. Every flower in the aurora borealis hue was present in wild profusion. Baskets of flowers hung from window ledges, balconies and streetlights; a cornucopia of colors: velvety greens, blood reds, luminous golds, sunflower yellows and pinks. The smells that wafted into the van were somewhere between sugary and spicy. Bright red rooftops with colorful flags made me dizzy with the beauty of it all.

Then we stepped into the hotel lobby.

The hotel had a Baroque look, and possibly had not changed since the Baroque era. It was dark, stuffy, and old-worldly. Plain lace curtains covered the open windows, while smells of cigarette and cigar smoke wafted throughout the lobby. Walls that might once have been white were yellowed with years of nicotine-laced smoke. Since I stopped that deadly habit years earlier, I'd become a pain-in-the-arse when around smokers. However, "When in Rome…" Paintings from the Masters lined the walls. Unadorned mahogany desks and rigid Scandinavian-style sofas filled the lobby. I longed for those homey touches such as gift shops, coffee bars and snack machines.

A tottering, elderly gent came forth to usher us to our rooms. He struggled to push our luggage through the narrow, darkened hallways, stopping every few feet to erupt into a thunderous phlegmy cough, then grabbed for his proper white handkerchief to relieve himself of the expectorant. I knew without looking that my kids were about to break out into shrieks of "Yuk!" I gave them the evil eye.

The company had reserved two rooms for us. The boys took the smaller room; Lauri and I took the other. The room was cold and dark as we entered, even with the one window shade open, which was the size of a small mirror. A very small, very hard bed occupied one corner of the room, covered by a beautiful antique quilt. I gently folded and moved the quilt to a very small and very hard armchair tucked away in a corner. What's with these Scandinavian types? I wondered if they'd ever felt soft, comfy furniture.

An ornate blue and white flowered water bowl and pitcher sat on the bureau with two embroidered towels next to it, all placed on a dainty white doily. The bathroom was not for bath taking, and probably should've been called the toilet room, as that was all it held; the bath was down the hall. We were required to sign up for a time to use the bathroom, but I decided a sponge bath would suffice. I certainly didn't want to get in the communal bathtub after some old geezer who may not have had good toilet habits. We're only going to be here overnight, I told the kids. We'll shower when we get to Iran.

I looked longingly at the bed…if I could just sleep for a couple of hours. Lauri sat quietly reading a book while I laid my head on the pillow. As I began to drift off, something hit the wall behind my bed with the force of an explosion—followed by wailing! I recognized the wail—it was Denny. It was not a good decision to put those two in the same room.

Oh please. Not now. I closed my eyes, but the noise escalated. I thought it best to go referee before we were asked to leave the hotel. I could see Denny under the bed as I entered, hands tied with his bathrobe belt, and yelping like a stuck pig. "I had to tie him up Mom," Jim said, "He wouldn't stop bugging me." To protect the rest of the paying guests, I allowed them to leave the hotel room with the proviso that Jim keep Denny in his sight at all times. I worried about the smirk on Jim's face as they left. Would he really try to lose his little brother who drove him nuts? I couldn't worry about it. I knew if someone tried to kidnap Denny they'd bring him back, pronto. Either he'd talk his captors to sleep or question them to death.

After sleeping for an hour and feeling refreshed, Lauri and I set out to meet the boys at the Tivoli Gardens, a short walk from our hotel. We joined them in exploring the city. Copenhagen was a beautiful, quaint city with welcoming people, happy to take our US dollars.

The next morning I was numb. The overwhelming effects of jet lag were in motion. We still had a flight of more than three hours ahead of us to Tehran, then another hour on to Esfahan, plus the wait between flights. I wondered what type of life awaited me. I was ready to relax and spend some quiet time with my husband.

I made a mental note: *No more trips.*

My eyes felt as though sand had replaced all the vitreous humour. I longed for some eye drops and a soft bed in which to collapse. I closed my eyes and the next thing I felt was the plane descending. I said a prayer of thanks to the Gods of Safe Trips, I'd soon be on solid ground. I raised the window shade, expecting to see a colorful patchwork quilt of farmlands or some type of agriculture, but was startled to see nothing but sand—a desolate, arid landscape of sand dunes, mountains of rock, and more sand. *Please, God, don't let my new home be down there.*

The pilot gave us our bearings: we'd flown high over Europe and were now over the southern tip of Turkey. We'd been descending for quite some time and the only color visible was brown; thousands of miles of brown barren desert. Would I ever see green again?

"Hey, look!" someone behind me called out. "There's Mount Ararat and Noah's Ark."

I pushed my nose into the cold glass and peered down. I suppose if I used my vivid imagination I could see something akin to an ark's shape nestled into a mountainside. Poor Noah! How did he feel when he found himself beached high and dry on that barren mountain? And how did all those animals, other than the goats, ever make their way down those craggy slopes?

And who stayed to clean up the ark?

1977 – Tehran, Iran

6

Culture Shock

O ur plane touched down at eight p.m., Tehran time, at Mehrabad
Airport. We were herded to a string of trams that delivered us to
the terminal. I heard no English in our tram, a smattering of French,
some Spanish, and the rest I'd assumed were Iranian or from somewhere
else in the Middle East. As I stepped off the tram I immediately felt
woozy. Still shivering from the plane's freezing interior, I was now
entering a sauna-like terminal. I wondered how long it would take
before I'd feel human again.

We were herded through Customs, where they checked our health
certificates and passports, then sent us to find our luggage and return
to Customs. As we headed for Baggage I searched the faces behind the
ropes for my husband, who was supposed to meet our plane. I didn't

want to think what I'd do if he'd missed that flight. I had no idea how to contact him. The kids clung to me tighter than my pantyhose.

A company van driver walked toward us with a sign: "CROSS PEOPLE" and boy did he have that right. "Dis vay pleez!" he yelled above the frenzy as he led us toward the noisy crowds behind the ropes. My body began to droop. My skin was dry and hot, not a breeze in sight, save for the garlicky breaths of the men screaming around and over my head. Men and women were shouting, laughing, and crying behind the ropes. Something looked familiar about a dark bearded man waving his arms. I thought he was Iranian so I turned away and began to scan the crowd again, and then heard someone call my name. Earl? Ohmygawd! It was him! He looked like all the other men behind the ropes, dark-haired, dark-skinned, bearded and mustachioed. I was never so happy to see this man. Lauri and Denny rushed ahead and jumped into his arms. I was next, but I was used to that. Actually at home our dog usually got the pat on the head before I got the requisite kiss. Earl gave Jim a bear hug, which warmed my heart. Maybe things would work out between the two of them.

After group hugs and kisses we untangled ourselves. It was then I began to look at my surroundings for the first time. To say I wasn't prepared for what I witnessed would be a gross understatement. Men were yelling at each other in what sounded like death threats, and in such menacing loud voices that I felt for sure a fight would break out any minute. I donned my sunglasses to hide behind as I checked out my new environment. Women seemed to be the majority behind the ropes, all the while screaming and crying as they greeted loved ones from incoming flights. Many of the older women were covered head to toe in black robes, called *chadors*. Some had their faces uncovered while others had pulled a tail of the robe across their nose and tucked a corner into their teeth, showing only their dark eyes. Many of the younger women seemed to prefer westernized clothes; suits, dresses, a hint above the knees, very high heels, and bangles of shiny gold bracelets adorning both wrists and halfway up their arms.

I made a mental note: *Buy gold bracelets.*

The majority of the faces of the unrobed young women looked exotic, with seamless creamy skin, jet back hair, bright red lipstick with matching fingernail and toenail polish.

I made another mental note: *Get a pedicure.*

What a huge contrast between those two groups. I wondered why some women were so free and flamboyant in their dress, while others seemed to cover every follicle of hair, neck, arms and legs, even to the thick, dark stockings covering their ankles. As the robed older women spotted their loved ones, I heard shrill, eerie noises coming from their mouths, similar to a barnyard full of turkeys. I looked around in amazement. Where was that noise coming from? It sounded like it came from their throats, like a yodel. I was told later that the noise was called ululation, which indeed came from their throats. By vibrating the tongue and uvula in a rapid motion—and yelling, the noise came out like I said: a barnyard full of turkeys. But only the women seemed to emit that strange noise. The men were busy yelling and embracing each other. I noticed the women kissed each other on both cheeks, while some men kissed each other smack dab on the lips, then the cheeks, then hugged, backed up, and yelled some more.

Earl left to find a porter, while I kept an eye on the carrousel. I thought I'd placed myself at a good advantage point to grab our luggage, but black-robed women swept by me, pushing and pulling as they grabbed for bags, elbowing me aside. WELL, EXCUSE ME! I wanted to shout. I thought it best to wait until my husband returned in case I needed backup. When our luggage did appear, I almost missed the largest one; it looked like it had been thrown under the plane. The case was dented, with one side completely split open along the zipper and held together by a length of twine. I guessed it could have been worse— like missing the twine. Most of our other pieces had obviously been opened, but were securely fastened. Black scuffmarks decorated most of them. I piled them at my feet and waited for Earl. Porters with empty luggage carts passed us with frowns. I had the distinct feeling we were *persona non grata*. By the time we cleared Customs, Earl had rounded up some friendly porters, grabbed the luggage and pushed us toward the exit.

Then we stepped outside.

Debilitating heat and deafening noise greeted us, which made the airport seem like a church nave. Minuscule European cars, old, over-sized American cars, pedestrians, mopeds, trucks and huge buses filled the landscape. Earl pointed to a tiny car as it passed us. At least ten people were scrunched inside, in a vehiclr clearly designed to hold only four. I thanked the Gods of Roomy Cars that we would have a van.

Earl and Jim helped the driver load our luggage, while the kids and I piled in and leaned back against the seat. Finally, I thought, on solid ground.

Then the driver got behind the wheel.

He gunned the engine and ripped away from the curb without even a backward glance. Our heads snapped backward, then forward. I grabbed for my husband and kids and held fast, eyes riveted on the path ahead of us. Four pale, white lines separated the lanes in the street, but I counted five lanes of cars. How did they do that? I looked at our driver. He didn't seem to notice cars speeding toward him. He deftly swerved out of their way, then back into his non-lane again. The absurdity here was the driver, who was in the "non" lane, had the *huevos* to honk at the car in the correct lane. Amazing!

Drivers honked, swerved and braked in a well-choreographed dance while autos, mopeds and pedestrians all moved together as in one group. Our driver never flinched as he averted a dozen collisions in less than a mile. No one seemed to notice the danger except my nervous little intestines. "Pedestrians have no right-of-way," Earl said, as our driver deftly missed an old lady who'd stepped into his path. "The drivers just dodge the people, cars, and bikes while they honk their horns and swerve."

Their apathy mesmerized me. We saw several accidents that clogged the street along our route. Our driver grumbled then found an opening to squeeze through. I noted that onlookers would gather around the fender-benders and add their yelling to the mix, then walk away chatting amiably to one another. Much later I heard the statistic that Iran had the highest rate of traffic accidents and fatalities on earth. Wish I'd known that sooner; I might have stayed in Copenhagen.

As we drove into the main area of the city, the traffic slowed, then we came to a complete stop. I watched as lines of men crossed the street in front of us, seemingly in a hurry to go somewhere. I wondered what was going on.

Then we turned the corner.

A theater marquee, standing at least ten feet high, pictured a female strapped to a pillar wearing a submissive look. She was wearing black fishnet stockings, garter belt, stiletto heels, black panties barely there, and black bra with cleavage pouring forth. Lined up on the sidewalk and spilling over into the streets were throngs of men waiting to enter the theater. The dichotomy of this scene was amazing: women walking by the theater, and on both sides of the street, covered from head to toe in the traditional black *chador*, eyes, nose and mouth the only indication they were female. Earl explained what he'd heard from his Iranian friend, Rallfe: devout Muslim women must hide every strand of hair and femininity to insure that they do not cause a man to have "unholy thoughts." I noticed there were no women in line for the show; only men and young boys. Odd, I thought. The women can't show any skin or hair, yet the men line up to watch a half-naked porn star. Incredible!

In the downtown area of Tehran were large groups of people walking on the sidewalks, in the streets, and milling about. I noticed that some men were holding hands or arm-in-arm, something we would never see in the States. I liked the idea that these men could show their affection for each other. Women do it, why can't men? Most of the young girls were hand-in-hand. I later learned that because young men cannot be intimate with a woman until they are married, and in fact, cannot even be alone with a woman until marriage, there was blatant homosexuality afoot.

With all the traffic and people on the street, it seemed like the middle of the day, but I knew it had to be near midnight. Cars, as if ready for a parade, were festooned with rows of small, multicolored lights strung around the top; gold tassels swung in car windows, while some were painted in crazy patterns of reds, greens and yellows. Many were crammed with bodies, some actually hanging out the windows, all swerving past us with lights blinking and horns honking. The noise alone was a culture shock for me. My nerves were on red-alert. The kids covered their ears. I could feel my spastic colon getting spastic again. Earl put his arm around me and promised I'd be okay. "They all drive like this, so they know how to miss each other."

Somehow that was not reassuring.

The company van, thankfully, had an air conditioner, but did little to camouflage the driver's overripe body odor as it blew back in our faces. My little ones were now holding their noses *and* ears. Their father put an end to that with one look.

I really never expected to live to see the dawn. Our driver had one thought on his mind: get the nose of his car into the first opening, never mind that the rest of the car didn't fit. He even scraped a few fenders, but no one stopped. They yelled out the window and drove on. *Who pays for these fender repairs?* In the States we'd be out of our car in a New York minute, with pencil and paper, and dollar signs in our eyes.

What was amazing to me was that most of the cars were midget cars, but still were filled to over-capacity, and then some. Many Peykans, the most expensive of the "midget" cars, could be seen around town, dented, fenders missing, and filled to over-capacity. Bearing down on those tiny cars were humongous busses and monstrous trucks. I wouldn't have been surprised to see a couple of those tiny cars being hauled along by a bus or truck's under-carriage. Later on in my stay, I did see several bicycles being dragged along on the bus's undercarriage as sparks flew behind the bus like a great fireworks display.

At one intersection we were rocketed forward and then slammed backward as the driver sat on his brakes, called a curse down on his fellow drivers and their ancestors, and sped off again. I looked at my daughter to see if she was ready to bail out. "Are you okay, honey?"

She was fixated on the road with a terrified expression. "No."

Thankfully, it wasn't a long drive to our destination. Earl had reserved the company condo for overnight guests. When I entered, the first thing I saw was a welcoming bed and knew I'd be face down in a matter of minutes. But after my shower I felt somewhat revitalized, so when the kids headed for bed, Earl served me a cocktail, along with some heavy breathing. I began to feel I just might live. After a shower, I fell into a deep sleep and dreamed women in black robes were yelling at me, chasing me while trying to cover me. They cut off my hair and put a black wig on my head, while screaming at me to become one of them. I woke up sobbing. Earl said he heard me yell: "Never! Never!"

The next morning we boarded the flight for our final destination— Esfahan—where I would set up housekeeping for my family for two years.

Esfahan airport was like Tehran airport: confusion reigned, only on a smaller scale. *Chador*-clad women outnumbered the western-clothed here. The affluent Iranian women I'd seen in Tehran, gold-bedecked and well coifed, were in smaller numbers in Esfahan. Travelers coming and going, hugging, yelling and kissing were in abundance. I had to admit as I watched this frenetic display; it certainly made the traveler feel welcome. In the States I believe most Americans worry more about appearances than letting our true feelings flow. But obviously these people were happy to see each other and didn't give two *rials* what anyone thought.

Finally the conveyor belched into action and the luggage began to roll out. Lauri and I thought we'd picked a good spot to grab our bags, when several black-robed women converged on us at the same time, as if we weren't even there. I lost my footing and had to back up. Now I was ticked. When they'd finally retrieved their luggage and moved away I stepped in, determined to hold my ground: *Come-on, sisters, make my day!* Something familiar caught my eye as it rolled and bumped along the opposite side of the conveyor. I watched it make the turn then realized what it was: My suitcase! But now it sported lengths of brown tape wrapped securely around all sides, which hadn't been there at the Tehran airport. I also saw a patch of pink as it rolled on. Fiery heat rose to my face as I heard my son yell: "Mom, your bra's hangin' out."

Two hot-pink size 36D-cups connected by straps were protruding from the torn zipper. Two men next to Denny stood transfixed as they stared at the bra. "Grab it!" I yelled to Denny, who took a step back as if it was a 220-volt live wire. Earl, back with a cart and porter, reached over Denny, grabbed the suitcase, tucked the bra back in and handed the suitcase to the porter. "Let's go," he yelled to Denny. "A bra never hurt anyone," he said with a laugh.

"Yeah, lame-brain," Jim added, "are you afraid of a bra?"

I'd noticed a few women staring at the case as it made it's way around. How embarrassing. Pink! Why not the white one? They probably think I'm a prostitute. On further inspection we found all our luggage had been searched, but only my zipper had been cut open. "Don't worry about it," Earl said. "This is probably what they do to all foreigners' luggage. A sort of rough and tumble Customs."

Air conditioning was nonexistent in the scorching, noisy airport, which reeked of sweat and other unpleasant odors. I spotted my two youngest holding their nose again as they walked along. I poked them. "Stop that! We're in a foreign country. We're their guests. Don't be an Ugly American." But, I did have to agree with them, it was unpleasant.

As I looked around the airport I saw men holding what looked like rosary beads. *Catholics, here?* But they couldn't be saying the rosary that fast. They seemed to be sliding the beads through their fingers, over and over. I later learned the beads were called *Tizbahs,* originally known as prayer beads. But they were now called Worry Beads, used in place of biting nails, or tapping fingers. In other words—stress relievers. This seemed to be a stress-reliever for men only, as I never saw a woman with beads in her hands. Maybe because she was so busy shopping, cooking, cleaning, washing, ...well, you get the picture.

According to the guidebook I'd read in the States, Esfahan was a revered city, the most visited by tourists, and the best place to live for foreigners. After reading that I'd felt a little better about the move. But as we drove through the rubble on the outskirts of the city, I wondered if the Esfahan Chamber of Commerce had written that book. The locale had fallen victim to neglect.

The company van driver seemed delighted to give us a tour and tell us about his city. No one in the car understood him, but he made a valiant effort. He spoke a smattering of English as he proudly pointed out various landmarks along the route, but that's where the education ended. I appreciated that he tried. Having memorized a few Farsi words before I left the States, I did understand about five words out of every twenty. But he spoke in sentences—and I only understood single words. I'd smile and say *khayli mamnoon*—thank you very much. He'd smile back, say "Velcome" then start all over again.

As we drove through town I was surprised to see all the brilliant flowers adorning the windows and shops, especially after the fields of sand I'd seen from the plane window. The dichotomy between the rubble-strewn streets and the variety of colorful flowers was remarkable. The red rose, Iran's national flower, was well represented, along with an array of colorful tulips and poppies. In every shop window a large picture of the Shah and Queen Farah was displayed. The Shah's portrait was impressive. He was quite handsome in his colorful uniform, festooned with rows of multicolored ribbons, while Queen Farah stood regal and beautiful beside him. I'd read she was a role model for the young girls; a sort of Iranian Jackie O.

Earl was eager to show me a famous Esfahan site, the *Naqshe Jahan* Square in the center of town, which was said to be the largest city square in the world. He also pointed out the city's most famous bridge, *Sio-se-Pol*, over the *Zayandeh* River in town, also known as the bridge of thirty-three arches. The bridge is nearly 1,000 feet long and 45 feet wide. Earl pointed out the impressive *Ali Mosque* and *Ali Minarets* that stood noble as they towered above the immense square, and had been standing guard over the city since the twelfth century; an outstanding example of historic Iranian and Islamic architecture. The tiny mosaic tiles gleamed golden as the sun caught their splendor, with flashes of turquoise, azure, greens and golds.

The city streets brought me back to earth as our driver drove on. Esfahan had been the capital of Iran at one time, but in the intervening years the city had been ignored and seemed to be falling in on itself. The population in the '70s was over a million, and the streets showed the scars from huge trucks, buses and cars with potholes, and crumbling roads.

Throughout the city, unfinished buildings with broken windows stood like old soldiers with missing teeth, while detritus of building material lay helter-skelter around the sites. Bricks, rocks and odd lengths of lumber were strewn about the landscape. Scaffolds stood as silent sentinels to work that might someday be completed. Lean-to shacks stood next to five-story apartment buildings. Old men and young boys swept the streets, but seemed to have no definite plan where the dirt and sand should go. Some left the pile of dirt and walked to another area and began to sweep. The brooms were constructed of a wad of straw, tied with string to a long wood pole. The straw at the end of the broom went in ten different directions as they swept, and missed most of what it came in contact with. Esfahan was a city with an incredible past, but the future looked bleak.

Construction work seemed to be going on everywhere. Five or six men stood idly by, leaning on their shovels as they chatted, while one or two men would be hard at work right next to them. I thought maybe this was the Iranian version of a coffee break. Earl didn't think so. He said in the six months he'd been there, nothing had changed on any of the construction sites. The buildings sat as skeletons; a promise of what was to come—that never came.

Cars, buses, trucks, motorcycles and bicycles sped noisily past as we drove into the main part of town. Most of the buses were in need of a good wash, and looked patched together with rope and tape. As in Tehran, they were also decorated with wild paint jobs of red, green, blue and yellow, while some had multicolored strings of lights strung from one end to the other.

This was truly a city of contrasts: Along the city streets, minarets gleamed under the dusty sunlight, while smartly dressed cosmopolitan women in suits and high heels stepped around curbside beggars as if they didn't exist. Everyone was in a hurry to get somewhere. Huge trucks, overloaded and listing to one side, wove in and out between oxcarts and crammed buses. In and out of this circus, Jaguars and Mercedes vied for room with sheep and their shepherd. Pedestrians, who seemed to have a death wish, stepped off curbs in front of oncoming cars, seemingly oblivious to the imminent danger. Traffic signals that worked sporadically didn't help with the chaos, and most times they were just ignored. I knew right then I would never drive in that crazy traffic.

Then I met the girl who would. Her name was Trudy* and we were to become great friends. She hailed from the Midwest and had the twang to prove it.

Our driver pulled to the curb and stopped in front of a gas station. I thought he was going to gas up. "This is it, Babe," Earl said, "Home sweet home."

"The gas station?"

"No, the apartment, next door."

I was a tad relieved, although the curb appeal left something to be desired. As we exited the van I could smell diesel fumes and my stomach did a quick turnover. The noise was unbelievable. Besides the clamor and fumes from the traffic on the street, the air around the gas station was filled with fumes from idling cars. Along with this, there was the constant beeping of horns while men shouted as if that would help move things along. I could see six pumps with barricades around two of them. Cars were lined up behind each other, snaking out the driveway and more idling at the curb waiting to get in. No one turned off his car's engine. No wonder I felt dizzy.

"Here comes Trudy," Earl said. I looked up and saw this petite, cheer-leader-type coming toward me with open arms. She immediately knew the look on my face was abject fear. "Hey girl, this ain't bad. Just be glad we don't have to drive in Tehran."

Earl introduced us as she made the rounds with hugs. "No thanks, Trudy, I'll never get behind a wheel in this crazy traffic."

"Oh, hell, girl, you'll change your mind once you get used to this place."

"I don't think I'll live that long."

"Hon, I'll drive us around so don't worry. Be right back," and with that she took off into the street. I couldn't believe it. I covered my eyes, and waited for the imminent crash. I heard the squeal of tires and men yelling oaths. I peeked through my fingers and watched as she blithely sidestepped around the oncoming cars. With her purse under her armpit, and her other arm in the air, she reminded me of a wide receiver racing for a touchdown. Trudy's husband, Cleve*, had joined us on the curb. "She's gonna' pick up some more liquor to celebrate you folks finally getting here."

"My God, I hope she doesn't get killed on my account."

"Nah, she does this all the time. I think she keeps track of how many times she side-steps death."

"Mom?" Denny whispered, "Does dad drive in this stuff or does he have a driver?"

"Not always," Earl said. "The company only gives us a driver for a few days when the family arrives. After that we're on our own."

"Our own?" I hadn't thought to ask how we'd get around.

"I told you about it in one of my letters. Steve and I bought a Jeep from a guy on the job. We're getting it next week. You can ride with Trudy to shop and go to the Clubhouse. She has no problem driving all over town."

Heaven help me if she drives like she crosses the street!

"Ah...I think I'll wait until you come home from work and you can take me," I whispered.

"Don't be silly. She's a good driver."

"But what if we get hit? Or hurt? Who's going to drive us to the hospital? Who do we call?"

"Why do you always worry about the worst scenario? I've been here six months and haven't heard of anyone from our job having an accident. Oh, which reminds me, I might get a Volkswagen from one of the guys on the job when he leaves, so you can use it for grocery shopping if Trudy's busy."

I knew I wouldn't drive. I'd be terrified in this traffic. "No thanks, VW bugs are like tin cans waiting to be crushed. I'll take a taxi if I need one. But, why do we need two cars?" I had hoped we'd have zero cars. I really didn't want to be the passenger in a car driven by my neighbor, or Earl for that matter; he didn't come from the "Kill or be Killed" school of driving, but I was sure Trudy did.

"Mom," Jim said with a condescending tone, "I can take you shopping when I get home from work. I plan to drive here."

"I don't think so," Earl said, "the kind of work you'll be doing, you'll want to come home, shower, and drop into bed."

"Dad, I'm not as old as you, I doubt that a day's work will send me to bed."

Earl smiled, "We'll see."

"I don't want anyone in my family driving in this chaos."

Earl sighed. He knew when I got freaked-out about something it took a lot of talking to un-freak me. "The Jeep's only ours part-time,

Cleve and I share it, and we can use it for trips into the country. The VW will be easier to drive in town, plus in the rainy season we'll need a top over our heads. But, believe me, I'm sure you'll find even my driving is safer than taking a taxi."

We'd been standing by the curb in the heat for too long, and I was suddenly hit with a wave of nausea. "I think we better go inside, I feel sort of dizzy."

Earl took my hand. "Okay, come on, I want you to see your new home."

As we walked toward the apartment, I was struck with the gas station scenario: When we left the States there were long gas lines, and here they were again, only here Earl said we'd be paying 80 cents a gallon instead of the 62 cents we paid in the States. I wondered what the price of gas would be when we returned home. I also wondered if I'd live to see that day, as I was sure carbon monoxide fumes would finish me off. I was hit by another wave of nausea. "Okay, lets get inside!"

I made a mental note: *Find a gas mask.*

1977 – Esfahan, Iran

7

New Home & New Friends

Earl led us up the stairs and opened the door. When I stepped in, the fumes hit me instantly. I stopped. "Why does it smell like gas in here?"

"Probably because it's been shut up for a couple days. It'll be gone once we open some windows."

I could see he was excited to show us the house, so I accepted his answer. But, I would check this fume-thing out later.

The kids followed us in. "Cool, Dad," I heard Denny say. "Yeah, Mom," Lauri chimed in. "Dad decorated it so cool."

I knew Earl would buy a few things for the apartment, but was shocked he'd made the place look so homey. It was more than I'd hoped for. The front room had a three-cushion sofa, two arm chairs and a coffee table, all sitting on the beautiful *Esfahani* carpet Earl had purchased. I flopped down on the sofa to give it a comfort test, and felt my spine shorten a few inches. The sofa didn't give an inch; it was akin to sitting on a church pew. The fabric on the sofa and chairs felt like horsehair, with the nap running the wrong way.

I made a mental note: *Don't sit on sofa or chairs with bare legs.*

Taped on the wall was a huge banner that read: WELCOME HOME TO MY LOVES !!

I began to look around. The apartment was small, maybe about a thousand square feet, less than half the size of our home in the States. I knew I had to make this work for Earl's sake, so I oohed and aahed as we walked through the apartment. There were three bedrooms; the largest we took as ours, Jim and Denny would share a smaller one, and Lauri's was the smallest—about the size of large walk-in closet. The kids and I took turns bouncing on the beds, and deemed the mattresses part concrete, part iron. Jim balked at the thought of having his pain-in-the-arse brother in the same bedroom with him. "Sorry, kids," Earl said, "It's all I could find that had three bedrooms. Otherwise, we'd all be sleeping in the same room."

We continued down the hall. Only one bathroom? This was insane. What would happen on work and school days when they'd all need to use the bathroom at the same time? I had visions of the gas station lines in front of the bathroom; down the hall, out the door and down the block. Our house in the States had two-and-a-half bathrooms, and we still had pileups and yelling: "…what's taking so long," and "put the magazine down," and "MOM!"

The bathroom looked to be about four by four, with a Western toilet, a shower, sink, and two feet of counter space. What more could a woman want?

Earl continued to play tour guide with the kids while I stopped in the kitchen to take a closer look. I could foresee a huge problem here. How was I going to prepare a meal for five people in this one-butt kitchen? Against a window was a bedpan-size sink with a two-foot countertop. The stove sported three small burners, which when lit gave off the heat of three votive candles. The oven would probably hold a meat loaf pan or two, but not much more. A small wood table with four small chairs completed the ensemble. In the corner sat a small washer and dryer, and I said a big *Halleluiah!* to that. I didn't know yet if Esfahan had a Laundromat, but I wasn't about to drive in that traffic to do the laundry. I'd scrub the clothes in the shower before I'd drive those streets.

When I joined the tour, I offered up a happy face for my husband. The kids watched me for signs of weakness. Would I say: "No, this won't do," or would I be a gracious mother and wife and say: "This is wonderful." The jury was still out. At least the place did have a television set, and best of all, air-conditioning, thank you AC Gods, or I would've been on the next plane home. My body's climate-control has always been genetically compromised, which left me in a state of heat exhaustion when temperatures reached 90 degrees. Southern California in July: 90 and breezy. Esfahan in July: 120 and sweltering. The only redeeming factor was that the air was dry instead of humid.

Thoughts of the gas station below played games with my head as we walked through the house. Did I smell diesel fumes? Could they actually be entering our apartment? Nah! Again, my Virgo imagination. I couldn't start bitching about things when my husband had taken such pains to make this place look homey. I'd have to find something to dispel that odor.

I made a mental note: *Get room fresheners.*

When Earl suggested we take a quick trip to the company Clubhouse to meet some of his friends, I asked them to wait while I made myself presentable. I couldn't meet anyone looking like an unmade bed. The shower was phone-booth size, but the water pressure was good and I was a happy camper. After cleaning up I felt better and was ready to take on the world. Earl told me when I finally appeared, what a revelation my son had experienced. Denny had flopped on the couch ready to watch the television, which was of an earlier era and resembled the first one Earl's parents bought in the 1950s. Denny looked puzzled. "What kind of TV is this, Dad? Where's the remote?"

"Sorry, son, no such niceties here. You'll have to get up and do it the old fashioned way."

"How's that?"

It dawned on Earl we'd had remotes since Denny was born. He had no idea you could go up to a TV and change the channel. "Just turn that dial on the front and it changes channels."

"You mean I gotta get up and do it?"

"Yep."

He walked to the TV and began turning the dial. "Dad, what channels do you get here? All these are fuzzy."

Earl said it was quite traumatic for my young son to learn there were no cartoons, no *I Spy, Wild West, Happy Days* or *Brady Bunch*. The English-speaking channel was NIRT (National Iranian) and offered such enlightening programs as: *My Little Margie*, *Rawhide*, and *I Love Lucy*. Earl said whenever any negative news began about Iran or the Shah, the stations, all government-run, went to black.

How democratic! "You mean if there's an uprising or something bad, we'll never hear about it on the TV?"

Earl laughed. "Welcome to Iran!"

The Club was more than I'd hoped for. As we walked through the gates I saw a large pool, a snack shack, a tennis court and a large clubhouse. I immediately cheered up. *This isn't going to be too bad.* Once inside, Jim spotted an assortment of kids and we lost him to a group of teens gathered by the jukebox. Lauri and Denny, already in their swimsuits, headed for the pool. Trudy was already in the water, beer in one hand and cigarette in the other. She introduced Lauri and Denny around. Most of the kids would be going to the same school in August. I was grateful they'd found friends their age.

The ache in my gut now had my full attention. I reasoned it had to be hunger since I'd last eaten on the plane. Earl had offered me some snacks at the apartment, but still nauseated from the diesel fumes I declined. However, the smell of food as we entered the Club was slowly eroding my resolve.

Earl introduced me to the Iranian gentleman who ran the snack shack. I couldn't tell his age due to his rugged face; dark and scarred like he'd tangled with a wolverine. He looked at least 80. Earl whispered that he was in his 50s, but had led a very hard life. He was spry with a smile that could have used a few more teeth. His pants were dusty and shabby, and held up with twine as suspenders. He wore an off-white dress shirt, covered by a dark sweater vest, and capped off with a dusty black wool jacket. I couldn't imagine why anyone would wear a vest *and* a wool jacket in this heat. Earl explained the reigning theory of climate control with workers: the more clothes you pile on, the more you sweat. The more you sweat, the wetter you become. So when a breeze hits that sweat, you're immediately cooled off.

I made a mental note: *Don't get too close to men in suits on hot, breezy days.*

I warmed to this little man immediately. He was friendly, happy, and it was obvious he loved his work. He took great pains to let everyone know he was the best cook in the country. Sadly, his options were greatly hindered by his inventory of only hotdogs and hamburger meat. His name was Mansoor, which he proudly told me meant he was protected by God. Earl told us to use the term *"Agha"* to address an adult man; a respectful way of saying "Sir." But he also felt we should use the person's name if we knew it. Obviously Mansoor appreciated Earl's manners, as whenever Earl approached, Mansoor would call out: "Aloo Meezter Crot, what you haf today? No problem, I get."

Earl and I shared one of his "best" hamburgers and fries, then found two chairs by the pool. Okay, I thought, as I leaned back and took in the whole vista, this will work out: a pool for the kids, a place to call home, and my husband nearby for the next two years.

Then I vomited.

I had no warning. I didn't realize I was going to do it until I did it. I wanted to die. Earl's face turned white as he watched me lose my lunch all over the pool patio. People jumped out of the way, Earl ran to find something to clean up the mess, and I jumped up and ran to the pool restroom. I could hear Earl asking for paper towels and water. After I'd sponged off and joined Earl again, I felt weak and shaky. I was in dire need of air-conditioning. My face turned as red as a baboon's arse and my head was spinning. My preference would have been to fall face-first into the pool, but I'd already made a spectacle of myself. I didn't think it wise to do this fully dressed, and also take the chance of polluting the pool.

Earl led me into the air-conditioned bar where I flopped down on a chair and put my red face between my knees. After a bottle of water I began to cool down enough to check out my surroundings. A dance floor took up the center of this cool, dark bar, with tables and chairs around it. A jukebox sat in one corner playing a country-western tune. An Iranian bartender and waiter were busy behind the bar.

"Hey, bring her over here," shouted a male voice. After my eyes adapted to the darkness I could see a group of people sitting at tables across the room and waving. "We didn't believe you even existed," one of the women said to me as we approached. "We thought Earl had invented y'all so's we'd feel sorry for him and invite him to dinner." This was Ronnie, and her husband, Bobby*, long-time expats who'd worked all over the world. Months would pass before I could remember which one was Bobby and which one was Ronnie. They hailed from Texas and were proud of it. Bobby did the spittoon thing, which I thought disgusting, while Ronnie sat around and looked beautiful. They were in their 40s, as we were, and we became fast friends; cards, parties and gossiping. There is a real need to bond with other expats when overseas, especially if you want to learn the ropes. I did.

We joined the group and before long I returned to a neutral color and felt I might live a few more hours. Earl introduced me around the group: Ben* and Brenda* looked like Barbie and Ken. She was model-beautiful, with a full figure men seemed to gape at whenever she walked through a room. Ben, tall, ruggedly handsome, enjoyed watching men gape at his wife. They'd been expats for over ten years. Without children, there was just the two of them to dote on each other, and dote they did. Then there was loveable Harry* and Sally*, salt of the earth types, except when Harry played Cribbage, then he turned into a competitive dervish.

I felt an immediate kinship with all of them. They'd all been through this expat thing many times. A couple of the men had been on overseas assignments for over twenty years. The women gathered round to give me tips on everything from shopping to shoplifters. I drank it all in while I enjoyed a warm, fuzzy feeling, obviously helped along by the gin and tonic one of the guys had handed me. What a great place this would be; a fun place to live for a couple years. I could now relax.

That is until I unconsciously reached into a bowl of peanuts on the table, threw back my head and tossed in a few. That's usually what I do. Hunger really has nothing to do with it. You put something edible in front of me and I go for it. It took less than twenty seconds for the peanuts to hit bottom and soar back up—very un-peanut looking. I wanted to die as the women quick-stepped away from me. A couple of them came forward and led me to the restroom. One stayed behind to clean up. I wanted to evaporate right there on the spot. "Hon, don't you worry none," Ronnie said (or was it Bobby), "you ain't the first one to lose your cookies in this country, and you won't be the last."

They explained the honeymoon phase for newbies: drink only liquids for a few days, and get used to the altitude and climate before you start gulping food. "Go home, take a nap, get over the jet lag and come back. We'll throw y'all a welcome back party."

I always wondered why some people used the term "y'all" when they were talking about one person. But in time I picked it up, and "y'all" became one of my favorite words. Or was it two words?

The sleep idea sounded good to me. As Earl led me out of the bar I could see my kids weren't going through a honeymoon phase. Lauri was racing a girl to the end of the pool, while Denny sat on the edge of the pool scarfing down another hamburger. Earl asked Jim to keep an eye on his sibs while he took me back to the apartment.

Two hours and one long nightmare later, I awoke to an empty apartment. I panicked. I'd been dreaming of cars, millions of cars, all racing around me while I choked on their exhaust. *Where the hell am I? And why do I smell gas fumes? Am I still in the middle of those cars?* I walked to the kitchen window and looked down on my nemesis: dozens of cars, motors running, were still lined up at the pumps.

Denny came running in while I was dressing. "Mom, you gotta come back," he yelled through the door, *Anna and the King* is gonna start in a few minutes. And next week they're showing *MASH*. This is a cool place."

Earl suggested I try the Club again: no food, just some bottled water and we'd relax and watch the movie. It was daytime in the States by now, and it was 10 p.m. in Iran. I had to get my body to catch up with the clock. Some part of me was happy that my kids weren't as miserable as me, but not every part. I hated to be the only wimp in the crowd.

The movie screen was set up on the grass, a little smaller than a drive-in theater screen. The speakers resonated loud and clear, but unfortunately because the screen sat on the ground, it was difficult seeing over peoples' heads. While Yul Brenner swung Deborah Kerr around the palace floor, I forgot about my stomach problems and was totally into the dance. Until, that is, I got a whiff of food from the snack shack and had to rush to the restroom again, but thankfully, I made it in time.

Hey! I was getting better!

I made a mental note: *Keep barf bags in purse.*

Because the men had to work on the fourth of July, the Club would hold the celebration on the 11th, the day after I'd arrived. I was still feeling puny, but could not disappoint my family. When we arrived games were going on in every corner of the Club. Tug-of-War between the fathers and sons was the favorite, with a huge muddy hole between them. Denny joined in late so they put him in the front. After being pulled into the mud hole he ran over to us to declare the game unfair: "Those guys were older and bigger than me and they stuck me in front."

Earl's reply: "Suck it up son."

Later in the day, Denny introduced me to his new friend, Reza, the son of the Iranian bartender. "Mom, I'll be right back, he wants to show me something." Denny followed his new friend to the back of the Club where two donkeys were tethered. Then he promptly ran back to give me the facts. I was sitting with a group of ladies, and was about to ask him if he needed some dry clothes when he blurted out: "Mom, you gotta come see this donkey's dong.

"*See what?*" I choked, not really believing what I'd just heard.

"A donkey's dong, mom, it swung back and forth, almost in the mud. You should'a seen it. It's humongous!"

The ladies around me immediately became busy with other topics, but I noticed grins as they tried to stifle their laughs. "He's a kid after my own heart," Ronnie piped in, "ya'll calls 'em as ya sees 'em." She threw her head back and cackled.

"Okay, honey, let's talk about this when we get home, it's not really a subject that should be discussed here."

"Why not?" He stood there waiting for an explanation that I wasn't sure how to give. "Well, first of all, it's not the proper name and..."

"That's what my friend called it," he interrupted in his outdoor voice, "and he should know, he's Iranian and they're Iranian donkeys."

Now, this kid hangs on details. I knew I didn't have a chance to stop him, so I stood up, reached for his arm and walked him away from the group. "No more about this. Do you hear?"

"Okay, okay. Jeez, what's wrong with a donkey's dong, anyway?"

A lavish barbeque was prepared using local lamb—kabob—and all the wonderful trimmings the women had brought from home. The day seemed no different than we would have celebrated at home on the 4th, and I found it hard to believe I was not in the States, but in a foreign country thousands of miles away.

Until the helicopters flew over.

Three of them were flying in formation, and each carried a long, heavily laden bag hanging from the struts. Earl told me later what he'd been told by the Iranians at the Club: that this was Iran's method of dealing with rapists. That three men had gang-raped a young girl. They were caught, shot, and their bodies were bagged and flown around the city as a warning for rapists. A fitting punishment, I thought. I wondered why the U.S. didn't use that type of instant justice. I know, I know, we are supposed to be a civilized country, but…it would be a great deterrent to rape—and save the courts and taxpayers money.

Before the fireworks started, the American flag was raised and we were led in the "Pledge of Allegiance," followed by our booming voices of "God Bless America." There wasn't a dry eye in the crowd of expats.

The fireworks show began at dusk. And what a show! The company had purchased the fireworks from China, which were magnificent and the most amazing show of fireworks I'd ever seen. Gigantic, flaming rockets ascended into the black sky, one, two and sometimes three or more at once. Each one mushroomed into a giant pattern, illuminating the sky for miles. The show went on for over an hour, while the fireworks continued to get larger with each blast. The Grand Finale was indescribable, as well as terrifying. There seemed enough firepower to blow up the country. It was a great day, and a sad one as my thoughts went back to the U.S. and our annual 4th of July picnics with friends. I wondered if they were missing me.

I made a mental note: *Write friends tomorrow.*

1977 - Esfahan

8

The Incredible Esfahan Bazaar

P romise me you'll wait to see the bazaar until my day off," Earl said. He was excited to show us this incredible place. "I want to see your reactions." He'd tried to describe the Esfahan Bazaar in some of his letters, but I had no idea what awaited me.

The following Friday we set off on our big adventure. Approaching the square, I was astonished at the site of the enormous Esfahan Bazaar. I couldn't take it all in. It was amazing. I could see some of the merchants had their wares lined up around the outside walls of the great edifice. Quite clever of these men, I thought: no overhead, and they could make a sale before the merchants inside had a chance to corral the tourists. On the ground and against the walls were hand-blown glass vases, bowls and platters, while copper and brass pots gleamed in the bright sun. Exotic-smelling spices and scents called to me: saffron, mint, tarragon, basil, cilantro, turmeric, and other spices I could not identify. Eagerly, I reached for my purse. "Hold off," Earl said, "wait until we get inside and see everything. There are over six hundred shops inside."

That got my attention. He herded us along.

Then we stepped inside.

Noise, odors and treasures! Oh, what a glorious, exciting place. Eardrum-piercing Persian and American music blared forth from every nook and cranny as it joined radios, tape decks, and the worst offenders of all, loud speakers affixed to the earthen walls. All came together in one huge reverberation. When I concentrated hard enough I could make out Neil Diamond, the Beatles and even some Rod Stewart, while Googoosh, Iran's most famous female singer in the 70s, wailed her disco sounds in the background. On every table—and on the dirt floor—some sort of player was present. All this music was mingled with a multitude of babbling voices as women in *chador*s, hell bent to get the freshest produce, shouted and shoved against each other, while merchants or *bazaaris* yelled out their prices.

Most of the *bazaaris*, men of all shapes, sizes, and colors, wore raggedy jackets with baggy pants that could have doubled for pajama bottoms. Some wore wool hats and suit jackets—and this was July, the hottest part of the summer. I later learned that most Iranian men wear these PJ-type pants under there street pants. Always ready must be their motto.

The bazaar was a cacophony of sounds with braying donkeys, bleating goats and ugly baaing sheep with fat, flat tails, clucking chickens, along with snot-nosed, howling kids—all underfoot and running wild. Pistachio nutshells lined the earthen floor as the *bazaaris* and the locals spit them out freely. I was enthralled!

The air was at once fetid and pungent, sour, and then disgusting. At times the odors were overpowering with meat that should have been tossed a week earlier, along with rotting fruit and rancid oils. Added to this assault was the rank smell of urine; stale and fresh, as some men chose to relieve themselves against any wall close enough. The biggest assault was from the occasional smell of animal excrement, as donkeys, sheep and goats deposited their offerings randomly throughout the maze. And, body odor inundated the bazaar, facilitated by the extreme dry heat outside, the humid air inside, and the mass of humanity.

Denny was intrigued by the animals that roamed freely, while Lauri hung next to her father, terrified of the leering men. Earl laughed at her, "Honey, these men will only keep you prisoner until they find a younger wife."

She didn't think it was funny. "Mom, it smells in here."

"Well of course it smells," Earl said, "look at all the animals running around in here. It's like a zoo."

"No," Lauri said, "I mean, B.O. smell."

Denny piped in: "It's not B.O., Dad, it's donkey poop. I just saw a man step in some and he just kept walking."

Earl became weary. He'd been excited to show his kids the bazaar and all they'd done was worry and complain. "Hey! This is a cultural lesson for you two. Some of these people have traveled miles to trade here. Forget about smells. Try to learn something from it. This is how they traded long before there were any stores. They'd carry all this stuff you see in here on their caravans and head out over the desert to trade with other countries."

"No way, Dad," Denny said. "You mean they'd carry all this stuff on camels through the desert?"

"Yep. The same way Marco Polo got around."

"Marco Polo? I thought that was a pool game."

I made a mental note: *Get son a history book.*

The bazaar was shaped like a huge honeycomb, a vast labyrinth of paths leading in all directions. Dark, unending lanes wound off to even darker places; dimly lit cubbyholes scooped out of rock and earthen walls. Every few feet a lone light bulb hung from a cord, while cracks in the dome let in beams of sunlight here and there. You could find everything from expensive art to spices, or vegetables—locally grown to imported. Some bazaaris seemed to have an eclectic sense of inventory: plastic books, silk brocade, silver tea sets, hand stitched lace, silks, cottons, bowls, tea glasses, shoes, boots, sneakers and music tapes. As we pushed and shoved our way along, I kept a firm grip on Lauri's hand, while Denny, begrudgingly, let Earl hold his. I noticed some of the men looking at me with disapproval. Did I imagine it? This ticked me off because I'd made a point of dressing modestly—a long blouse over jeans—yet I could feel them undress me with their eyes. They made no secret of it. I told Earl to get in their faces.

"Really, Dodie? Are you serious? We're foreigners here, this is their country and I'm not gonna start an International incident because some old geezer finds you nice to look at."

"It's more than just looking at me," I said. "They're gawking right at my breasts."

"Can't blame 'em."

"The next time we come, I'm wearing a long Levi jacket. Let's see them check out any body parts then."

"Not me," Lauri said, "I'm never coming back to this scary place." And she didn't. She much preferred shopping uptown where all the gold stores and carpet shops were. *Wonder where she got that?*

Other than the lechers staring, I loved the place. Everywhere I looked was something I couldn't live without. Beautiful hand-woven carpets were everywhere, some hanging from wobbly wooden racks on earthen walls, some piled on the earthen floors while peddlers cajoled you to buy the carpet of your dreams. I gravitated towards the carpets woven with exquisite colors of turquoise, indigos, red and golds. Earl had to pull me away or I would have purchased all of them. There were stalls were artisans made picture frames of camel bones with intricately carved stories of Persia's history. The brush contained only one cat whisker, so fine was the painting and engraving.

After I'd recovered from the shock of the noise, crowds and odors—wet yaks came to mind—I loved it. How could you not love a place that called out to sell you something wonderful? I'd find a way to get around the ogling men, smells and noise. It's amazing what a person can endure when they're besotted. And return I did, with anyone I could drag along as a driver. I knew just where to find the wonderful produce that hadn't been picked over, such as pomegranates, oranges, tangerines, strawberries, watermelon, grapes, bananas and kiwis, as well as eggplant, red cabbage, cucumber, lettuce and green beans. The bazaar begged to be explored, and I was ready. However, I've been called directionally compromised in the past, so I knew I needed help to navigate this place. I'd always drag an experienced bazaar-shopper from the club along with me, and hopefully she'd find the way out. I returned many times, but found that you could walk forever and never quite see it all. Dozens of peddlers hawking their wares called to me from stalls no bigger than a small closet.

One of my greatest finds was Copper Alley. Every type of copper and brass work known to man; it was one of my favorite places to shop. The first time Trudy took me there I knew I'd found a home. At one of the stalls, sitting on a stool, was a small boy not much older than six years, his hand barely large enough to hold the tool as he worked on a copper pot. His spindly legs dangled at least two feet from the floor. He seemed to know exactly what he was doing as he pounded away. When finished with his project he proudly showed his work to the merchant. The boy obviously did a good job as the merchant smiled, patted him on the head, and handed him another pot. I wondered as I saw this: is this child labor? or is this man his father? I sincerely hoped he was the merchant's son. Of course I had to buy several pots from this precious boy. I found out later that it was the boy's grandfather; that made me feel a tad better.

At another stall I found more glorious copper. The merchant was a frail, ancient man who looked like he might blow away in a mild wind.

Squatting on a dirt floor, he etched out wondrous engravings on copper and brass pots, platters and vases. I was in awe of the work coming from such an old man, who looked as though his sight had left him in his 90s. His cataract-fogged eyes stared off into space as he worked on his fine etchings. Could he possibly be blind? I saw him trace his work with his bony fingertips, over and over, always ending with a finger on the spot he'd just finished. I tried to get his attention: "*Salam, Agha,*" but he never looked up. I squatted beside him and touched his emaciated arm. "*Agha?* These are beautiful. *Che ghadr?*——how much."

He stood, reached out and plucked a pot from the earthen wall, then held up five fingers.

"Huh?" What did that mean? I looked around for Trudy who'd left me to check out another stall. I found her and dragged her back, along with the copper merchant who wasn't about to let a prospective buyer get away. "Would you please ask him how much for this copper pot," I asked him.

"No problem, Ma-dam" he said. He rattled off something in Farsi and the old man again raised five fingers. "He say you buy five pots and he gif you good price."

I'd heard about this game. Only a rube takes the first price. Did they not know with whom they were dealing? Dodie, the master haggler! "I don't need five pots. Please tell him I want only *this* one," I said as I handed him a small copper pot from the floor. "And I need to know the cost. If it's a good price I'll return and buy more." I was extremely excited. I could envision my house glowing with copper and brass treasures.

Again with the chattering from the merchant, but only a quick nod from the old man. "He say you take five or he not sell."

"How can you say that when he didn't even move his mouth?"

Trudy nudged me. "They all work together to fleece foreigners," she whispered, "tell him you'll return another day and maybe he'll change his mind."

"Okay, *khayli* mamnoon." I turned to leave. "*Farda.*"—tomorrow, I said.

I took another step. Nothing!

I looked back. No movement from the old man, but the copper merchant had pulled Trudy by the arm towards his stall. Well, *damn*! I thought I had this haggling thing down. I must return with a seasoned haggler. And, return I did, many times, so much so that the old man knew me by my cough, and would begin to pull out his treasures for me to admire. The sly old fox got what he asked for originally, and I was happy to oblige. Of course I told everyone who asked about the lovely copper in my home that I'd bargained for—and won.

I loved going to the bazaar, but one day in particular I found it very annoying. Trudy and I had stopped outside the bazaar to check out some great-looking fruit. As I bent over a box of pomegranates, I felt a hand on my right butt cheek, followed by a firm squeeze. At first I was so surprised I wasn't sure what had happened. I'd worn my tight Levis and a long blouse that covered my arms and my butt, so why would anyone venture there? When I realized someone had just taken a handful of my cheek, I swung around, definitely blurred the line between bravery and recklessness, and backhanded the man behind me, again and again, as hard as I could. Really hard! For an instant the man looked terribly confused, then I lost him in a cloud of dust from his jacket that I'd just pummeled. When the dust cleared he still stood there, as if asking for more pummeling. An Iranian woman standing nearby wagged her finger: "No, no him. He no touch you, other man. He gone."

I was furious. I had taken special care to dress modestly, not a pore of skin showed save for my hands, neck and face, and still the creeps had to take a feel; so much for showing skin and causing men to have impure thoughts. I think they just liked to feel foreign women. As we entered the bazaar, I was on alert for any lechers that got too close.

Our shipment from the States finally arrived. Amazing! I'd gone three weeks without things I thought I couldn't live a day without. Eagerly we opened the boxes and were thrilled to find things I'd forgotten we'd packed. Jim had done his own packing and only used one box. Most of what I'd packed everyone enjoyed; the games, the tapes, the books. When I packed the household things we'd need in Iran, I also threw in my eight-track player and some of my favorite tapes, but when I'd finished unpacking, only Neil Diamond had made it through Customs. I knew our shipment was checked as it entered the country, (first hint: everything disheveled) but never thought Customs would be interested in Credence Clearwater, the Beatles or the Eagles. As a result, my kids, husband and neighbors had to listen to Neil Diamond day and night. A few weeks later I found some ABBA and Beatles tapes at the bazaar. I played them nonstop while I worked around the house, which gave me a feeling of being back in the States.

But going grocery shopping brought me back to Iran.

9

Grocery Shopping & Food Prep

Ladies! You need to kneel down and kiss the ground in front of your local supermarket." This was the start of my first letter home. Esfahan gave grocery shopping a totally different meaning. In the '70s, no *supermarkets* existed in Esfahan. Grocery shopping wasn't just a hot and torturous job, it was all time-consuming when you had a large family to feed. There was no such thing as a one-stop market. We had to visit multiple stores to get what was on a simple small list, such as bread, milk, eggs, vegetables, fruit, and toilet paper (now that was a non-starter), and a lot of miscellaneous staples that were not available.

Compare this to what most Americans are used to as they walk into a sparkly clean, well-lit, fully stocked, air conditioned supermarket, along with ever-helpful salespeople groveling at your heels, eager to help you find an item, and happy because you might have gone to a dozen other stores of the same caliber, but you chose them. Well, okay, not all supermarkets. Here, I felt faint, hot, unclean, unwelcomed, and unloved.

Okay! I admit the big corporations stateside have the money to spend on all the wonderful accouterments they offer the happy housewife shopper, but still, a little neighborliness goes a long way. I did try to keep in mind I was a foreigner, and not everyone was excited to have me here. But I was bringing money into the community, especially the way my family devoured food. There were a couple of small Mom & Pop stores on the main drag of Char Bagh, but again, nothing you needed at the time was available. Very frustrating! Also, you could actually find liquor stores in those days: Mir Street Liquor and Nazar Liquors, both stores had excellent wine, and very inexpensive. Vodka from Russia was about two dollars a fifth, and smooth as velvet. Much later, at the start of the revolution, all those places would be burned to the ground.

Dressed in what I thought was very modest for my first day of grocery shopping, Trudy and I entered our first produce stall of the day. Trying to make some points with the merchant I thought it would be neighborly to use what little Farsi I knew. I walked up to him, smiled and said: "*Salam, Agha, hale shoma che towreh.*"—Hello sir, how are you? He looked at me as if I'd just flown in from Mars. Oh, oh! Did I use the right words? I felt like a fool as he walked past me without a word.

Trudy pushed me forward. "We have got to talk! First off, they don't recognize what you're saying because you don't have the right accent. And, you're not an Iranian, so I'm sure he thought you were speaking some type of foreign language he'd never heard."

That ticked me off. I'd practiced the pronunciation as *Ms. Dour* had taught us. I was sure the merchant just didn't want to acknowledge me. I would keep trying to use the language, and if it didn't work, maybe I'd dye my hair black and wear a *chador*. Anything to feel loved.

Store after store it was the same thing. The merchants were not happy to see me, or the horse I rode in on. I soon learned from an

Iranian friend of my husband's that Iranian men don't feel it's right to get too friendly with a foreign woman. Earl said the grocer probably didn't understand me, so I shouldn't take it personally. He said most of the merchants in town are grouchy guys because someone's always trying to rip them off—either shoplifting or trying to argue the price down.

My foray into grocery shopping was everything my expat friends had warned me about, truly a descent into hell. First off we had to start early in the morning because of the torrid heat. Trudy would fire up the Jeep just after dawn and off we'd go. The produce stalls were dreadful—small cubbyholes, dimly lit with fly-larvae-encrusted light bulbs hanging over everything. Rusty, medieval scales hung from the tin ceilings to weigh your produce. The skin of the fruits and vegetables were normally bruised and broken, sometimes with fissures large enough to drop a dime into, which was exacerbated by being manhandled by the customers. I witnessed Iranian women taking bites of the fruit to make sure it was sweet enough for their taste. If not, the fruit was dropped back into the bin from whence it came. The grocer would witness this, yell at the women, they'd yell back with fruit juice flowing down their chins. I'd grab my stomach and rush out.

Trudy had warned me about the vegetables and fruit. I was to examine each piece closely to make sure no one had taken a bite. Also, she gave me the protocol for using the scales: the second you see an empty one, drop your produce into it. But of course, likely as not, your stuff could be yanked out and someone else's deposited, followed by a glaring woman who might elbow you backwards, butt first, into the cucumber bin in her quest to get to the scales.

I'm not exaggerating. At first I thought: hey, I'm getting the bum's rush here because I'm a foreigner. Then I noticed the snub really wasn't personal. The women were on a mission: get the grub and head home before those black robes became ovens. However, I did notice the merchants had a problem waiting on foreign women, or I should say anyone who couldn't speak Farsi. I finally realized I did indeed need to learn this push-and-shove routine and possibly more Farsi if I was going to get home before dark. Not knowing the language made it a bit difficult to converse, such as saying: "Hey, kiss my grits!"

After spending twenty minutes trying to find produce that wasn't ready for the compost pile, I'd have to wait at the scales for the grocer to weigh them and give me a price. Another twenty minutes could pass before he'd reluctantly walk over, *tsking* me as he did. *Tsking* is a theatrical gesture of disgust whereby the *tsk-er* sucks in air, loudly, while he throws his head back denouncing you as *persona non grata*. When that happened, the old-timers told me, grab your stuff and head for the door as if you're going to leave without paying. I tried this, and as I put a foot outside the shop the grocer came running, "Ma-dam! You mut pay!" At that point I was told to say: "Oh, sorry, I thought you didn't want to wait on me." Then he'd grab my produce, toss them into the scales, give me a price, take my money, and *tsk* me as I left the store.

The fruit and vegetables were seasonal. In the summer we had more than we could handle, but in the winter the produce was scarce. Most grocery items had their own store, i.e., the egg store, the milk store, the paper goods store where you had to hunt for toilet paper—along with the requisite disgusting looks you got from the merchants for using that vile stuff—the flower shop, and the butcher shop. These shops were open air, without windows or doors, which welcomed the hungry flies the size of 747s to set up housekeeping and lay their eggs on inert objects. Most shops had corrugated metal doors that were pulled down at night to keep out dogs and thieves. The flies were always welcome.

We tried to hit the milk store last so it wouldn't turn to buttermilk before we got home. Keeping my house supplied with milk seemed to be the hardest battle to win. The milk came in small bottles, a tad smaller than the kind our milkman delivered in the 60s, and about six ounces per bottle. They also were sealed with the same type of round cardboard lids we used to play "Toss" with as kids. Lauri and Denny could drink their weight in milk, but Jim, going on 19, 5'11" and weighing close to 200 pounds, could empty those bottles in rapid sequence. He'd pull the cardboard lids from about ten bottles, guzzle them dry, wipe his mouth, and ask what was for dinner. My husband could down quite a bit of milk also, although in the States he never cared for it, saying milk was for toddlers. But here the milk was excellent. I was told it was not pasteurized, ergo the good taste. I'd always heard unpasteurized milk could lead to milk fever and eventually death, but as I looked around at the throngs drinking the stuff I had to wonder if it was an old wives tale. I just hoped we wouldn't all end up with colitis; that wouldn't do in this town with a shortage of toilet paper.

Getting enough milk to keep my family happy required hitting at least three milk stores every day. Sometimes you could only purchase one or two small bottles at each store. I needed about thirty bottles a day to feed my family's addiction. Trudy would pick up extra bottles for me on her solo runs.

Eggs posed a huge problem as well. Coming right from the nest, sans washing—chicken shit and all—the eggs were piled high in wooden bins. By the time the eggs had journeyed over camel and goat trails to get to the merchants, a good percentage of them were cracked. I'd have to pick through the pile to look for undamaged eggs—trying to miss the chicken shit—and then place them tenderly into the thin plastic bags the store offered. No nice egg boxes with cardboard inserts were available, giving each egg its own comfy little nest. Oh no, just vulnerable little eggs, stacked in a pyramid with the pile teetering on the countertop. It reminded me of a game we played as kids called pick-up-stix—trying to pick up one egg out of the pyramid. If you spotted a clean egg anywhere other than the top of the pile, you were a little reticent to grab it and cause the whole pyramid to collapse onto the floor.

Next was the walk back to the car with the eggs, which resembled a high-wire act, and one I tried to perfect. Slowly! No jerky movements lest two eggs bump each other, cracking their shells and oozing out over the other eggs. Sidestepping other pedestrians was an art as well. By the time we drove the corduroy roads back to the apartment with the eggs wedged carefully between my thighs, I sometimes had to toss the whole freaking bunch then throw my soiled clothes into the washer.

Thus it went day after day. Sometimes the stores were out of milk or eggs, or anything you'd expect a store to have in stock. So off you'd go, walk another block and try to find the next store just to be told they were out. "Nah! No haf." Sometimes the grocer didn't like our looks and just ignored us. Sometimes the things on my list required ten or more stores. Did I mention I was on foot with temperatures nearing the century mark? Add to this having to walk against the blistering wind that kicked up at times and would blow sand into every orifice—covered or not.

To further the shopping nightmare, the pathetic little bags available were made of plastic thin enough to read through. Sometimes they would only support two anemic bottles of milk. Sometimes. If not, we would hear the dreaded familiar sound as a seam separated and the side of the bag gave way. Or, sometimes the handles would shred, break free of my grasp, and everything would shatter on the sidewalk, splattering shoes, toes and/or passersby. No one was immune from the carnage. When this happened, as it did about once a week, I'd try to look as inconspicuous as possible as I slid the glass over to the gutter with one bloody foot, and then walked on as if I hadn't a clue where all that mess came from.

The butcher store was the first place I scratched *off* my list. I thought I'd hurl the first time I passed one. The rancid smell first got my attention. I made a mistake and looked right at the skinned corpse of a lamb and felt my gag reflex jump. There, in the glassless window, was a small, skinned lamb hanging from a hook, a few defrocked chickens, and who knows what else. Skinned and gutted, with heads still on, while playing host to a family of flies. Women were actually in line to buy a cut from those sad carcasses. Later I learned that a few stores sold frozen imported beef and veal from England and Australia. This was where most Brits purchased their meat. When I heard this I was overjoyed. Though extremely pricy, I could not let that deter me. I had no plans of giving anyone in my family a nice fat parasite to take home to the States. I didn't think our Anglo antibodies were ready for an onslaught of foreign bacteria. Because Iran was a Muslim country, I couldn't recall seeing any bacon, sausage or pork chops lying about. And, of course, I craved them. I'd been told that the Korean restaurant in town served pork, but Earl was afraid he might be served a *joub* dog fried up to look like a pork chop.

I made a mental note: *Find frozen imported pork.*

Another of the frustrating things about shopping was that you had to be finished before one o'clock in the afternoon. At that time the merchants pulled down their corrugated metal doors in your face. It was *Siesta* time! Most Iranians took this time very seriously. Everything closed from one o'clock to four o'clock; all matter of stores, banks, and even the airport. You would not be served during those hours, even if you were desperate. Even if you begged. Even if you offered them a bribe…well maybe then.

The first time I witnessed this abrupt closure was at a street stall. I'd hoped to grab some fruit while Trudy waited in the Jeep. The grocer must have had his watch set ahead of mine, because as I walked up to grab a handful of fruit, he yelled, "Nah!" and threw his prayer rug down behind a counter, curled up, and fell fast asleep. *Okay, I can take a hint.* I wondered if I'd had an armload of food to pay for when he was ready to flop down, would he have taken my money? But, they knew exactly how to get this all done and everyone out of their store in time for *Siesta.* Who could blame them?

After my two hour shopping marathon, I still had the formidable job of cleaning and sterilizing everything that would go into our mouths. Seasoned expats had warned me about the bacteria and dirty produce, supposedly fertilized with questionable fecal matter, so I was prepared for the amount of work required—or so I thought. After dumping the bags on the counter, I'd have to scrutinize closely for breaks or tears that I might have missed in the market. If an egg was cracked it was contaminated and had to be tossed; no keeping it for a nice omelet in the morning. Same thing with the produce; one tiny cut, slice or dent, and it was tossed. Earl said I could forget about the potatoes and eggplant because they had thick skins that would be removed before eating. However, the ladies in the know warned against this folly, so I ignored my husband—the man with the cast-iron stomach.

Then came the tedious and time-consuming job of sterilizing everything that had made the cut. Trudy gave me the recipe: Fill the kitchen sink with water, add one cup of bleach, a handful of veggies and let them soak for thirty minutes. Then repeat same until all were soaked. Wonderful! Now we had sanitized vegetables and fruit that smelled and tasted like the YMCA pool. The problem was, my sink was the size of a hospital bedpan, and only a few small veggies would fit in at a time.

One of the more frustrating aspects of cooking in Esfahan was the *naft* (kerosene) running out, or the *barq* (electricity) being turned off. This could happen anytime, and it was the bane of every expat who entered the kitchen with the hopes of cooking a meal.

Sterilizing the water had to be done every day as well. I had no less than three pots on my stove at all times: boiling water for drinking, ice cubes and tea. But, if a burner went out, unless you'd sat and watched the stove, you couldn't be sure whether the water had boiled the requisite thirty minutes. So I'd have to start all over.

Besides getting the food ready for consumption, we had the oft-occurring demise of the stove and/or oven when it ran out of fuel. Until it actually ran out of *naft* (fuel that was delivered to our tank in the basement,) I'd be unaware of the shortage. I'd invited some friends for dinner and made my prize-winning carrot cake for dessert. I put the cake in the oven while we ate. When the buzzer sounded I walked into the kitchen and immediately knew I had a problem: the kitchen was *cool.* The small kitchen was always hot when the oven was on. I had no idea when the fuel had run out, so the diners politely ate carrot cake pudding instead. Another night I'd invited some friends for dinner and the electricity went off just as we sat down to eat. Luckily I'd packed some candles in my shipment so we ate by lavender-scented candlelight. Quite nauseating to say the least. That is until even the bloody candle fizzled out.

When I did bake, it was an in-and-out job—as fast as possible. I didn't bake anything that would take more than a half-hour, and then it could very well flop before it was done. Nothing seemed to work. Baking bread was out of the question, so I picked up a loaf at the store for sandwiches. Earl had warned me about the packaged bread—obviously made only for foreigners—it was like eating crumbling Styrofoam. No self-respecting Iranian would ever eat that stuff, he said. As soon as the wrapper was opened the bread would fall apart in a million little pieces. Trudy offered to take me to find the best bread—Iranian bread. The Farsi word for bread is *nan*, or as the expats called it, minibus bread: by the time you got it home it looked like it had been run over by a minibus, but so incredibly delicious I knew I'd never want any other kind.

We watched as the baker cooked the bread to order. His oven was a hole dug into the ground, about three feet deep, with hot coals at the bottom and red-hot sides. After he shaped the dough to resemble pizza dough—only a little thicker—the baker literally threw the dough against the sidewall of the earthen oven, where it stuck and began to bake. When he thought the bread had cooked long enough on one side, he used a long pole with a pick at the end to loosen it, flopped it over and slapped it onto the wall again. When he felt it was just right he pulled the bread from the hole with his pick, placed it onto a piece of brown paper, and folded it in half like a giant taco. It was baked to perfection. All I needed was a slab of butter to toss inside.

We could have owned stock in this man's business for all the *nan* we purchased. We all had trouble keeping ourselves from tearing off hunks to eat on the way home. Several times the kids and Earl walked in with only half a piece, or even less, looking contrite, but happy.

My refrigerator was also bad news. So small I needed a Global Van & Storage man to load it so food wouldn't fly out when the door was opened. Nothing stayed cold. But I reasoned my family ate the food so fast, there wasn't time for it to go bad.

Ramazan was celebrated in August that year. I had no idea what the Iranians were celebrating, but we were told not to eat in front of them, i.e., on the bus or in public, as they were fasting. Also, we were told not to wear red. The reason behind these taboos was that when the people were fasting, the sight of food or anything red would cause them to be angry. I asked one of our English-speaking Iranians at the Club what was going on. He said the religious people were celebrating the Muslim holiday of *Ramazan*. It was a time for spiritual purification achieved through fasting, self-sacrifice and prayers. They are required to fast each day from sunrise to sunset. At the end of the month the celebration begins with a three-day festival known as "*Eid*," which means, "to break the fast." It is the culmination of the month-long struggle towards a higher spiritual state. That explanation made sense to me. We could all do with some spiritual purification, and for sure it wouldn't hurt any of us to try the fasting track for a month.

One important fact I learned from my new expat friends when I arrived was the taxi system: *Su-san* taxi was the mode of transportation used most by foreigners. This was a private company you could call for pick-ups at your home. The rate was reasonable and the interior didn't reek. Also you could rely on being dropped where you asked to be dropped, and not a block further. You could also flag down a *Su-san* taxi on the street if you were lucky enough to spot one. They would stop for you, with only one or two other fares, but no more than that, so at least you had room to breathe.

The alternative was the private-car taxi, wherein *anyone* who drove a car could instantly morph into a taxi service and stop for you—and as many bodies as he could squeeze in—for five *rial* (twenty cents, American). To flag down the private-car taxis you had to step off the curb into the street, wave your arms and yell out your destination. The first time I witnessed this I was shocked. Not only did the natives step off the curb, but also walked a few steps further into the dreadful traffic.

After a few trips around town I realized pedestrians had no fear of moving cars. And in fact, would sometimes walk right in front of a moving car to get it to stop. To add insult to injury, the pedestrians would yell at the driver, who'd swerved to miss them, but failed to stop. If a driver slammed on his brakes to avoid a person, the pedestrian might then bang a fist on the taxi's fender in indignation.

One Saturday, the kids wanted to go to the Club for a swim. Trudy was busy so I called a *Su-san* taxi and off we went. On the way, my kids pointed to an elderly woman standing in the street. Noting that we were on a collision course with her small body, I yelled at the driver. "*Ist!*"—Stop!

"No problem, Ma-dam, she vill moof," he said, then swerved when she did not moof, so our driver had to swerve to miss her. Watching from the rear window I saw another car coming at her. Unable to stop, and not quick enough to miss her, the driver clipped her and down she went. I watched in amazement as the woman stood up, pulled her *chador* tightly around her, grabbed her ankle and hopped on one foot while yelling at the driver. He waved his arm in a dismissive way, and drove off. She then moved a tad further out into the traffic, ready to take on another car.

"What is going on here?" I asked the driver, "Why didn't that man stop? He hit her."

"No vorry, Ma-dam," he said, smiling, "no problem."

Adding to the traffic snarls were the pushcarts that terminally blocked traffic, along with a shepherd and his flock—the ugliest sheep

I'd ever seen. They definitely didn't look anything like Mary's Little Lamb. They were filthy, with ugly square faces and short, fat tails. Not a pretty picture. And, they always seemed to be herded right in the middle of the busy streets, while drivers screamed at the shepherds from their cars, honked incessantly, and were completely ignored by the shepherds—and their ugly sheep.

I knew I had much to learn about this country, its people and their driving habits. I did have a giggle over their obscene gesture though, which I learned was a "thumbs up" sign. I assumed that carried the same message as our middle finger salute.

After I'd been in country for nearly a month, Trudy called to say she would be going to Tehran for a few days with her husband. Grocery shopping would now be done solo. Feeling I'd learned the skill well enough to go it alone—all I really needed was milk and eggs—I called for a *Su-san* taxi and felt like an old-timer as I instructed the driver in Farsi: *"Lotfan, mi khaham tokhm e morgh* and *shir."* I'd practiced that sentence for an hour, and hoped I'd said it right. He nodded his assent and off we went. When he pulled up to the egg store I was elated: *Hey, ain't I the one. He understood me.* I stepped from the taxi and asked the driver to wait. When I exited the store he was nowhere to be seen. Had I used the right phrase? Did he take a quick fare and would return for me? I could see I needed more Farsi lessons. I knew I could find another ride, but I didn't want a private-car taxi where I'd have to squeeze into an already crowded, hot, smelly car. I pondered this as I walked another block to the milk store and picked up six bottles of milk.

Loaded down with a bag in each hand, I stood on the center divider waiting for a break in the traffic to cross the street. I was preoccupied with thoughts of reaming out the *Su-san* driver if he did show up, when I heard a motorcycle very close and slowing down. I turned to look as I stepped into the street. Three young men, all packed onto one seat of the motorcycle, were slowing down as if to stop. I distinctly remember they were grinning at me. I wondered why. Surely they weren't going to offer me a ride. Coming alongside of me, one of them reached out and grabbed my right breast—and didn't let go for a block—or so it felt to my right breast. I let out a surprised yelp, dropped both bags, which clattered and then shattered onto the curb, the street, and my feet, as the creeps sped off laughing and yelling something I couldn't understand—and probably wouldn't want to.

My fight-or-flight reflex was to run after them and slap the snot out of them. Then I felt a throbbing in my right breast. I looked around and saw several men standing by grinning, while two *chador*-clad women shook their head with disapproval. Were they thinking: *that's what you get for not covering yourself, you infidel!* I resented their looks of disapproval and returned the look. I'd turned my attention back to the mess at my feet and began to pick up some of the glass, when I realized that both women had walked up. They offered me a sympathetic smile as they bent to help me pick up the mess. "Never mind," one said, "no good boys."

I immediately felt ashamed for thinking the worst. As I bent down with them and began gathering shards of glass, I realized there was more than one way to bond with the natives. These ladies were no different than me, other than being covered in black robes; they were still women and sisters underneath. I must have said *Khayli mamnoon* a dozen times, and meant it. "No problem" they answered. I wondered: if this had happened to me in the States, would women have come to my aid?

After that episode, I looked for those three creeps every time I went shopping. Not that I'd recognize them of course, as I really didn't get a good look at them. They all wore dark jackets, even in the blazing heat, and with dark hair—and on motorcycles—looked pretty much like ninety percent of the population. I reasoned that I couldn't go around slapping every male on a motorcycle, so I'd better get over it. I knew I wasn't the only woman who was being manhandled. I learned that this was a national pastime for these creeps. I couldn't help but wonder: if these women hadn't been covered from head to toe all their lives, maybe their male offspring would grow up without that morbid curiosity of needing to grab a woman and feel her. Dunno', I'm just sayin'...

I made a mental note: *Stand back from curb.*

1977 – Esfahan

10

Acclimating & School Days

Trying to get through the month of August was like watching a slideshow of a friend's vacation; it dragged on and on. Since I'd arrived no rain or cooling breeze could be found. Hot nights and hotter days, with no relief in sight. The mean climate in August was 100 degrees, and when coupled with the altitude of over 1,500 feet, I felt like I was pushing against a block wall, especially after I'd spent my life at only 300 feet above sea level. When I showered I could not get my body wet enough, plus the hard water felt like an exfoliate. Before long my skin began to flake and cake, while my heels looked like a cicada in metamorphosis. Old-timer expats at the Club would grin at my husband: "Ain't she cute," they'd say, as I'd wheeze and limp by. "Just wait, she'll acclimate before too long."

I ignored them. I didn't want to acclimate. I wanted to get out of that hell-hole and return to my nice clean home in the California burbs, my swimming pool and air-conditioned ranch-style abode, where the weather accommodated humans, not camels and goats. Then I remembered. And it hurt! I had no home to return to.

Eventually I could walk a whole block without getting dizzy, seeing double, or tossing my lunch, which made it a little easier to walk and talk at the same time. Slowly I felt like I might live to see my kids grown and married after all. The ladies at the Club cajoled me into playing some tennis early in the morning. Hey, come on, it's only ninety-five degrees today, they'd say. Of course, they'd been in this hot country for over a year and had already acclimated. I was a real weenie and didn't care who knew it. I don't perspire, I told them. I'm missing the normal body thermostat most people have. After one set they all looked like they'd been sprayed with a fire hose, while I looked like a red-faced baboon, head throbbing—but every dry hair still in place. Then the wooziness would begin and I'd head for the pool, fall in, tennis clothes, shoes and all. The gals who had me as a partner knew ahead of time that at any moment I might go running towards the pool and that would be the end of the foursome.

I did talk them into playing a little earlier when the temp was only about 85. I'd ride with Trudy to the courts and play for an hour. Trudy, being of the gossip-mill ilk, would sit with the non-playing ladies to pick up the latest problems. She'd listen to their woes: diarrhea, the shopping nightmare, the sterilizing process, the terrible living conditions, and the heartbreak of psoriasis. I'd get all the gossip on the way home. Some of these women never got used to the weather or the country, and eventually would pack and leave. I felt sorry for their husbands, but I was sure these women would have issues anywhere they lived.

Eventually I felt I'd made some progress; now I could walk without fainting. I also learned to live with the dust and dirt. I knew if I didn't vacuum every day I'd have enough dirt to build a mosque in a week. As we settled in and put our familiar things around the apartment I began to feel more comfortable, however, I never learned to live with the diesel fumes. I began to spend more time at the Club for tennis, cards, and enjoying the absence of fumes. Strangely, they didn't seem to bother Earl or the kids—either that or they didn't want to admit it. I knew it wasn't healthy for any of us to inhale that poison day after day.

I made a mental note: *Find another apartment.*

We visited the Club every chance we got. Jim enjoyed the teen dances and cute young girls. He worked with one of the Super's kids, Lyle, and they hung out together. Lyle was from California, so they had many stories to share. Jim received accolades from other men on the job, and I'd hoped that Earl would give him a pat on the back. I don't think it ever happened.

Wednesdays at the Club were movie nights. Most of the movies were ancient, some we'd already seen, but we watched them again anyway. I think it was the enjoyment of sitting on the cool ground like kids and mingling with new friends. *The New Centurions*, which I'd missed at home, and the old favorite, *Fiddler on the Roof* were still exciting to see this far from home. Thursday was poker night, which I did attend later, and every day was tennis for the brave of heart.

School began for Lauri and Denny in the middle of August: Denny in the 6th grade and Lauri in the 7th. They attended the American School of Esfahan, started by the Shah in the early '70s. The Shah enticed teachers from other countries with offerings of large salaries and inexpensive housing. The classes were small and lively, and the teachers were young, bright and energetic; the cream of the crop. Lauri attended the middle school, while Denny was in grade school. The tuition was $4,000 per school year, per child, which was tacked on to our W4s. Even though the price was exorbitant, Earl and I felt it was well worth the money. With such low enrollment, the kids felt like they were attending private schools. Lauri had three other children in one class, six in another, and fifteen in the largest. Denny's class had a few more, but still way below the number of students in his class in the States.

The first day of school was a much-dreaded day for me. My children would be out of my sight and on the highways with insane drivers. I was sure the school bus drivers were no different then their taxi counterparts. At over 100 degrees it was not a day I wanted to walk the streets to the bus stop. The Shah had allocated several of the Government of Iran buses or "GOIs" as we called them, to transport the company children to and from school. These buses were in a little better shape than the local transport buses, which was not a compliment.

"*August?*" Denny wailed. "School's not supposed to start 'till September. How come?"

I didn't blame him. It was hard to even step outside in the blistering heat, but I was told the schools had air conditioning so I knew he'd survive. To prepare for school Lauri arose each morning at five o'clock, just as Jim and Earl were leaving for work; thankfully, there were no long lines to the bathroom. Her routine: shower, wash, blow dry and curl her hair. Denny awoke at five-thirty. His routine: roll around in his bed while he moaned he didn't need to get up until five-forty-five. He'd then throw water in his face and stagger to the kitchen. After eggs or cereal, they'd be ready for the harrowing trip across the dreaded streets to wait for the school bus.

That first morning I realized it was not the transportation that I needed to worry about as much as crossing the street to get *to* the transportation. As we made the trek to Lauri's bus stop I realized I should've geared up for the event like an athlete prepares for a big match. Stoplights, crosswalks and sidewalks were nowhere to be seen. Funny, the word "sidewalk" to me implied concrete and maybe even a curb. But not where we lived, and certainly not where I had to walk to cross the kids in the middle of the busy city. Some areas were laden with what must have been rocks from the third century lying about. Other areas were just plain dirt. Some had hunks of concrete lying in our paths, as if the area had once been a construction site they forgot to clean up.

At six-twenty-five Lauri and I were out the door. I began the trek by grabbing her hand in a death-grip. She, of course, would try to wriggle free lest one of her new friends see me holding her hand to cross the street. *Horrors!* That didn't work for me. No hand, no cross.

I'd scan the street for fast cars, slow cars, donkeys and sheep. When I thought it safe, I'd step into the street, only to see a car coming around a corner with no intention of stopping. We would shriek, jump back, and then carefully try again. Once across the street we had to walk over a half kilometer of starved dogs that hadn't the strength to bark, rocks, sand and brick piles, then jump over the *joubs*—irrigation ditches (quasi garbage disposals) that ran down both sides of the street.

After she climbed aboard the bus, I'd head back to get Denny, whose bus was thirty minutes later than Lauri's. Avoiding the catcalls, honks, jumping *joubs,* stubbing toes on rocks, I'd finally stagger in the door only to be met by a wild-eyed kid who knew the *joub* had swallowed me up. "What took you so long?" he'd demand in his hyper voice, while I reached for a salt pill and leaned into the cool tile wall. "I was scared you got hit or something."

It wasn't even seven in the morning, but the heat was oppressive. The wind was dry and blistery which caused the road dirt to cling to me, and even managed to lodge in my teeth and anywhere else it wanted to go. "Okay, give me a minute to cool off, will ya?" I flopped down on a chair and leaned my head back.

"Mom, c'mon, I can't miss the bus. Where's my *joub*-dog stick?"

Denny had pilfered a sharp stick from an abandoned construction site and proclaimed it as our protection against the wild beasts on the road. Actually, the dogs did look as though they might need a bite of something, and I'd hoped they hadn't had the taste of human blood and wouldn't be drawn to my stubbed and bloodied toes.

It was a heartbreaking sight to see the proliferation of stray, mangy dogs. It appalled me to see those pathetic animals trying to exist on scraps along the *joubs*, where they'd scratch and drink, and hope a tidbit would fall their way. I had to look away from their hollow eyes. My son saw the dogs as marauding beasts, ready to tear us apart limb by limb. "Honey, I really don't think they'll hurt us. They're malnourished and just look scary." I never saw one with the energy to bite its own fleas.

Denny's bus corner was in the opposite direction of Lauri's. As we walked I noticed a *joub* dog following us. His scraggly little tail seemed to wag whenever I turned to look at him. *Is he giving me a sign?* I told Denny I thought the dog was trying to protect us. When we reached the bus stop the poor cur dropped down on the ground, but kept his distance. His eyes never left us while his tail feebly etched a swish mark in the dirt. When my son was safely on the bus and I began to wend my way homeward, the *joub* dog stood up and followed at a respectable distance, still half-heartedly wagging his tail. He followed me to my apartment, then wandered off and I didn't see him again that day. The next morning as Lauri and I stepped out our door, we found him curled up on the front stoop. My daughter froze. What now? Do we step over him, walk around him, or call for help? The dog jumped up, moved away to allow us to pass, then followed again, waited for the bus with us, then followed me home. He did the same when it came time to take Denny. Only this time as we approached the bus stop, an old man came by sweeping the street. I heard a low throaty sound coming from the dog, which turned into a savage snarling growl. I wondered where he got that energy. I knew it. He *was* protecting us. The dog followed us home that day and I put out some scraps for our little protector. However, it also brought twenty more mangy dogs to our doorstep. Our *joub* dog accepted the treat only after I'd put it on the ground and walked inside. Denny named him Jouby. He stayed faithful to us until a few days later when I noticed him following someone else to the bus stop. I guess she provided a better doggie treat. I learned much later, and it broke my heart, that police are sent out on poison patrol to slow down the dog population.

Denny joined the swim team at school and we attended all his competitions. According to my son he was the swiftest and strongest swimmer on the team. Well, I like that in a child. Be positive. Wonder where he got that? Lauri immediately joined the track team and we attended her meets as well. Earl was happy she'd chosen track, as that had been his sport in school. We were amazed at her speed, but mostly by her endurance. The temperature hovered around the 100-degree mark, yet she ran and always finished in the top three. She was particularly excited about an upcoming meet in the spring. "If I make the cut, we'll be running against the American School in Cairo, Egypt, and we get to spend three days after the meet to do some sightseeing."

We'll see about that.

1977 – Esfahan

11

Schmoozing Iranian Style

While living in Iran I wanted to learn everything I could about the country's customs. I felt all expats had that duty, if for no other reason than to avoid embarrassment. The first custom I learned was to be patient and gracious when purchasing a carpet, especially from *Agha* Hanasab, the carpet merchant on Avenue Saltanabad. Earl had purchased an *Esfahani* for our living room from *Agha* Hanasab before I'd arrived. It was lovely, but rather drab. The carpet was dark browns, beiges and creams, but I wanted a bright, colorful carpet for the dining room.

Before we left for Hanasab's, Earl explained the rug-buying custom: A good rug merchant has no intention of selling you a rug until he's served tea, and chatted about the weather, if you liked Iran, and possibly discuss the state of the union. "Don't insult him by trying to get down to business the minute you walk in the store. Then after you've finished your tea, he'll expect you to discuss and rave about his glorious carpets *before* you get down to business."

Well, I'm not much for doodling around. I wanted to get in, find what I wanted, and get out. But again, When in Rome… When we entered the store I had my first lesson on the art of Schmoozing—Iranian Style. Hanasab, a rotund, red-cheeked man whose beard and mustache joined in one great push, met us with open arms. His enormous girth seemed to fill the small shop. He gave Earl the normal greeting in Persian, which Earl repeated, and they shook hands. He then led us to a desk and pointed to two chairs. "Sit, sit," he ordered with a smile. We sat. He then clapped his hands and a young boy appeared holding a tray with gold-rimmed glass teacups, about the size of a two-ounce shot glass. Hanasab filled the cups with hot tea from a beautiful silver samovar and passed them around. I hesitated. I wasn't sure what the Iranian custom was for drinking tea, so I watched him for my clue. The sugar came in an elegant sterling silver cup, but looked like miniature chunks of icebergs. He placed two small chunks between his front teeth, then sucked the tea through them while making very slight sucking sounds. I chose to drink my tea the American way, passed on the sugar and just sipped. Earl, who has never used sugar in his tea, took two chunks and placed them between his teeth as he watched Hanasab. He would have done quite well had he not decided to say something while in mid suck. Out came the sugar chunks and tea down his chin and onto his shirt. He shot me a quick look of embarrassment, shrugged, put the sugar chunks back between his teeth, and went right on sucking.

When Hanasab finally finished his second cup of tea, he began a diatribe about crooked carpet merchants in the bazaar, half-knot carpets, and machine-made carpets that were sold as hand-made. Next he talked about the weather, did we like his country, and then looked at me for the answer. "Oh, of course. But the driving…"

Earl cut me off, "What she means is she doesn't drive here because she's afraid she'll get lost."

"No problem. You must take taxi, voman should not drive."

"Exactly," Earl shot out. "That's just what I told her." He looked at me with a pained expression that seemed to say: Sorry; we'll talk later.

Hanasab stood and motioned for us to follow him. While I half listened to his broken English extolling the benefits of owning hand-made rugs, the years it took to make one, and what a great bargain he would give us, my eyes took in the exquisite carpets around his tiny shop. They were strewn all over; on the floor, hanging from wooden dowels, and nailed to walls. I found them all so beautiful I didn't know which pile I wanted to start with.

"Vere vould you like to start, Meezter Crot?"

I started to answer, then realized he'd addressed my husband. I whispered to Earl that I'd like to pick out the carpet this time. He nodded. I turned and faced Hanasab. "*Agha,* I think I would like to see some large rugs, at least a fourteen by twenty." I pointed to a pile on the floor near us. "I like this size."

Hanasab was still looking at Earl, while Earl looked rather sheepishly at me. "Go ahead," I whispered, "tell him."

"*Agha* Hanasab, if I may, I would like my wife to pick out the rug. I picked out the first one I bought from you, now it's her turn."

Hanasab looked a bit disproving, then said to Earl, "As you vish, Meezter Crot." He then gave me a quick little bow, but I could see he was not happy "Vhat is your pleasure?"

It was obvious that *Agha* Hanasab felt a woman had no business picking out such an expensive item, and that the decision should be left to a man. I gloated in the fact that I would be the one to pick out the rug. I pointed to a stack of large rugs near me, and asked him to pull them apart so I could see all of them. He called his assistant, a young boy of about twelve, to turn the carpets for us, while Earl and he continued discussing the world at large. Thirty minutes later I'd found exactly what I wanted: the most gorgeous hand-made Tabriz carpet—purples, burgundys and golds, with the Tree of Life pattern. I was ecstatic. *Agha*

Hanasab made a sale, but he still wore a pout that peeked out under his hairy face.

The next thing I learned was that Persians consider the soles of the feet or shoes the lowest and basest part of the body. Therefore, it's an egregious insult to show them, i.e., to put your feet up on someone's desk, or to put one's leg up on one's knee—things that show the soles of your shoes. I also learned that to offer a Muslim your left hand is a huge faux pas. They shake with their right hand, and eat with their right hand. This is because Muslims use their left hand to splash water on their behinds after evacuation, rather than using toilet paper as we do.

A duty, rather than a custom, is the morning call to prayer, in which devout Muslims must partake. The prayers are recorded on tapes and played through a sound system that defies credulity, and blares out from minarets all over the city. I remembered reading in the travel books that there were more than 20,000 mosques in Iran. I think I heard them all that first day.

Each morning at four o'clock we were jolted awake by an unearthly sound. The first morning I heard the noise I flew out of bed in stark terror. *"Oh, my God, what's that noise?"* I yelled to my husband over the din.

"I thought I told you about that in one of my letters. It's the "Islamic Call to Prayer.""

This was the wake-up call to all the faithful—as well as all the expats—and I never got used to it. The noise was a jolt, like an electric prod stuck in your ear. Sleep had left the building. A narrow asphalt alley separated our apartment from a group of two-story Iranian homes, in fact they all seemed connected as they ran the length of the whole alleyway. Each home had its own courtyard; some large enough to park their cars in. The buildings were old and weather-beaten, and in a bad state of repair—not too different from other buildings in town. But their courtyards were awash with green plants and colorful flowers. Most had a large fountain in the center, and from my second story view this was a welcome sight from the otherwise dingy grey of buildings and streets.

Not able to sleep after the Call to Prayer, I noticed my neighbors moving about in their courtyard and stopped at my window to watch. I wasn't really being a snoop, I told myself, just learning about their customs. I was amazed at the piety of the men as they prepared for morning prayers. Shoes were removed, then face and hands were washed with water from the fountain. They would then kneel on a small prayer rug, and with head to the ground and rear in the air, they would pray. Sometimes I noticed them weaving back and forth, but always so reverent. I was told they must pray five times a day as the Koran dictates.

Since sex is considered unclean by the very religious, a man must shower after sex before he can attend the call to prayer. I wondered if our neighbors thought we might be sex maniacs as I sometimes took two or three showers a day because of the sweltering heat. Then add to that the showers the kids and my husband took.

Later in the mornings I might catch the men splashing water on their face before heading off to work. Wow, I thought, men really do have life easy—here as well as the rest of the world. They splash a little water on their face, maybe run a comb through their hair, and off they go. Somehow that has never seemed fair to me, especially considering what women must go through before they step out the door. Oh well, that's another book.

In the heat of the hot summer nights I saw that many of our Iranian neighbors slept outside on their balconies, while many slept on their rooftops. Bedrolls were thrown down and Mom, Dad and the kiddies bedded down, clothes and all. I could not imagine how hot the women must have been in those long black robes, without a breeze to cool their sweaty bodies. I sincerely hoped they were allowed to remove the robes at night. I was very thankful for my hard bed, occupied only by my husband and myself, a cool cutesy little nightie, and a blessed air conditioner.

During the daylight hours, young children played in the alleyway between the homes. I came to see how alike all children are, whether in Iran or the US: no matter how small the alley, the Iranian children always had enough room to run, play ball and ride their bikes. We really aren't that much different, we humans, just born in different parts of the world.

I made a point to get to know our Iranian neighbors. The women finally came around, but their husbands would only nod and look down. I would greet the women if we passed in the alley, and speak to their children in what little Farsi I knew: *Hale shoma che towreh?*—how are you. That was about all I could handle at the time, but I felt the women knew that I tried, and in time they made a point to greet me as well. They were kind and very helpful, even if we couldn't understand each other. A lot of arm waving and pantomiming usually did the job.

12

Dorothy Hamill & The Accomplice

To reward myself for the misery of the heat and fumes I had to endure, I decided to get my hair styled to lift my spirits. My last cut had been a week before we left the States, and now it fell in a muddled mass around my face. I asked around at the Club for a recommendation to an upscale hair salon, one that didn't just cater to long, straight hair—which seemed to be the style worn by most westernized Iranian women.

"Oh, I know just the place, and you'll love Farid, and he speaks English," one of the expat ladies offered. "He'll do wonders with your bad cut."

Well, thank you very much! It wasn't a bad cut per se; it had just grown out to look like a bad cut. But she was right. I made an appointment with Farid the next day. My Dorothy Hamill "do," which I'd been so happy with in the States, now resembled a Howard Stern "do." Trudy offered to drop me at the salon. She did the hair cutting in her family, and she wasn't about to take the chance of getting scalped. Good for you, I thought. Even if I wanted to cut the family's hair, the kids would never let me touch them. I used to cut their bangs when they were very young, and every time they saw those old pictures they wailed: "How could you do that to your own children?" Okay, not everyone has a barber's eye. Lauri declined to go with me, saying she'd pass until she saw if my Hamill Wedge turned out okay.

The shop looked upscale from the street, but as I entered I found it rather rundown. Some of the style chairs were in need of upholstery, and the walls could have stood a coat of paint. The smell was foreign to me. Maybe they used a different solution for perms than we did in the States, or maybe the smell was hair dye. I sincerely hoped the shampoo didn't smell that bad.

A handsome young man, possibly in his twenties, approached me at the front desk. His hair hung over his shoulders in a sort of mullet shag. His clothes were very G.Q., right down to his shiny penny-loafers.

"Mee-sez Dotie?"

"Yes! *Salam.* Are you Farid?"

"*Baleh. Hale shoma che towreh?*" he said, offering me the usual Iranian greeting.

"*Khob.*" —good—I replied, hoping I'd feel that way when I left the shop.

"*Khob.* Please come vith me."

I followed Farid past several empty stations. *Where is everyone?* "Are you the only one working?" I asked, nervously.

"*Baleh*, I stay for you."

Stay? It wasn't even noon yet. When I made the appointment, I'd assumed he'd be done with my cut by one o'clock. Was he giving up his Siesta for me? Had I found the only Iranian in town that didn't sleep between one and four p.m. "Oh, *khayli mamnoon," I think.*

I followed him to his station, all the while worrying about the empty shop. Did an empty shop mean customers didn't like his work? I had to make a decision, and quick. Maybe if I told Farid I'd just remembered another appointment, or had a headache, or anything that would get me out of there, he might be relieved, and close up for his *Siesta.* But as I began to plot my escape, two young girls entered from a back room and stopped at Farid's station. They smiled at me and took their place on either side of my chair. *What does this mean? Are they going to tag-team my hair?* One girl pulled scissors from her apron pocket while the other wrapped a white plastic sheet around my neck. *Oh, please don't tell me they're going to dry-cut my hair.* "Um, don't you wash hair first?" I asked the girl with the scissors. She smiled, not having a clue what I'd asked her, either that or she didn't want to upset me with a "No" answer.

Farid then asked me to follow him to the shampoo bowl. "Not to vorry Mee-sez Dotie. You sit here and assistant vill vash your hair and vill bring you back to my chair."

That was a relief. Well, this might work out, I thought. At least they're going to wash me before they cut me. After an exuberant shampoo, in which Farid's assistant appeared to be deaf to my yelps of pain—I'm very tender-headed—she wrapped a towel around my head and led me back to his cubicle. I watched with apprehension as he meticulously arranged his weapons of choice on a roller stand by my chair: two combs, two very pointed and lethal-looking scissors, a blow dryer with several tips, various sizes of round brushes, and a vanity mirror. I wondered how this young man would have any idea what a Dorothy Hamill Wedge was, or for that matter, had even heard of her. Nah! He didn't look the type to follow World Championship Ice Skating. I prayed he wouldn't send me home resembling Phyllis Diller.

"How vould you like your hair cut today, Mee-sez Dotie?"

I thought for a minute. How do I say this? I know he'll think I'm nuts if I give him a girl's name instead of the name of a hairstyle. "Uh, well. I know this sounds crazy, but have you heard of Dorothy Hamill?"

"*Baleh*. Is this vhat you vant, the Hamill Vedge?"

Oh my God, he knows! I could not believe this. "Oh, yes, that's exactly what I want. Have you done that cut?"

"*Baleh*, many times?"

Many times? And I thought I'd be the only stylish one in town.

I was in for a wonderful surprise. Farid was a master at his craft. Not only did he know who Dorothy Hamill was, but he also knew just how to get that great style. As he parted and layered, then cut my hair, he would look at my hair in the mirror, then look at himself, smile at his cleverness, then back to the cutting. When he was satisfied with the cut, he called his girls. With an assistant on either side of my chair, and holding the hairdryers as if readying for a gun battle, Farid shot off orders in Farsi and they took their stances. He then carefully took a well-measured section of hair, rolled it up on a large round brush and slowly brought the hair down as the girls aimed their dryers at the layers of hair on either side of the brush. When he felt the hair had had enough heat to get just the right bend, he would slowly unwind the brush, move to another section, and then wind up again. As he let the section of hair fall from the brush, it made the most beautiful bounce, exactly like the woman in the TV commercial whose long, lustrous hair sways in slow motion. I couldn't keep the grin off my face. I'd never seen this method of using two assistants to blow-dry hair. Stateside, a hairdresser normally holds the brush in one hand, and the dryer in the other, and works them together, along with increasing her chances of carpal tunnel syndrome. What a clever way to achieve this hairdo. Of course…now there were three people to tip, instead of just one.

But, never mind. I was amazed! One minute I looked like a wet Lhasa Apso and the next, *Voila!*—I looked exactly like Dorothy Hamill…give or take twenty years and a few added wrinkles.

I had much to learn about this country and its people. Before I'd moved to Iran, I never considered where my drinking water came from, other than my kitchen faucet. I never considered where my electricity came from, other than the switches on lamps, walls, various and sundry plugs located at convenient intervals throughout my home. I never considered where the heat and air conditioning came from, other than the cutesy little louvered registers at ceiling level all over the house that blew out the required heated or chilled air. I never considered what made them all work; how the gas went into the furnace, was heated by a flame that warmed the heat exchanger, which in turn warmed the air, and then circulated through the vents, forcing warm air throughout the house.

But as a new expat to Iran, I now found I was flummoxed about everything I'd taken for granted—until I had to worry about it. The heating pump in the basement: how to keep it full of *naft* to keep us from freezing in 20-degree weather. Or the cooling system that most times worked arbitrarily when the weather reached 120 degrees outside. This all depended on when the "AC" or "*naft*" man came to town to make it work. Some days he was busier than others and couldn't get to our house. Busy also meant taking his three-hour *Siesta*, prayer time and various obligations that he must attend to before he showed up at someone's house, if indeed, he came at all. I also had to fret about the water that came through our rusty pipes. Well, either the pipes made the water rusty, or the water came to us plain rusty. Where did it originate?

One of the first things they tell you before you travel to a third-world country is: "Don't drink the water!" Always keep a jug of sterile water in the kitchen, and also on the bathroom sink for brushing your teeth, taking medicines, and to quench your thirst during the night. Sterile water meant boiling our water with a couple capfuls of bleach added to kill the little bastard germs. But the sterilized water always tasted like drainage from my Maytag. But, after a while you become more comfortable in your environment and forget the rule and rinse—and *swallow*—from the faucet! Just when I thought I had everything under control, I screwed up.

A few months after arriving in country I did the unthinkable—I got comfortable. I forgot the rules. Could my stomach be that weak? Was I in for two years of pain? I was in a hurry to get to the Club for cards and swallowed a gulp of water from the faucet after I'd brushed my teeth. I swallowed without even realizing it, a habit I'd acquired since birth.

The first time it happens: "OHMIGAWD, DO YOU KNOW WHAT I JUST DID?" you scream from the bathroom. You fret and worry and when nothing comes of it, you forget again. Then, after a time, when nothing happens, you feel very *expaty* and figure you've built up enough antibodies, so you go for it!

Then one day you feel them: the tiny little fingers of pain that start in your upper abdomen. Your eyes get wide. It's got your attention. The pain increases in intensity as the nasty little buggers work their way down the miles of intestine to the middle of your gut; twisting and turning, cork-screwing again and again until they are stopped in their tracks, momentarily, as they come head to head with THE MIGHTY COLON! DA DA DA DUM-TA DUM! And you drop to your knees, writhing as your abdomen explodes in spasms of pain. T*hen* you remember. Oh, yeah, don't drink the water!

A brief walk through town revealed *joubs* running down both sides of the street. A *joub* is a small, hand-dug channel filled with questionable water and questionable refuse, in which numbered trees have been planted by order of the Shah. Because Iran has a definite shortage of trees, and therefore wood, the word was out: if you disfigured one of the trees the Shah would have your head. These *joubs* were used for many conveniences: rinsing the vegetables that merchants sold from their street carts, a receptacle for rotting produce, a urinal used by the merchants—or any male passing by if the urge to purge hit them, and a quick lap or pee by the scabrous dogs who prowled the streets. Earl had warned me about this: "Don't buy anything off those street guys. They wash the produce in that filthy *joub* water, and they also take a leak in it." I'd seen the merchants bend over and swish their produce in the *joub*, but I'd never witnessed the "leak."

While shopping one day, I exited the store to see a merchant fiddle with the front of his pants and relieve himself in the *joub*. I turned to shriek at Trudy who was behind me talking to a friend. "You're not going to believe what that merchant just did!"

"What? Pee in the *joub*?"

Okay, I was warned. But from then on I kept a wary eye on the merchants to make sure they didn't step outside to do some *joub* swishing.

One excruciatingly hot day after Trudy had dropped me at home with bundles of groceries hanging from every appendage, I sat down at the kitchen table to have myself a little pity-party. How can I do this? I'm exhausted, I feel a heat stroke coming on, and now I have to wash, bleach and put away all this food. I scanned my rabbit warren of a kitchen. Where was my beautiful California kitchen with its Magic Chef range and oven, my huge Kohler sink, my eight-seater Thomasville maple table?

Gone, girl. Get over it.

My eyes stopped mid-scan and focused on an answer to my exhaustion: my washing machine! How had I missed this incredible opportunity? It could work! Why wouldn't it work? How could a Permanent Press cycle do any more damage to this sad produce than was already done? And I was sure the swishing would do a more thorough job of getting into those undetected nooks and crannies. And why stand there and wash fruits and veggies for hours when they'd be eaten in less than five minutes. Why not try it? And so I went for it. If it worked the whole expat community would hear about it from my rooftop. If it failed, my lips were sealed.

I filled the washer with cold water, then added two cups of bleach. I checked for cuts, holes and bruises on all the produce, then gently layered them in the water, pushed the gentle cycle, and set it for thirty minutes. Then I prayed. How could I lose? If it didn't work, then the family would eat pureed vegetables and fruit for dinner.

Well, it did work. Sort of! Some of the veggies looked like they were in a state of decomposition after their thirty minutes on Mr. Toad's Wild Ride. I noticed the tomatoes looked the worst for wear. Okay, so I'll make catsup. No big deal. The eggplant seemed to stand up to the rigors of the Permanent Press cycle, but the onions shed their skins and left an awful mess. The lettuce came in bunches, rather than heads, with nothing holding the leaves together, so they became tangled up with the onionskins. The cucumbers seemed to fare pretty well, a tad softer than when they went in, but by the time I peeled them and placed them in a vinaigrette dressing, no one would be the wiser.

I made a mental note: *Put loose lettuce and onions in pillowcase.*

The washing machine became my secret accomplice. I'd fill it with the requisite water and bleach, add fruits, tomatoes, potatoes and cucumbers, then add the lettuce and onions in a pillowcase. I put the eggs in the little blue basket that sat on the top of the agitator. It looked safe enough, but it took a tub-full of broken eggs and scrubbing out the washing machine before I found the secret to adding eggs to the mix. I dressed each egg in one of Earl's work socks. Why not? They needed a good bleaching, and the thick socks kept the eggs from banging against each other. Earl was always amazed that his work socks were so white. Just a thoughtful little wifey, I'd say.

My routine was great. I'd set the washer for Permanent Press and then settle down with a great book. Among some of the books I'd packed in our shipment, Zelda was the one that most fascinated me. I was eager to read about her life with F. Scott Fitzgerald. His life was most amazing and I wanted to understand what type of woman could live with a self-absorbed man like him. I had plenty time now, in fact I could read *and* listen contentedly to Neil Diamond or the Beatles, accompanied by the gurgling and sloshing of my secret accomplice. I was so into the book that the whole process was one happy adventure: one wash and a spin dry and *viola*! By the time my family got home, the kitchen was clean, produce were sanitized and in the refrigerator. Boy, I was good! I'd found the perfect solution for the mess that had cluttered my kitchen and my life. Now I had time to do important things like visit the bazaar, make a run to the Club for a quick game of cards, or just curl up with Neil and a good book.

The photos on the following pages are from our stay in Esfahan over thirty years ago, and are not of the best quality. However, my photos of Esfahan's amazing architecture do not do them justice. To see them in color and the incredible mosaic work of those artists, please go to:

http://www.bamjam.net/Iran/Esfahan.html

1. Copper Alley: My Favorite Artisan

2. Elaine And Steve, AKA Conan The Barbarian

3. The "Powdered-Milk" Cow.
We're On The Second Floor, Fresh bread In Hand And Drooling

4. Now-Ruz: Carpet Cleaning In The Muddy River Water

5. Six On A Cycle, With A Goat In The Sidesaddle.

6. Gypsy Children in their finery

7. The Amazing Gold Stores I Kept In Business

8. Our Home in Khaneh

9. Taking A Break From The Faithful VW

10. Earl Trying His Hand At Carpet Weaving

11. Martial Law Comes To Esfahan

12. Bored Martial Soldiers

11-10-78

Dear Dodie & Earl:

We got 2 cards from you at work - sounds like you had a good vacation. Things are wierd over here. Curfew is still on. They had some bad trouble in Tehran ~~yester~~ last week - Tehrans' curfew is back to 9:00p.m. We are still being advised to keep a low profile. Wish you were still here Dodie - ole Ethel doesn't tell us a thing. They have another new guy up in security they are suppose to increase the dept. until they have _23_ people.

God knows where they are
going to put them.

████████████████ are leaving
the 27th & not coming back.
████████ and her family have"
moved out to Shahin Shahr.
She's still working in the
office for ██████ Everything
is pretty much the same.
█████████████████████ are sending
there families home. ████████
keeps asking ████████ is she
wants to mess around! yechs.

The shah put military
personnel in all the key
positions in the government.
Hopefully this will cool
things down, I hope so I

don't want to have to leave
yet. The only things that have
happened have been the BHI
bus bombing - no one really hurt,
youth Hostel, La Fontaine, Old
American Club, destroyed. Picnic Box bombed
A few American homes rocked or
fire bombed & quite a few cars
burned. A couple of isolated
incidences women being
attacked around the pas part
area. Grumman offices got rocked
last week - so Bell gave us the
next day office. That's about it.
Everything has been on strike — car
gas, Iran & Pars Air, Telephone,
Mail, bottled gas, naft etc.
That's what has been happening over
here aren't you glad ya left?
Well I gotta get busy. Sorry this
is so. sloppy but I'm suppose to be
working. I'll keep you informed
WE ALL MISS YOU —

Preceding page letter transcribed here for clarity

11-10-78

Dear Dodie & Earl:

We got 2 cards from you at work – sounds like you had a good vacation. Things are weird over here. Curfew is still on. They had some bad trouble in Tehran, curfew is back to 9:00 p.m. We are still being advised to keep a low-profile. Wish you were still here Dodie – Ole Ethel doesn't tell us a thing. They have another new guy up in Security, they are supposed to increase the dept. until they have 23 people. God knows where they are going to put them.

██████████████ are leaving the 27ᵗʰ & not coming back. ██████ and her family have moved out to Shah in shah. She's still working in the office for ██████ Everything is pretty much the same. ██████ are sending their families home. ██████ keeps asking ██████ if she wants to mess around! Yech!

The Shah put military personnel in all the key positions in the government. Hopefully this will cool things down. I hope so. I don't want to have to leave yet. The only things that have happened have been the BHI bus bombing – no one really hurt. [The] Youth Hostel, La Fontaine, Old American Club [all] destroyed. The Picnic Box bombed. A few American homes rocked or fire bombed, and quite a few cars burned. A couple of isolated incidents: a woman being attacked around the bazaar area. Grumman offices got rocked last week – so Bell gave us the next day off. That's about it. Everything has been on strike – car gas, Iran & Pars Air, telephone, mail, bottled gas, naft, etc. That's what has been happening over here, aren't you glad you left? Well, I gotta get busy. Sorry this is so sloppy but I'm supposed to be working. I'll keep you informed. We all miss you - ██████

1977 – Esfahan

13

Trips, Gypsies & Opium

E arl was famous for making friends, no matter where they came from, or if they even spoke English. He just liked people. So I was not surprised when he came home one Thursday night with plans to meet new friends. "How'd you like to take a trip to the countryside and have a picnic in the mountains?"

"With who? And do they speak English?"

We would be going with Rallfe*, an engineer on my husband's job. I'd heard Earl rave about this smart young Iranian who spoke excellent English and received his Engineering degree from Yale. He was excited about working for such a large company, and in his own country. I was relieved to hear that Rallfe spoke English. I enjoyed meeting new friends, too, but I wanted to know more about this guy before I entrusted our lives to him. "How does he drive?"

"Good. He learned to drive when he lived in the States, so you can put that worry to rest."

"Can he protect us if something happens?"

"What do you mean? Nothing will happen. Rallfe knows the country. He has cousins in some of the small villages. He says we'll stop and meet his family and maybe if we're lucky get some fresh homemade bread."

I'd heard some scary stories of foreigners who were never seen again after they took a trip to the country, but these stories came from women at the Club, of course, most of whom never left their home other than to visit the Club. So I had to take that into consideration.

"For God's sake!" Earl bellowed when I brought up these wives' tales. "Some of those women have nothing to do but sit around and tell tall tales because they're afraid to venture outside the Club fence. We'll be fine, and besides, I think it'd be good for the kids to see how the country people live." He pulled me to him for a hug, "Come on, we'll get to see the country, get away from the noise and, pollution."

Rallfe told Earl he'd take us up in the mountains where we could drink pure ice-cold water from the snow-fed springs. And, it would be at least fifteen degrees cooler up there. When I thought about the noise and heat here in the city, and the noxious fumes in our apartment, all of a sudden being sold to slavers didn't sound so bad.

Jim had plans that day to meet some kids at the Club, and Rallfe's wife, Dorri* had other plans, so it would be just the three of us and Rallfe. Earl said we'd be taking the Volkswagen as Cleve and Trudy would be using the Jeep. I did wish our old Volkswagen had been a tad larger as the kids and I squeezed into the backseat, along with a box filled with luncheon snacks, drinks, blankets and Denny's well-honed *joub*-dog stick.

Heading out of the smoggy, traffic-filled city, I was excited now with the idea of this trip. Before long we'd left the noise behind and entered a tranquil countryside, alive with flowers and streams. We'd left dry, arid deserts, climbed mountains, and descended into lush, verdant valleys. The outing was only supposed to be a half-day trip, but ended up being eight hours as Rallfe drove through rugged mountains and steep goat trails. For one of those eight hours, we drove over a paved highway. The rest of the trip was over rock, gravel, dirt and-boulders. I can't believe we lived through it, and marveled that our old Volkswagen did, while it groaned and creaked but kept right on trudging ahead. But the beauty of the day made it all worthwhile. The scenery was stunning, even the dry desert.

Rallfe was everything Earl had claimed. He was a bright young man with dark eyes that danced when he talked. He was full of stories of his ancestors and regaled us with the history of his country. He was excited for us to meet his country cousins, which we certainly did, as he seemed to have relatives in every village we came to; if they weren't relatives, they were long-lost friends. In spite of my worries I enjoyed meeting them all. Of course I had no clue what was said, but from their smiles and invites into their homes for tea, we knew we were welcome.

When gurgling sounds of empty stomachs filled the car, Rallfe suggested we stop at the next village to get some fresh bread. He spotted an old man squatting in the dirt next to a dilapidated storefront. He asked the man where we could get some fresh bread and butter. The man waved at us to follow him. We all piled out of the car and trailed behind as he jabbered on to Rallfe. Through side alleys and turn-backs we walked, until we came upon a small rundown two-story hut that looked as if it was held together with mud and straw. The top floor was the living quarters, the bottom a barn. An emaciated cow stood tethered to a drooping fence next to the barn, munching on what little grass sprouts could be found after the goats had had their fill. She raised her head long enough to see what all the commotion was about, then went back to her munching. The cow's udder was small with thin, elongated teats. They looked to be sucked dry and I wondered how she could produce anything other than powdered milk. Her ribs rose up under her hide like rows of bamboo sticks, and a bell hung from her scrawny neck. We all patted her bony flanks as we walked by.

Rallfe said that owning a cow and goats showed this family to be in good standing in the community. They sold milk and bread to the locals, and also had their fill of fresh milk and butter daily. Rallfe's statement got Denny's attention as well. He looked back at the skinny teats and asked: "How can fresh milk come from those dried up things?" A scalding look from his father was all the answer Denny needed, but actually I'd had the same thought.

We followed the old man up cracked and uneven steps, where the smell of baking bread wafted out to us. Three *chador*-clad women were busy with bread and butter production in the kitchen. A small girl sat on the floor with her legs wrapped around a ball of dough. Flour was sprinkled liberally on her face, hands and dress. She smiled up at us as she stuck a hunk of dough in her mouth. Flat slabs of baked bread were randomly stacked around the room; some on a counter, others on the floor. That raised my hackles.

I made a mental note: *Get bread from counter.*

Tables and chairs were noticeably absent. In the corner of the room sat an old crone on a stool. Her eyes had the white sheen of cataracts, but she was still able to eye us suspiciously. I smiled. She eyed.

After Rallfe handed over 30 *rial* (forty-five cents) the old man and little girl handed over four slabs of bread, folded them like taco shells and slapped a hunk of freshly made butter inside. Thankfully I didn't have to cause a scene as the bread given to us came from a stack on the counter. The old man bowed and thanked us repeatedly for our purchase and told Rallfe where we could get some fresh honey further on up the road. Denny had his bread half-eaten by the time we got to the car. We all dove in and ate a huge hunk of the bread, then Rallfe walked back to the house and purchased more for the picnic.

We followed the old man's directions, and there in the middle of the desert we found a little old dried up moth of a man with his worldly possessions stacked around him: his bevy of bees, water pipe and prayer rug. He also had a sagging tent with a rug thrown inside for sleep. The old man was excited to see potential buyers. He told Rallfe the only people who passed him were villagers on donkeys or caravans who only wanted to trade. He took apart his stacked boxes containing thousands of bees, and with Rallfe translating, he told us how the bees got all their pollen from the beautiful desert wildflowers. We bought four plastic bottles of honey from him and off we went.

The day was long and tiring, but enlightening. Some of the villages we passed through looked like pictures out of history books. The women and older girls wore the *chador*. The little girls, maybe four to five years old, played by the roadside while the older girls were bent over a small stream, along with their mothers, washing clothes. They pounded the clothes with a small rock, then rinsed them in the dirty water. I felt this was a great lesson for my kids and should be viewed by all expat kids to see how easy they have it. Children were sweeping streets, pushing carts, and working in their family's store. Earl pointed this out to our kids who were watching in awe. Denny was the first to speak: "How come the kids are doin' the wash? Isn't that a mom's work?"

Lauri said: "No, Denny, Dad means we're lucky we don't have to do the wash in a stream or sweep streets."

"I hope they get a big allowance" Denny said, then leaned back against the seat and said: "Dad, speaking of allowance…"

Rallfe drove further up into the mountains over rocky terrain and terrifying roads until he found just the right place to stop: a large grassy plateau with a stream nearby, replenished by a small waterfall from the mountain. I spread the blankets on the ground while the kids ran to the waterfall. "Go ahead, taste it," Rallfe yelled after them. "You'll never get such clean water. It comes right from the snow."

Denny squatted down, scooped a handful from the stream, and exclaimed: "Wow, it's cold, and good, too! The water in our apartment is never cold and tastes like bleach."

After we'd had our fill of the warm, moist bread and drinks from the startling cold stream, we set off again. Rallfe said some of his relatives lived about an hour away, and they had donkeys the kids could ride. That got Denny excited, but Lauri said she'd pass. I think she had visions of the disgusting donkey she'd seen at the Fourth of July picnic. As we came over a small hill, I spotted something off in the distance. Circus tents came to mind, except they were black. Rallfe said they were Gypsies and slowed the car. Denny was excited. "We read about Gypsies in school, Dad. The teacher said sometimes they never leave the desert and wander around all their lives, and never stay in one place. Can we go closer so I can see them better?"

Rallfe said they were called a band of Gypsies and it was best just to ignore them. "They will want you to take their picture and then want something in return. I would suggest you stay here by the car."

I could see that the Gypsies were camped along a riverbed, underneath giant black awnings, which were open on all four sides. The awnings were held fast to the sand by ropes and wood poles, with about three feet of canvas hanging down on the four sides. Earl asked Rallfe to stop so he could get some pictures. Rallfe said he'd walk over and talk to them while we took pictures from the car. He said most Gypsies speak a common language based on Farsi, and normally nomads can communicate with each other, even though they may come from entirely different geographical areas.

Earl began to attach his zoom lens when we noticed some children running towards us. They stopped about ten feet from the car and indicated they wanted their picture taken by posing with subdued smiles. Earl clicked away. The smaller children of the tribe ran right up to the car. They were a sight to behold—disheveled hair, dirty faces, barefoot with ragged clothes. One little girl, about twelve, ran up to Rallfe and whispered something in his ear. "She wants you to take her to America," he said with a laugh. That's when I noticed how different this little girl looked from the rest of the tribe. She had the same almond-shaped eyes as they did, but her hair was reddish-brown, while the rest of the children had dark brown to black hair. Her eyes were green rather than brown, and her skin was not as dark as the other children. While most of the children were dirty and unkempt, her clothes were clean and her hair neatly combed, and shone as though she'd just washed it. She ran to me and hugged me. I was taken aback for a moment.

What should I do?" I asked Rallfe.

He walked over and pried her arms from my waist. "She knows you can't take her with you, so now she's hoping to get you to give her something, which she will then give to her mother. They all do this to foreigners. She's the one who was assigned this job today."

What a charmer. I wanted to give each of the children some money, but Rallfe stopped me. "Don't do that. They are born beggars and you will be laughed at when you leave. They have no need for money. They never leave this desert. Everything they have, they barter for."

I didn't care. I felt we should pay for the pictures we'd taken. I handed her a couple Iranian coins, she smiled, hugged me again, giggled, then ran off to the group under the tents. I grabbed Earl's camera and zoomed in on the parents. I could see women under the awnings, most turned in our direction. Some of the women sat cross-legged on the ground, some holding babies as they walked in circles. Others looked to be tending smaller children. The women were dressed in long flowing bright skirts and blouses. They appeared to have on several layers of clothes, with vibrant colors of red, green, purple and yellow. Colorful beads hung from their necks and were also strung through their hair and on their wrists. The men were quite drab compared to the women and children—blacks and browns, billowing pants and what looked like suit jackets. Some had dark rags on their heads and sat cross-legged on the ground in their own little circle. Some were walking around the perimeter of the tent.

Leaving our Gypsy band behind, we headed up the rugged mountains for another village of Rallfe's relatives. The ride was a dazzling and terrifying drive. Up steep mountain trails and down into green valleys and lowlands with sheep and goats wandering freely. As we drove into the small village, Rallfe stopped in front of a butcher shop. "Freshly killed lamb," he announced. "You won't find it any fresher than here."

The shop had just slaughtered a lamb and its limp body hung in the window, with its head still attached and intestines lying nearby. Denny jumped from the car to take a closer look at the corpse, then ran back vowing never to eat lamb. "Mom, it still had its eyes open, and it looked sad."

Rallfe purchased some lamb, and off we went. We stopped along a beautiful stretch of the river for our lunch. A small waterfall gushed from the side of the hill near where we sat, never touched by human hands (feet, I'm not so sure about), and so sparkling clean and cold it was a shock to the throat. We washed the meat, tomatoes and onions in the waterfall and Earl cut the meat into chunks. Rallfe made a fire and skewered the meat on sticks, laying them over the hot rocks. The kids had been off exploring the stream while Rallfe cooked the lamb, and when they returned, overcome by hunger, they readily ate what was on their plate. They had no idea what they were eating, but as they yummed and ate more, Rallfe decided the kids should know that they'd just eaten the dreaded lamb. "See, that lamb cooked up good, yes?"

"Yuk," yelped Denny. "That's the thing that was in that window?"

"It was lamb," Earl interjected, "and you just finished gulping it down and saying 'Yum.'"

"Yeah, but I didn't know it was that bloody thing with flies all over it." He dropped his plate and tried his best to look sick.

"Hey," Earl said. "It's too late to get sick. The fire killed everything on the meat, and you ate it and you liked it. I don't want to hear any more about it."

Denny ran off swearing he'd never eat another poor lamb. Lauri echoed his sentiment, but didn't seem as disgusted as her brother.

Our last stop was a grape vineyard owned by more of Rallfe's cousins. They were excited to see him and welcomed us with open arms—and three empty wooden crates. We were then led to the vines to pick and fill all three; a compliment, Rallfe said, to trust us with their grape picking. Somehow I didn't quite swallow that line.

They were the sweetest grapes I'd ever tasted. And, yes, I ate them right off the vine. I wondered what the "company" wives would think of me as I stuffed them in my mouth with abandon—sans bleaching.

I made a mental note: *Take Imodium when you get home.*

As we headed for home, Rallfe called our attention to a line of camels in the distance. "It's a caravan," he said. "The nomads take the same route from one outpost to another, trading their wares for provisions along the way. They've been doing this for centuries."

"What are their wares?" Denny asked.

"The things they want to sell," Rallfe said. "Pottery, silks from India and China, spices of all kinds. Remember, when caravans crossed the desert, no other ways to import and export products were available. No planes, trucks or trains; all done over land."

"Wow! But if there are those ways now, why do they still go by camel over the desert?"

Rallfe seemed happy to be our history teacher: "This is all they have ever known. It's been passed down from father to son for centuries. They see no reason to stop because they can still sell whatever they carry. And they still find buyers, such as the *bazaaris* in Esfahan and Tehran."

Rallfe told us of the huge barns, built centuries ago, called caravanserais, which were built just for the camel caravans, and where everyone slept; camels, goats, and families. And, speaking of families, Rallfe told us some of the men had several wives, which I imagined could cause a little ruckus between the women: *"What do you mean she gets the padded bed roll and I have to sleep in the hay!"*

A new rumor in town had me excited. Hollywood was to shoot a movie called *Caravans* in Esfahan, and I didn't want to miss the opportunity to see it filmed. I do have a vivid imagination, and I'm curious to the point of being obnoxious (I've been told), or maybe I'd seen too many movies. One way or the other I would find out where this movie was being filmed.

Hollywood did come to Esfahan, albeit very hush-hush. If it weren't for my nosiness, we might've missed it altogether. I'd asked the managers at a couple of upscale hotels if they'd heard that Hollywood would be shooting a movie called *Caravans* in Esfahan. No one had a clue. I reasoned that they'd have to film the movie near or in the bazaar, so if Trudy and I hit the bazaar every morning, we were sure to see something going on; trailers brought in for the stars, more camels than usual, lighting and sound equipment in boxes labeled *Caravans*—something different than normal.

"How about getting on as extras?" I said to Trudy.

She looked at me as though I'd gone round the bend. "Why would they want two American women as extras? They'd want locals. Iranians."

"So? We could darken our makeup and find a *chador* to throw over us. It might work."

Trudy wouldn't go for the *chador* bit, but we did use darker foundation on our faces. With a redhead and a blonde, we felt our chances were slim but decided to check it out, anyway. After about a week of scouring the bazaar for an area that might hold a large group, we found them. That was the first time we'd gone so deep into the bazaar, and it was a bit scary. I kept a vigilant eye out for anyone who might be following us, and prayed we'd be able to find our way back if we were chased. I became a tad nervous as the area became darker the farther in we walked. Finally we began to hear voices; faint at first, then louder. My imagination ran amok. There definitely was something going on up ahead. When we turned a corner it was as if we were on a Hollywood sound stage: Dozens of people, running here and there, Iranians in colorful tribal dress standing in separate groups. English could be heard now and then in the crowd. No one seemed to notice us among the throngs of extras and Hollywood people. I figured as long as no one stopped us we could pretend to be part of the production. I just knew someone from central casting would run up to us: "Wow, two perfect women as stand-ins for our love scenes with Anthony Quinn." But, alas, we were ignored. They did hire locals though, however only if they had the right qualifications: dark-skinned, black hair and spoke the language. *Picky, picky.*

We stood back and watched all the excitement. Soon a man in shorts and wearing a Hawaiian shirt that screamed "Hollywood" approached us and asked if he could help us. I was about to ask for a job, when Trudy spoke up. "We're excited you're filming here and wanted to watch."

"I'm afraid not. This is a closed set. How did you get in?"

When we told him there were no signs and no one there to stop us, he said he'd take care of that, and waved us on our way. Well, we tried. At least we could tell everyone we watched the filming of *Caravans* and also chatted with a production guy.

Fridays were days off for the men, which they irreverently called: TAIFF—Thank *Allah* it's Farsi Friday. As a rule our family would go into town on Fridays, shop around, hit the bazaar and have dinner at one of the beautiful hotels. This Friday, Earl had other plans: "What you got planned for tomorrow, Babe?" Earl asked.

"Nothing, why?"

"Well, Mohammad, one of my workers, has invited us to dinner at his home."

"Where's his home?"

"Oh, some village in the country," he said dismissively, "not too far from here."

I frowned. "Who'll be driving?"

Earl shook his head. "Me! Come-on! I've driven out there before you got here. Besides, it's in the general direction of where Rallfe took us on the picnic. He gave me directions so I won't have a problem finding it."

"But that was so remote." I knew I'd not win this one, but was nervous about venturing out without an interpreter, or for that matter, without someone who knew the area.

"Wouldn't you like to see how they live out there?" Earl asked. "The village people are very hospitable. Mohammad said it would be an honor to have us visit his home."

I thought about what some of the company wives had said after our last trip. *You were just plain lucky the Gypsies didn't rob you and leave you for dead,* and, *they could have tortured you as well.* I'd heard tales of bandits in the remote villages, and I sure didn't want to be on winding country roads in our clunky Volkswagen, or be chased by Gypsies on camels. I was sure the camels could overtake our Volkswagen. But to go alone? At least with Rallfe along we'd had a translator, and maybe someone to keep us from being robbed and left for dead. But now this would be a trip with only my husband whose Farsi was sketchy at best.

The kids looked at me for a reaction. They knew their dad was always up for anything exciting and new. He believed when you lived in a foreign country you should take an interest in the people and try to fit into their culture. Well, on one level that was probably a very noble idea, but when the people he wanted to visit lived in remote areas where we had a huge opportunity to get lost, I worried. "Can't you get an invite from someone on your job who lives in town?"

Earl often related stories about his laborers. Most of them were illiterate country people; most couldn't write their name in their own language, signing their paychecks with an X. Many of his laborers were so poor they didn't even have electricity or running water. He felt they were hard workers, were thankful for a decent-paying job, and above all, were faithful. I'm sure they respected him because he respected them.

Earl said Mohammad—age unknown, but probably around sixty— was one of his favorites on the jobsite. He understood quite a bit of English, but kept his speaking to: "Hello Meezter Crot, are you good?" and "No problem." He was always one step ahead of the other workers, always smiling and willing to do anything asked of him. "Besides that," Earl added, "his uncle is a *mullah* and will be joining them for dinner. Wouldn't you like to see a *mullah* up close?

"Not really." The *mullahs* I'd encountered around town were ragged and scary looking, and always gave me the evil eye. But, here was my worry: my husband spoke no conversational Farsi. He used his foreman, an English-speaking Iranian, to give the orders on the jobsite. He did know enough street-Farsi to greet his workers, ask about their families and such—however he had no idea what their answers were—but they liked that he cared enough to try.

I decided to think positive. I would go—and have a good time.

It was a beautiful day, the beginning of autumn, and a cool chill was in the air. The kids had opted to stay with friends. Without the usual back seat quibbling, the ride was intoxicating. I even looked forward to meeting Mohammad and his family. After we'd driven for quite a long time, I became a bit nervous. "Are we lost yet?"

"Thanks for the confidence."

"Sorry, but you didn't answer my question."

"No! I'm not lost. I'm just not where I expected to be."

I was pretty sure that meant we were lost. But I knew better than to push this male-ego thing about getting lost. I've never understood why men have a problem with admitting it. It's okay. It's human. What's the big deal? I do it all the time.

Another thirty minutes of Earl driving, with me biting my tongue, we began to see signs of life—a goat here, a donkey there. A slight bend in the road found us in front of a small, wooden lean-to. An ancient-looking man sat on his haunches on the front stoop, his head drooped in slumber. I said a silent prayer of thanks to the God of Travelers. "Is this Mohammed? He sure doesn't look like he's expecting company."

"No, this doesn't look right, but maybe this guy knows Mohammed."

Earl parked the car on a dirt patch and approached the man. He gave a slight bow as if the man were a Crown Prince. "*Salam, Agha.*

Bebahkshid,"—apologizing for waking him. He handed the man the crumpled scrap of paper with directions to Mohammad's house written in Farsi.

The old man grunted, ignoring the piece of paper, then patted the floor next to him for Earl to sit.

What the heck? I watched in amazement as my husband sat on the stoop as if he had all the time in the world to visit. But then I recalled that Iranians are very hospitable; they want to chat and drink tea first. I could see a wide smile on Earl's face as he accepted something the old man passed him. *Now what's he doing?* From where I sat, I could swear my husband was sucking on some type of hose, which was attached to a tall, skinny vase. Oh, this is great, I thought. He's happily smoking and visiting while I sit here in the car, it's getting late, I'm cold, and people are waiting on us for dinner.

Wait! Earl doesn't smoke. I sat there in angst for another ten minutes. At that point I figured politeness had its limits. I was about to get out of the car and grouse when I saw Earl pass the vase back to the old man. With bony fingers, the old man drew something in the dirt, which I hoped was directions and not a game of tic-tac-toe. They both stood. The old man pointed a feeble, crooked finger toward the north. Earl bowed, said his *khoda hafez's*—goodbyes—and headed for the car with a huge smile on his face.

"Well, did you enjoy your smoke?"

"What was I supposed to do? He offered it as a sign of welcome. I had to take it."

"But you don't smoke."

"It wasn't tobacco. It was hashish."

"What?"

"Hashish. It's a mix of grass and opium."

"What? In that vase?"

"It's not a vase, it's called a hookah, and you suck on the pipe. Stateside the kids use grass in the hookah, here they use opium."

"Opium? How can they afford to buy that?" I'd heard that it grew wild along the country roads, and rumor had it that the old people could help themselves to it, but I'd thought it was just that—a rumor.

Earl laughed: "It's the Shah's answer to Social Security. It keeps the old guys happy, and it's not illegal for them."

"Wait! You mean you smoked opium just now?"

"Well it sure wasn't tobacco."

Ohmygawd! "Can you drive okay? Do you feel woozy?"

"No, but life does seem a lot sweeter."

I kept a close eye on my husband as we headed for our destination. He seemed a tad too relaxed. I prayed he'd find Mohammed's house without stopping again. I didn't think he could take another hit of politeness. Miraculously, Earl found his friend's home. I exited the car with a knot in my stomach and a full bladder, and Earl with a huge grin on his face. Mohammed met us at the door with welcoming arms, a kiss on each cheek for Earl and a bow for me. He rattled off some Farsi I'd hoped didn't mean we were too late and the food was gone. I was famished. He put an arm around Earl and led him into a large room. I followed, feeling like the uninvited guest. When they entered the room I hesitated at the doorway. Was I supposed to follow them into this room? I wasn't invited to sit with them, and I saw no women on the floor, which I assumed was the custom. No one seemed to notice that I still stood in the dark hall.

The room was immense. Persian carpets covered the floor. A white sofreh—a type of tablecloth—had been spread on top of the Persian carpets and was laden with heaping plates and bowls of food, looking like a stateside potluck, only on the ground. I later learned that to an Iranian, the more food offered, the more prestige the family has. It looked to me like Mohammed must have been very prestigious.

Several men and young boys sat together, cross-legged, forming a circle around the food. At the far end sat an ancient white-bearded man. His head wrap and robes signaled he was a *mullah*—a holy man—and all seemed to defer to him whenever he spoke, which was generally with a mouthful of food. I also noticed most of the men were shoveling the food into their mouths with their fingers—a sight that made my stomach lurch. Even as the bowls were passed around, the men would reach in with fingers, grab a handful and shove it in their mouth, then politely pass the bowl on.

Okay, so this is how the country folk take their meals. I'd said I wanted to see how they lived, so who am I to lurch? But I was relieved I wasn't sitting among them. I looked around the room. Antique brass and copper pots held prominent positions on the walls and floor. I saw no "sitting" furniture such as sofas, easy chairs, or the like. Also missing were a dining table and chairs. I wondered if I was limber enough to get down on the floor and up again without help. When you haven't pushed your quads or hamstrings into submission since childhood, how can you possibly expect them to expand? I watched Earl take his place in the circle, and was amazed that he sat without a hitch. I reasoned it had to be the opium that made him so limber. I could see he had totally immersed himself in the introductions all around. Even though I knew he would never remember any names, or what was said, he definitely seemed like he understood every word with a look of total interest in what everyone was saying. What more could a host want?

Mohammed looked up, smiled at me then yelled something in Farsi that made me jump. Two *chador*-clad women appeared in the hallway. "*Bia inja, bia,*"—come here, they said as they took my arm and led me down the hall. I felt a little better about this whole thing, but stopped grinning when I stepped into the kitchen. About ten women, some standing, others squatting, were eating from bowls they held in their hands. I covertly scanned the room and could see no place to sit. Then it dawned on me. This must be the cultural thing I'd heard about; men eat first, women eat when they're through serving the men.

Before I took a plate offered me, I knew I was in serious need of a bathroom visit. "*Meekham dastshoo'e?*" I said meekly, hoping I'd used the right pronunciation for bathroom.

"*Baleh, baleh*," one of them said as the others giggled. She took my arm and led me outside. A bright moon revealed a small lean-to. She took my hand and pointed to the shack. I looked at her quizzically. "*Baleh*," she said, then headed back to the house.

"*Khayli mamnoon,*" I mumbled, sorry to watch her leave. I would have preferred her to stand outside and wait for me, but she probably didn't like being out there in the dark anymore than I did. Inside the shack it was cold and smelled like a cesspool. A small window let in the moon's glow. I stood for a minute to get my bearings, but none were there. I ran my fingers on the wall where I thought a light switch might be. Nothing, except a sticky feeling. I shivered as I wiped my hand on my slacks. Okay, maybe a pull-cord of sorts. I ran my hand over my head to feel for some sort of cord, then got the heebie-jeebies when a sticky web attached to my fingers. I let out a yelp. This was no bathroom! Rather it resembled an outhouse, only a bit larger. The floor was dirt, which I could feel as my shoes scraped across it. The walls were corrugated tin and pinged as I touched them. The roof was…I couldn't even see a roof, but I had a wild feeling it wasn't red ceramic tiles. I also wondered how many species of spiders were about to pounce on my bare butt if I dropped my knickers.

No! It wasn't going to happen. The stench had me reeling as I staggered out. My bladder would have to hold out for a few more hours. I'd heard brutal rumors that had to do with holes in the ground, and the odor, but so far I'd not had to use one. This was not going to be the day. I walked back to the house and tried not to notice the questioning looks at my rapid return. I did hear a few giggles, so I giggled back.

A few bowls piled with food waited for me on the counter. I assumed that meant I'd be eating my meal in the standing position. The women had finished their meals, while one of them was squatting on the tiled floor washing the dishes in a plastic tub. I noticed the floor tile had a drain hole in the center of the room, next to her dishpan, and was surprised to see her toss the dishwater around the floor, and push it towards the hole with a broom. Handy, I thought, just throw a bucket of water on the floor and scoot it down the drain; dirty water gone from the dishpan, while shining up the floor.

I smiled and emptied my bowls like a good little guest.

The food was incredible. When I'd first come to Iran I was introduced to what the expats called "burnt rice," an Iranian dish called *Tah-deegh*. I wondered why this hadn't caught on in the American diet. It was heavenly! The rice was cooked first, then poured into a separate pot that had been heated with oil and spices. When the rice on the bottom turned brown and crunchy, the pan was upended and served with a golden crust of rice on top. After I'd had two helpings of the *Tah-deegh*, string beans, red cabbage, radishes and lamb, I thought it prudent to stop. The women were genuinely pleased that I ate so much. Next came fresh fruits and yogurt. I was so busy eating I didn't even realize I was still standing. Oh well, as they say, When in Rome…

On the drive home Earl waxed on about the wonderful evening, and wasn't I glad I'd come, and weren't they the perfect hosts? Yes, I agreed, but when I asked him what the men had talked about, he said: "Beats the shit out of me, but I sure had a good time."

I was not surprised at his answer, especially after his appetizer of opium.

Less than a mile down the road my bladder began to push against my waistband. "Can you pull over, please, I have to pee."

"What? Are you sure? It's pretty dark out there."

"Pull over, please!"

I opened the car door, unzipped, squatted down as far as my tight quads would allow, and let go. *If the company ladies could only see me now*!

14

Cheating Death

A few weeks had passed since our last outing to the country, when Earl came home from work with another trip planned for us. I opened my mouth to protest, but he held up his hands to silence me: "Don't worry, it's with a couple I know from the jobsite, Steve and Elaine, and they've done this river trip a couple times."

"River trip?"

"Sounds fun, huh? They have an eight-man raft, plenty room for all of us."

As my eyes widened, Earl said: "No need to get all excited. It's not rapids or anything like that. A small current, not whitewater."

"But what about…"

"I said not to worry. You know I wouldn't take my family any place that wasn't safe. You'll love it, and you and Lauri can wear your bathing suits. Steve says it's in the middle of the boonies. In fact it's so remote there aren't any homes in sight, so no country people to deal with. Doesn't that sound like a fun trip?"

"Uh, well, I…"

"No worries about the driving either. Steve has driven all over this country on his days off. He's sort of a hippy-type, you know? Long hair, long beard, but he's sharp as hell, and knows his way around these roads. He also speaks fluent Farsi. Whatdaya say?"

What could I say? He was hyped. The kids were hyped. I couldn't be the bad guy here. Considering we'd made two previous trips to the country without being kidnapped or slaughtered on the roads, I felt I should give it a try. "So you trust Steve? I mean, you know him well enough to trust his judgment?"

"I do."

According to Earl, Steve had been on the job for over a year, taking R&Rs to Thailand and Viet Nam. "He's a real explorer. You'll like him. He looks like a Hell's Angel, but he's a teddy bear."

As I prepared for the trip, I remembered the wives' orientation. We'd been told not to wear bathing suits in public. Going to the country seemed rather innocuous, but I was a born worrier. I did concede we girls could at least wear tank tops and cut-off jeans. The weather was still warm most days, but cooled down in the evenings. The thought of going swimming in a clean cool river did sound appealing.

Friday turned out to be a beautiful, cloudless day and I was eager to get out of the city. Lauri invited Trudy's daughter, Melanie, as Denny had already made swimming plans for the day at a friend's house. We packed some bread, fruit, cheese and wine and headed out to meet up with Steve and Elaine. When we pulled up to their apartment, Steve was standing outside to greet us. My first thought was that Steve could've starred in *Conan the Barbarian;* all he needed was a headband and leather jock strap. He was huge! Over six feet, with orange hair billowing out around his face and shoulders like he'd just stepped from the eye of a hurricane. Eyebrows that resembled Andy Rooney's, and hands the size of baseball mitts. On his feet, which looked the size of swim-fins, he sported Conan-type sandals.

Then he opened his mouth. "Well, here's that pretty little lady I been hearin' about." His voice sounded like what the nuns told us we'd hear on Resurrection Day: Booming! Thunderous! He walked toward me with open arms that looked like they could easily span a few telephone poles. I steeled myself for the hug, but was surprised; it felt like being engulfed in a huge, hairy sleeping bag. All of a sudden I felt safe. No one would mess with us with this tank around. His wife, Elaine, was the antithesis of her husband: small, petite, long golden hair that nearly touched her waist. I immediately knew I wouldn't like her. Well, it would have helped if she'd been a tad larger and not so beautiful. I felt like one of Cinderella's stepsisters.

The trip sounded exciting as Steve waxed on about it. He and Elaine had done this before with another couple and had no problems. He'd seen no homes or people. He'd found a perfect place to launch the raft where the current was swift towards the middle of the river, but slow near the shore. He would help Earl inflate the raft, then he and his wife would take the Jeep down to a spot where the current slowed, and we would come ashore. We'd then all get in the jeep, drive back up to the launching site, drop off Steve and Elaine with the raft, and then Earl and I would drive downriver to pick them up when they came ashore. Wow, I thought, he's really got this thing planned. I couldn't imagine doing this with anyone else but Steve.

Steve drove out of town for about an hour, when we came to a beautiful, secluded area on the river. As I looked around I had to admit it was definitely "remote" as he'd promised. Tall, gangly trees were canopied over the riverbank. The sand was clean and compact, as if no foot had ever touched it. A forest of trees could be seen off in the distance, but beyond that were mountains and blue sky. We threw down a blanket, put up some sand chairs and polished off the picnic lunch we'd brought. Steve pulled a bottle of wine from his Jeep, which the men promptly emptied, while the girls splashed in the water in front of us. We sat around and gossiped about the jobsite for about an hour or so: the marriages, who'd left whom, and who'd cheated on whom—an expat tried-and-true time-waster.

Everything seemed to go smoothly.

That is, up to the point where Steve and Elaine drove off.

Earl told Steve to go on ahead, he didn't need help inflating the raft. This worried me. The raft was huge, and I really didn't want to be alone that long, anywhere, much less a remote stretch of the river. *Please don't go, please don't go* I silently prayed as they climbed into their Jeep. I felt suddenly very vulnerable, but I didn't share that with my husband.

"Goodbye, good luck," they'd yelled as they drove off.

I sincerely hoped that's what we'd have.

While the girls and I jumped around in the frigid water further downstream, Earl was in the water up to his knees while he set about inflating the raft. We were about fifty yards away when I thought I heard Earl yelling. I looked up to see him waving both arms at me as he screamed my name. I couldn't hear what he said, but by the tenor of his voice I knew I'd better move. I grabbed the two girls by the arms and we began to run toward him.

"What is it?" I yelled, as we got closer.

He pointed toward the trees. I glanced over my shoulder. That's when I saw them. A few men were walking in our direction, each waving something over their head.

"Run, Dodie, Goddammit! Get the girls and get in the raft!" His voice terrified me. It was a tone I'd never heard from my husband. Feral! He was our protector. How could he be afraid of anything?

As I ran with the girls, I took a quick look back. Now I noticed many more men. They seemed to be walking faster and picking up things from the ground. We ran as long as we could on the sand, then crashed into the water, legs pumping, and jumped into the raft. Earl threw me an oar and told me to use it if anyone got too close. He pushed the raft out farther and jumped in. We seemed to be moving in slow motion. For every oar stroke, the men seemed to get closer. Then they jumped into the river and were swimming after us, and their numbers had increased.

An adrenalin surge seemed to suck all the air from my lungs. How could this be happening? We hadn't hurt anyone. What had we done to cause this? I began pushing the oar against the water with all my strength, but I could see they were gaining on us. We weren't yet in the fast current and I prayed we'd reach it before the men got any closer. How could those men swim that fast while encumbered with suit jackets, slacks, shoes and sticks?

"Look out," Earl yelled as our raft approached a railroad trestle. I looked up and saw several men standing there. I watched helplessly as they reined rocks down on us. Earl had the girls lie flat on the bottom of the raft and cover their heads. I was still rowing frantically and had no way to cover myself, when a rock the size of a tennis ball slammed into my thigh. I let out a yelp, which incited the men in the water, and at one point, one of the faster swimmers got his hand on the edge of the raft and tired to pull himself in. Earl, cursing, stood up and slammed the oar down on the man's hand several times, then onto his head. The man let go, grabbed his head and disappeared under the water. I thought he'd killed the man, but then he surfaced. He had a stunned look on his face, as though he didn't know what to do next. The other men, witnessing this, came to a stop, and then began to swim back toward the shore.

I now know what it feels like to be on "autopilot." I had no knowledge of what I was doing. I worked that paddle in and out of the water like a robot. My heart beat so hard I thought it would burst through my chest. Earl finally brought me around by yelling my name. "Dodie! You can relax now. They're gone."

I dropped down into the raft and began to sob, my cries converging with the girls'. "My God, Earl, we could have been killed, drowned, and no one would ever know what happened to us. Why did this happen? I want to go home, not just home here. I want to go back to the States."

"Stop!" he yelled. "They were just a few ignorant fanatics. I'm sure they were only reacting to you wearing shorts."

"Fanatics? They're lunatics. Why would you want to kill someone because their arms and legs are showing?" I could still hear myself as I sobbed and gulped for air. I knew I was near hysteria, but somehow couldn't stop. I could hear the girls' sobs. Both of them were in the fetal position, arms wrapped tight around their heads with their faces stuck against the wet, smelly bottom of the raft. I vaguely remembered hearing them cry throughout the ordeal, but couldn't stop oaring to comfort them. I reached down and pulled the girls up. I tried to soothe them but my daughter would have none of it. "I want to go home too, Mom," my daughter whimpered. "There are mean people here."

We finally reached the spot where Steve and his wife had parked the jeep. When we came ashore, we didn't have to say a word. They could see the fear in our faces.

"What happened, man? You look like ghosts."

"Your rafting trip almost turned into a drowning," Earl said, as he pulled the raft to the shore and helped us step out. "I thought you said this place was remote, nobody around for miles."

Earl's accusatory tone was a shock to Steve. "It was, man. I never saw anyone here both times we'd come." Steve turned to me. "What the hell happened to your leg?"

I looked at my leg for the first time since the rock hit me. The skin was angry and red, about the size of a grapefruit. "A well-placed aim," I said. "Can we just get out of here before they come looking for us?"

We rode in silence for the first half-hour. Then Steve began to chat with Earl, saying he just couldn't figure it out. He'd never seen anyone near the river. Earl told him to forget about it. He didn't blame him. He blamed himself for putting his family in jeopardy. The rest of the trip was quiet, as we all had our own thoughts of that terrible experience.

I called Rallfe and Dori for dinner the next night. "Rallfe," I started, "I have to ask you a question about your countrymen."

"No problem," he said. "but I can't always give an answer for some of my people. They seem to be changing right in front of my eyes."

"Rallfe, we were attacked by a mob at the river."

"What? What river? Why were you there?"

Earl told him about the river raft trip, and what had happened. "Rallfe, the girls didn't have on swimsuits, they were wearing cut-off jeans and Tee-shirts. We were told there were no homes or people up there. There were no villages in sight."

Rallfe looked down as if studying the patterns on the tablecloth. Finally he looked up at me. "I apologize for the backward ways of some of my countrymen. But I can tell you why they were furious with you. You were in the water."

"Of course I was in the water! What else are rivers for?"

"No! Not for women."

I didn't understand what he meant by that, but then remembered the river in town, how men and small boys would be splashing away, but no women. I was always curious why the women stood there on the shore, covered in black on a hot miserable day. "Why do they want to keep women out of the water?"

Rallfe looked truly apologetic, as well as embarrassed. Dorri spoke up for the first time: "Some illiterate men believe that women are dirty and pollute the water."

"Because…?"

"Because of their menses."

"You mean anytime, or just during their menses?"

"Anytime!"

Here was an answer to my question, but I was stunned into silence. It would take me a long time to get my head around that one.

Rallfe explained that many Iranians want their Islamic religion back; which supposedly the Shah had nearly eradicated. They firmly believe in the Holy Koran, which says a woman must cover her body so as not to tempt a man with unclean thoughts.

Unclean thoughts? Didn't these men have any more willpower than that? "In other words you're saying for a man to look at a woman's skin or hair can cause them to want to jump her bones, or the next woman to come along? I find that hard to believe!"

"That's the thinking."

"What about those men who watch the French porn movies in Tehran?" I asked. "What about those sinful thoughts watching that trash? Are the porn stars to be killed because they caused such thoughts?"

"That's different," Rallfe said. "They can't stop the theaters from showing those movies. And most religious men would not go to see them. Only the unholy."

"Whoa! There were hundreds of men lined up to go into the theater when we drove by. Does that make them sinners?"

"I guess that's the general feeling. But the thought held by the Islamists is the woman is at fault, not the man."

I wondered at the dichotomy: here were men running around pinching foreign women, grabbing their breasts and standing in line to watch porn movies, but were incensed about a woman showing a strand of hair.

"I personally think it shows poor restraint on the man's part if it leads him to sin," Rallfe continued, "but then I'm westernized. I lived in America too long, and the women in my family have never worn the *chador* or even head scarves."

I asked Rallfe why some women still covered their hair. He said when the *chador* was first banned by the Shah's father, older women who'd worn the chador for years fought this restriction, and couldn't imagine going without one, while younger women were delighted to remove it. But now with the way the country seemed to want to return to Islamic law, he doubted women would be allowed to go without one. Freedom for Iranian women has a long, sad history, he said: In 1962, women finally received the right to vote, and in 1967 they got the right to divorce. However, if the wife divorced her husband, she gave up the rights to her children.

Why didn't they tell us this at our company orientation? I wondered. Nothing was said about women not allowed in the water. I'm sure it would have sent a few wives home to unpack. "I wonder if it's time to pack up and go home."

"We can make sure that never happens again," Earl said, giving me a look, "but I'm sure not going to let one isolated incident send us packing."

After Rallfe and Dorri left, I had some serious thinking to do. I was thankful we escaped with our lives, and also vowed we would never go near a river, or any body of water outside of the Clubhouse for that matter. I wondered what the Iranian employees at the Clubhouse thought of us in our brief tennis outfits and swimsuits. They always showed us respect, no matter how we were dressed.

When I thought about this whole scenario of women tempting men, I thought back to my catechism days in grade school about the Adam and Eve story. I have to believe that while writing Genesis, some ancient misogynist suggested: "Hey, let's write that the woman tempted the man with the apple, then we can always blame her for our sins."

1977 – Isfahan

15

A Stoning

The sky loomed dark with brooding, heavy clouds. Wind whistled through the dank alleyways as Trudy and I walked deeper into the bazaar. I shuddered as I pulled my parka tighter around me. *Should I be doing this? Should I turn back?*

I had put out the word that I wanted to purchase a silk carpet. They were sold all over town, but I wanted to find one that was incredibly beautiful *and* incredibly inexpensive. My Iranian neighbor, Bibi*, told me of such a place in the bazaar. She said the merchant sold exquisite silk carpets that were intricately woven by his wife and daughter, and he sold them much lower than the rug merchants in town because his was a family endeavor. I was ready to go. Bibi* drew a little map for me, which at the time looked clear as mud. "Don't worry," she said. "You'll find him."

I really didn't need another Persian carpet, but the thought of a silk one was overpowering. I could ship the carpet home and then find a room to put it in later. But, wait, I thought, I don't have a home to ship it to. I couldn't think of that now. I'd mail it to my sister to keep for us until we returned and found a home.

Trudy agreed to go with me to the bazaar, and hopefully, between the two of us we'd find the rug merchant. The bazaar stretched forever as we made our way deeper into the dark passageways, lighted only by an occasional crack in the mud roof, and a few light bulbs hanging from strings. We passed long-deserted buildings, walls covered with crumbling mosaics that opened onto secret courtyards. While walking through the labyrinth of honeycomb alcoves, Trudy asked, not for the first time, "Are you sure you know where this rug guy is? I could swear we're going in circles."

She was right. I knew I'd seen a couple of these buildings before. I'd followed the map Bibi had drawn, but all of a sudden the alleyway petered out. Maybe I'd taken a wrong turn, but I couldn't admit that to Trudy. "She did say we had to go into the bazaar quite a ways. I'm sure we're okay." I had a creepy feeling about being so far into the bazaar, and I knew Trudy was right. We were lost.

We were now well past the cacophony of the entrance. It was eerily silent. We kept walking. I was about ready to admit defeat and turn back, when we heard voices. We stopped. "Did you hear that?" I asked. "There's someone up ahead."

We stood still as we tried to fix on where the voices came from. "They sound angry," Trudy said. "Maybe we..."

Trudy was interrupted by a shrill scream; the unmistakable wailing of a woman. My heart thudded and my skin rose up in goose bumps. What had we heard? I had to find out. I led Trudy by the hand as we picked our way through the myriad of alcoves deeper into the bazaar. "Stay close to me," I whispered. I hugged the sides of the old, crumbling walls as curiosity pushed me forward. We could hear men's angry voices as we crept closer. Trudy stopped dead in her tracks. She was not going another step. "Let's get out of here."

I peeked around the next alcove. At first I wasn't sure what I saw. It was a group of men circled around a writhing figure on the ground. Then it hit me, "Oh my God!"

"What!" she hissed. "What did you see?"

I turned back toward her. She stood stock-still, afraid what my answer would be.

"Ohmygod, Trudy, I think they're stoning a woman!"

"No!" She tried to turn but her feet seemed frozen.

I could feel my legs weaken. I wanted to turn and run, too. If they were stoning a woman, what would they do if they found us here? I'd heard the rumors that the practice of stoning a woman to death for adultery was commonplace in this chauvinistic patriarchal land, but I still had to see it to believe it.

"Come here," I hissed. We inched closer. From a distance of about thirty yards we could see a group of men circled around a woman lying on the ground. Several *mullahs* were in among them, and one particular *mullah* seemed to be calling the shots. He'd yell something out in Farsi, which seemed to rile the men as they picked up another rock to hurl at the prostrate figure in the center of the circle. As the men stooped to pick up rocks, we could see a small woman in the center, curled into the fetal position, and covered in black. Her screams pierced the air above as men heaved rocks at her. My heart thudded in my ears. My legs felt like they would crumble under me. I grabbed Trudy's arm and we turned to run.

And ran right into a black body!

"Vhat you doink?" she hissed. "No place for foreigner. How you find here?"

A woman covered in a black *chador* stood in front of us with a menacing look as she waited for an answer. I could feel Trudy's body go limp. I firmed up my hold on her arm. *Don't faint on me Trudy.* I surely didn't want to face this alone. "*Salam kanoom*, we got lost," I said. "Can you tell us where the exit is?" My voice sounded like I had a mouth full of helium. If I hadn't had to hold Trudy up, I think I would've fainted.

The woman's steely black eyes glared at us. I knew I'd not convinced her of our innocence. "Go!" she ordered as she pointed in the direction we'd come.

"*Khayli mamnoon*," I mumbled as we took off running. I had no idea where we were headed, but I knew it was in the opposite direction of that horrible scene. We stopped to catch our breath when we heard the unmistakable babble of merchants and the banging of coppersmiths. I wanted to scream, to cry, to kill those men. I don't remember how we reached the front of the bazaar because my mind was awash with thoughts of murder, but the entrance was a most welcome sight.

Trudy was staring straight ahead as she drove us home, her jaw set. I couldn't blame her for being upset with me for dragging her into the bowels of the bazaar. But I was overcome with the sickening sight we'd just witnessed and needed to talk about it. I finally broke the silence. "What kind of archaic beliefs do these people have? To kill a woman because she had an affair? And what about the man she slept with? Where the hell was he? Why wasn't his cheating arse stoned by a bunch of ticked off women?"

"Good point."

"Can you imagine the terror and fear she must have felt?"

"Well, maybe she should've thought about that before she crawled into his bed," Trudy said, philosophically. "Women here know the rules they have to live by."

"He must've swept her off her feet and right into bed," I said, "but I don't think any man is worth dying for—I don't care how good he is in bed."

I apologized to Trudy for getting her into such a dangerous situation. I knew she would never have gone so far into the bazaar on her own. She'd been here longer than me, and other than her crazy driving, and running across busy streets, she had much more sense. She said she was amazed at how I kept forging ahead. She thought for sure I knew exactly where I was headed. We were silent for the rest of the trip home, each with our own sickening thoughts of what we'd just witnessed.

For months that scene invaded my dreams. What happened to her? Did she have a family? And what about the man she was adulterous with? This was a man's country, a man's religion. It seemed that women were only here for their husband's needs, procreation, meals, and housekeeping. What these women needed was a big dose of Gloria Steinem!

16

Shah & I Go To USA

We heard through the grapevine that the Shah and his wife were traveling to the U.S. as guests of President Carter. When we finally received the newspaper in our care package—always two weeks late—we read the headlines with some relief: "*Rosalynn Carter and Jimmy Carter host welcoming ceremony for the state visit of the Shah of Iran and Shahbanou of Iran, 11/15/1977.*

That came as good news to all of us. We thought it meant everything was still copasetic with the U.S. and Iran. We'd heard some new rumors flying around about the Shah getting his butt in hot water with the *mullahs*, as well as ordering SAVAK to do away with dissidents. But the problem with rumors is that they are exactly that. No one knows what's going on, and everyone has something to add: "Did you hear the Shah is going to be run out of Iran?" or "Did you hear SAVAK is turning against him?"

And so it went. Basically, I tried to ignore any talk of the Shah or his country. I figured it wasn't my business and really nothing seemed different, other than I'd noticed a few extra *mullahs* skulking about. Esfahan is a big city, and I thought they might be having their yearly convention. Days would go by and I wouldn't see a *mullah,* then one day I'd see them group in the square or shuffling along near the mosques. They always had an evil eye for the Western women, but I still didn't connect the dots. Because I'd half-heartedly accepted Rallfe's explanation of why the attack at the river had taken place, I realized I'd better put that terrifying day behind me and try to go on with life in this sexist country.

The weather finally began to cool off, and so did I. Life was so much easier now that I could walk without passing out. Shopping was now old hat. I was considered a regular and most of the shopkeepers knew me as the lady with the red face and determined look. I could keep up with the best of them now. I knew when to approach the scales, toss whatever was in them into the bin below, and put in my own stuff. Now, I would only do this when I noticed the Iranian women arguing over the price of something, or, who knows, they could have been discussing their husband's erectile dysfunction. All I knew was they were paying no attention to their scales and I had an opportunity. Of course, I'd get screamed at, but by the time they were through calling evil spirits down on my ancestors and me, I'd called the shopkeeper over to give me a price.

I took this as a sign of fitting in, of being a force to reckon with, and also a kindred spirit to these feisty women. In time I think they respected me for standing up to them. In fact, as they got more familiar with me I'd even be offered a piece of fruit they deemed edible. I had to take a bite, didn't I?

These women were meticulous shoppers, and I watched them to see where the best fruit or veggies were stacked. Most times the juiciest fruits or sturdiest veggies were hidden under the old and bruised produce, similar to the markets in America where they stack the oldest goods in front of the newest.

However, I knew I'd never acclimate to the traffic and *kamikaze* drivers. In fact, I felt lucky to be alive after one glorious day of tennis in the country, followed by a terrifying ride back to the city. One of the girls I played tennis with at the Club had invited me to her home in Khaneh for lunch and tennis. Denny was off school that day and decided he'd like to come along and play tennis with her son. Khaneh was a good forty minutes from our apartment in town, but most of that time was spent getting out of Esfahan. I was delighted to get away from the city noise and continuous noxious fumes at my apartment. I called for a *Susan* taxi, but when I saw the driver I had second thoughts. He looked to be about fifteen years old, extremely handsome, and from the moment he floored the accelerator and yelled out the window at a couple of pretty girls, I knew I was in trouble. Denny and I looked at each other, gulped and tried to smile. I told the driver several times "*Khayli baad*" but he only winked at me in the rear-view mirror, pushed the pedal to the metal and let her fly. We were thrown all over the back seat with his radical turns. When we arrived at my friend's house I tipped the crazy driver out of gratitude for getting us there alive. We made Khaneh in twenty minutes and left a trail of honking, irate drivers.

For our return to Esfahan, I was able to flag down a company driver who'd just dropped off a passenger in Khaneh. Usually the company drivers drove fairly safe because the wives would report any reckless driving and they could lose an easy job. I guess our driver took one look at me—red-faced from tennis, clothes disheveled—and assumed I'd probably pass out and wouldn't notice his erratic driving.

"*Agha!* Slow down, please," I pleaded, as he got more reckless. He didn't acknowledge my pleas. At one point we were flying down a narrow street—room for maybe one-and-a-half cars—when Denny let out a yelp and told me there were two cars coming right at us. I slunk down low in my seat; I couldn't bear to look out the window.

"Look, Mom, you have to see this!"

I took a quick peek and screamed, "*Agha!* Slow down, you're going to get us killed!" Then I slid back down into the fetal position.

Denny was still at his post at the window giving me a blow-by-blow account. "No way!" he exclaimed, "Our driver's going down the middle of the road."

Just as I was sure we'd be dead in a matter of minutes, Denny broke in: "Mom! Both cars moved over at the last second." According to Denny, our driver had sailed between them like they were pylons, never flinching, and continued on at break-neck speed while he yelled oaths at the cars he left in the dust.

"Wow! Mom! That car was so close I could've touched it."

I wondered how we'd escaped death. There didn't seem to be any safe mode of travel. If I took the private-car taxis, I'd be stuffed in with unpleasant odors and evil looks. If I took the bus, I'd have to worry about collisions with trucks. So, it had to be the company van, if at all possible, but first I'd check out the driver's age. He'd have to be much older and wiser. I had to put my fate in the hands of *Allah* and forget about it. Either that, or never leave the house—but that wasn't an option. There were too many places to go and money to be spent.

More sad commemoration days were upon us: the tenth day of the month in the month of *Moharam,* and were considered days of sorrow and mourning. During the two days, people primarily wore black clothing, and joined their neighborhood congregations of mourners. Usually they gathered in a mosque in the morning hours and chanted mournful lyrics while they beat their chest by hand, or beat their back with a bundle of chains. There was also, in each group of mourners, a musician who beat the drum or cymbals. At their homes they served "holy" food to guests as a sign of respect and allegiance to *Emam Hosien* and the other martyrs. There are many sermons delivered by religious leaders in each neighborhood, and no happy music is allowed during the two days. No weddings are planned during the entire month of *Moharam* out of respect for the *Emam*.

What was most unnerving to me was the parade I witnessed down the middle of the city streets. Men were walking, holding hands, crying. Some were shirtless, periodically swinging a heavy chain over their shoulders and lacerating their bare flesh. Blood ran down their backs but they continued the lashings. When I asked Rallfe about this he said it was a time to show their sorrow and reflection, and mourning the prophet's grandson.

I made a mental note: *Never let daughter marry a muslim.*

Clouds, gray skies, and homesickness arrived along with the month of December. Missing my son, homesickness for Christmas carols, for the smell of fir trees and fireplaces, for the friendliness and excitement that emanates from people on the street as the holidays draw near. I wasn't homesick for the house I'd left behind, but for family and friends, presents for the kids under the tree and familiar surroundings. I wanted to go back to the States for Christmas in the worst way, but of course leaving my husband at this time of year didn't seem very wifely. I'd already found a sad little artificial tree, decorated it with the colored lights Iranians hang around their cars, and an assortment of sad-looking red balls and bells. Hey, you do what you have to do when you have to do it!

Then the phone call came.

It was from my sister, Margie. "You'd better get back here soon," she said. "Chris is having problems."

My body slumped. "What happened? I thought things were going okay. Cliff never called me." I'd called and talked to Chris, then to Cliff and his wife at least once a month, and things were going fine. Chris was working towards getting his Carpenter's Union Card, which would give him more money and health insurance. He was pumped up about that when we'd talked. How had things deteriorated so fast? Margie said Cliff had called her because he couldn't get a call through to our house.

He asked her to pass this on to us: Chris was not working for Cliff anymore. Cliff caught him smoking pot on the jobsite and fired him.

"Is Chris still living at Cliff's?" I asked, dreading the answer.

"Yes, but he says he's going to move in with a buddy. And Cliff is worried."

"I'll call you right back."

Earl had walked up as I took the call. He knew by my expression that it was bad news. Chris, right? Drugs, right? I knew this would happen. Thank God he didn't come with us. We'd all be thrown out of the country by now."

This was not what I wanted to hear. Earl, as a stepfather, had given up on Chris a long time ago. But as a mother, you never give up hope that your child will find his way. I had no way to help my son. Since he was ten years old he'd danced to his own drummer and I wasn't privy to that beat. I'd thought if I left him in the care of his uncle, whom he got along with, he would make sure Chris worked every day, and everything would miraculously work out. I'd hoped. That wasn't enough.

When Earl calmed down, I told him what my sister had said. "You need to fly home and take care of this. We can't expect my brother to be responsible for Chris if he leaves."

We agreed that I'd take Lauri and Denny with me as they'd have no supervision during the day while Earl and Jim worked. I was sick with worry about my son, and eager to go home, take care of him, and see my family. Maybe just my being there would help pull Chris together. I had to believe this. Earl called the office and asked to have three tickets ready for us. There was no straight flight to LAX, so the company would have an employee meet us at the Frankfurt airport, take us to a hotel for the night, and then shuttle us back to the airport for the flight on to LAX, where they would have a rental car for us Everything sounded too organized. I wondered if I could be that lucky.

Two days later we left for the States. The company tried to make sure I had a seamless trip, however, the weather didn't cooperate. As the plane approached Frankfurt, the pilot announced that the airport was fogged in and we would be landing in Cologne, instead. From there we would be bused to Frankfurt. Hopefully the next morning we would be on our way to LAX without too much delay.

When we landed at the Cologne airport, Lufthansa employees herded us to buses. Our bags were thrown in the bottom of the bus, and we were off. In good weather the drive from Cologne to Frankfurt is normally two hours, so I was told. But if anyone has ever taken a five-hour bus trip in zero visibility, then you know what it's like to want to surrender to death.

"Mom, how can the driver see the road?" Denny asked with concern, "I can't even see out the windows on either side of the bus."

"Don't worry. If it were not safe the airlines wouldn't have put us on the bus. And I'm sure the driver faces this kind of weather every winter." *Liar!* I was paralyzed in my seat, silently plotting how to grab my kids and escape through a bus window before it careened off a cliff. Actually, I found out later it might have been easier to jump out the window than to try to find accommodations in a deserted airport in the middle of the night, in Frankfurt, Germany. It was surreal. For most of the people on our bus, Frankfurt was their final destination. The others seemed to know exactly where they were going, and disappeared from the airport in short order. We found a stray cart and dumped our luggage into it. The echo from the cranky cart bounced off the walls. It was spooky. I expected the Phantom of the Opera to come swishing by in his cape.

We walked the cavernous building, which by now resembled a ghost town. Not a single agent behind the desks. All gates were closed. Vendors had closed their shops and gone home with no reason to stick around in the fog.

"Mom, where is everyone? How come no one's here?"

Look causal, I thought. *Don't let the kids know you're terrified.* "Honey, it's foggy outside. No planes will be taking off or landing here tonight, so all the merchants have gone home."

"But what about Dad's company guy? Do they know were stuck here?"

"Maybe the guy was here five hours ago. I'm sure they were notified about the glitch. Don't worry. Somebody will show up any minute to take us to a hotel. Just relax."

"I'm hungry," whined Denny.

"I'm tired," whined Lauri.

"I'm tired of your whining," I whined. "Just relax will you?" But I could not relax. We'd walked the airport for almost thirty minutes and I was worried. I had no German Marks to use the telephone, and I also had no idea how to get anyone on the phone if I did have Marks. Now I was tired, hungry and grumpy. I saw some movement up ahead. "Run kids, go find out who that is. Maybe it's the company guy."

They both took off running. I saw them stop, then heard them talking. Hallelujah, I thought, saved by my kids. They waved for me to come. Thank you Gods of Stranded Travelers! It's about time. But when I got closer I could see the man was an airport janitor. A mop hung from a metal bucket on wheels that he pushed ahead of him as he walked. He spoke little English, but by way of arm waving and shouting, I let him know we had no place to sleep. I pantomimed closing my eyes and snoring. My kids were instantly embarrassed and gave each other the eye roll. He smiled and motioned for us to follow him.

I made a mental note: *Purchase a German phrase book for flight back.*

We walked for what seemed like a mile, through several doors, which he opened with a key from a massive, jangling key ring hanging from his belt. Then he opened the final door. He looked at me and smiled as he motioned for us to step inside. "Es goot?" he asked.

I looked around the room. "Goot?" I don't think so. Obviously this was a boardroom for airport executive meetings. A long mahogany table that could easily seat twenty people occupied the center of the room, with chairs strewn around it. A credenza on a sidewall held an empty water pitcher and glasses. Against a far wall was what looked like a sofa cut in half.

"What?" I asked. For all I knew he wanted us to approve of this huge room.

"I get choo cofer." And with that he was gone.

"Ohmygawd, I don't believe this."

"Believe!" said my daughter. "At least the room has a sofa and some chairs."

"A sofa? It looks like a taco," offered Denny.

The kindly janitor returned with two burlap blankets, then apologetically backed out of the room. "Wait," I pleaded. Where's the bathroom?"

"*Das badezimmer?*" he asked.

"I guess." I pantomimed throwing water on my face, bending over a sink and brushing my teeth. Again the kids did the eye-roll thing. Hey, they were lucky I didn't pull down my slacks and squat.

He looked at me with such pity. "*Ja. Das badezimmer*" and pointed down the hall.

"Oh, *danke,* I said, which was all the German I knew.

I took the taco, without a blanket, and the kids curled up on the floor with the itchy burlap bags. I guess today you would call what I slept on a Futon, but I'd never seen such a thing. I didn't like it and it didn't like me as evidenced by the way it kept closing down on me all night. When I tried to turn over it would fold up around me, leaving me only enough room to breathe before enveloping me again. How I longed for a soft Sealy, with silk sheets and a down pillow.

I couldn't sleep anyway. My thoughts were full of my son and how I was going to solve his problems. What would I find when I got home? Would I be able to remedy everything in two short weeks? I doubted it. Maybe I could find a good family therapist that could help. He needed someone that wasn't emotionally involved in his life to help him. I never was able to get him to confide in me. I decided a therapist was needed, and I'd make that call as soon as I got home. With that problem solved, I thought I'd be able to sleep.

However, my bladder had a different idea. Padding down the dark, spooky hallway to find the *badezimmer* was not conducive to sleep. I've always had nocturia—the medical word for having to pee three times a night. At home it's a pain, but at least it's familiar. In that deserted airport it was scary. Please let there be a plane out of here in the morning, I prayed, I couldn't spend another night like this.

At some point, I must have fallen asleep, only to be awakened sometime in the early morning hours by people talking. I panicked. I could see it in my mind: twenty businessmen in black suits, red ties, polished black Van Heusens, all carrying leather attachés entering the room, and the shock on their faces as they see a body rolled up in a taco, and two bodies on the floor covered in burlap sacks.

I woke the kids and we crept out of the conference room. We could see some activity up ahead and I said a silent thanks to the Gods of Good Weather. Pushing our luggage cart ahead of us, we ran for the *badezimmer,* freshened up, then headed for the ticket counter. I was so happy to see the airport was up and running, I didn't even get crazy when I was told the flight wouldn't be ready for two hours. We had no Marks, but I did have an American Express card and about five American dollars. Denny was appointed to find us a restaurant or snack bar; I knew if anyone could find a place to eat it would be my son. He found a small cafeteria just opening, and we gratefully plopped down at a table. I caught the eye of the waitress. "Is it possible to get some breakfast here? I only have an American Express card, but…"

"*Nine,*" she said. "Ve only take Wisa."

That was the last straw. I wanted to cry, but I thought I'd take the pitiful tack. "Oh, well, we were stranded here over night, and I…"

"Chewst a minute, I go see." She returned carrying a tray with two cups of hot chocolate, one strong cup of coffee and two pieces of day-old apple pie, which she apologized for.

"*Nine*," I said, "*Is goot*." I thought I sounded so continental.

Denny offered her his dollars, but she refused.

"*Nine*, no problem. Enchoy."

We found our way to the departure gates, only to find our flight would be delayed for an engine problem—maybe an hour, maybe four. I had no problem with that…as long as that taco and I would never touch each other again.

When we finally boarded, I did wonder who dropped the ball here? No one met us at the Frankfort airport. Would there be someone at LAX?

And, …*what awaits me at home?*

Sleep! Oh glorious sleep! The three of us slept nearly all the way back to LAX. I caught up on some much needed rest and felt like I could handle anything that was thrown at me. I'd take care of my son's problems, which didn't seem so horrific now that I felt rested.

According to my sister, Chris told her it was no big deal. He'd been offered a joint by one of the other carpenters, and as he took a drag, Cliff walked up. He was busted! However, knowing my son, I knew he hadn't told her everything. Chris knew that screwing up on the job would get him fired yet he did it anyway. He had never been able to say "No." Now he would be without a place to stay if Cliff would not take him back, and without an adult to keep tabs on him. My sister also told me that Chris had bought a motorcycle off one of the guys on the job. I wondered where he got the money. It must have been a real dog because I knew Chris would spend every dime he made. He'd have no insurance, so the possibilities for more problems were staggering.

After clearing customs in LAX, I called Cliff. No answer. I left a message for Chris to call me at my sister's. The company man who met us at the airport apologized for the Frankfurt mishap, but said he knew nothing about that part of the trip. But he was there and I was happy. He'd arranged for a car for us, but I was a tad nervous. It had only been five months since I'd driven, but I felt like a beginner as I drove down the L.A. Freeways like the Little Old Lady from Pasadena.

That night I called Cliff from my sister's. He had no idea where Chris had gone. He'd called around but no one had seen him. Lauri gave me a couple names of Chris' old friends. I finally ran him down at Tony Savio's* house. Mrs. Savio* answered the phone. I'd not met her but her son had been to my home many times. She told me that Chris was indeed staying at their house, worked with her husband and Tony on a construction job, and as far as she could tell, he was doing fine. She would have Chris call me when he returned from work. Relief swept over me. I'd pictured picking up Chris in some gutter in the ghetto. Thank you Gods of Worried Mothers!

Chris called later that night. He sounded down, missed us, but was still adamant that he would not go back to Iran with us. "I've got a good job now, it pays good, and I'm doing okay," he said. "Can you come over here tomorrow when I get off work?"

The next afternoon I met Mrs. Savio. For some reason I'd envisioned a run-down place with the boys sleeping on cots in empty rooms. But I was happily surprised. The house was neat, the yards were lovingly tended, and she was warm and motherly. We sat and sipped coffee while she filled me in on everything. She told me she had five sons, all moved out but Tony, and her house seemed so empty. She said she was happy to have Chris around. "He's so helpful, and full of stories that make me laugh. I told him he could stay as long as he kept to my rules."

I asked if her sons had ever been into drugs. Yes, she said, they experimented as most teenagers do, but eventually they grew out of that phase and were doing fine. What relief I felt. I told her I was going to find some sort of therapist for Chris, but she pooh-poohed the idea. "He's doing fine, don't waste your money."

When Chris got home from work that night, we hugged, cried, and hugged again. We drove to my mother's house, where my sister and family were waiting for us. I couldn't believe I had only been gone five months; it seemed like years. Chris and I talked all the way to my mother's house while he tried to convince me he'd only smoked a couple joints and was not "into" drugs. He liked his job, had saved some money for a car, and everything looked rosy. Too rosy.

Then he dropped the bomb on me.

"Mom, I messed up Jim's car."

My mouth dropped open, but before I could speak he said: "Mom, wait until you hear the whole story, it wasn't my fault." As he began, I wondered if my son would ever take blame for anything in his life. It had rained the night it happened, he said, and his motorcycle's tires were slick. He needed a car. And, besides, he said, Jim was gone and wasn't using it, so why not? He'd broken the lock on our storage garage and hotwired the car. When he drove down the hill by our house, a guy ran a red light and Chris slammed into his car. The driver of the other car was drunk and ran off. It was 2 o'clock in the morning, and no other cars were around. He said he panicked because he'd had a few beers, and was afraid the cops would come by, so he and his buddy pushed Jim's car to the curb, called a friend who had a truck, and they towed the car back to our storage garage.

"How could you just take his car?"

"Mom, he wasn't using it. I figured I'd put it back when I was through and no one would know the difference. It wasn't my fault that drunk ran the light."

"Stop! What do you mean it wasn't your fault?" Again my son with all his sociopathic reasoning. "Chris, you have to know that the blame lies with you. You literally stole your brother's car. Now instead of you saving for your own car, you're going to save up and give him the money to fix his car, or buy him another one."

"I will, Mom. My job pays good. You'll see. But don't tell Jim. I want to surprise him with the money when he gets home."

"You'll surprise him all right. He'll probably take your head off." I knew I'd have to tell Jim, and I knew he'd be mad as hell, as well as hurt. He wanted to trust his brother, but he knew his brother too well.

For the next few days I was behind the wheel running errands. I dropped off the kids at their friend's homes, and shopped for things I couldn't find in Esfahan. Chris and I met up for dinner every night and he seemed fine, working every day, and loved it. I wanted to believe that the worst was over. *Could it really be over?*

Christmas day was what I'd hoped it would be. My mother fussed over me, friends and family came together to welcome us home. The table was set for twenty, and the mouth-watering scents of holiday food and familiar, heart-warming smells of pine filled the house. My sister played the piano while we harmonized our traditional Christmas songs, while I hung tight to my mother. Then the phone rang. Chris told me he wouldn't be able to make it. He said the company had asked him to work on Christmas day. His words were slurred and he seemed confused.

"Where are you? I'm coming to pick you up."

"No, Mom, gotta go to work. Merry Christmas."

I called Mrs. Savio. The boys had gone out. She'd have Chris call me as soon as they returned. I headed for the kitchen where my brother-in-law was tending bar: "One double eggnog please."

"Don't worry about him," was the unanimous feelings from my family. "He'll come home when he's ready. He's too old for you to worry over, and besides, Chris has always done what he wants." How old is "too old" I wondered? A mother never quits worrying about her kids. But I knew they were right. I couldn't ruin everyone's day. I'd worry about it tomorrow.

I finally got a call from Chris the day before we were to fly back to Iran. He said he was fine. He'd gone camping with some friends and was now back at work. I picked him up that night and we drove to my mother's. We talked into the wee hours of the morning, with both of us crying. He finally made me realize that no matter where he was—in the States or in Iran—he'd still be Chris. "Mom, I'll be fine. I know you love me and worry about me, but I know how to take care of myself." He loved me. But did he love himself?

Our two weeks flew by way too fast. The kids and I spent our last night with long-time friends, Joe and Gail, who lived about thirty minutes from LAX. Gail wanted to hear all about the gold stores in Iran, while Joe wanted to hear about the belly dancers. I just wanted to sleep. I'd spent a sleepless night at my mother's worrying about my son, so I'd planned to get to bed early for some much-needed sleep. We had an early morning flight and would have to be up and ready for the shuttle by 4 a.m. It was after ten before I got settled down on the sofa.

Sometime during the night my friend's dog, who had a terminal case of eczema, decided to camp by the sofa where I slept—and scratch. The scratching noise was irritating enough, but the dog also had a collar around his neck with several metal tags that clanged together with every scratch. I tried desperately to ignore the noise. I buried my head under the covers, but to no avail. I finally got up, bitching and moaning, grabbed the dog, tossed him into one of the bedrooms down the hall, and shut the door. Just as I began to slip into REM, I heard some grumbling, heard a door open and then heard the dog hit the floor. I assumed one of the kids slung him out of their room. Oh, no! Please. I can't do this. I'm so tired and have to get up soon. I listened, but I didn't hear the dog. Thank You, Gods of Sleep, he must have gone into another kids' room. Soon I heard more grumbling, a door opened and four furry feet hit the ground, then a door slammed. I could hear the dog's nails clicking on the hardwood floor as he headed for the front room, then a doggie sigh as he settled down next to the sofa. All was quiet for a second or two, then the scratching and clanging began again. When you're tired, somehow sounds are exaggerated; it sounded like I was inside a tambourine! This time I picked up the dog, walked through the kitchen and opened the back door to toss him out. But as I did, their cat came scooting in between my legs and into the kitchen, with the dog racing after it. Please, God, I can't do this.

Around and around they ran: kitchen, front room, hall, kitchen… well you get the idea. I finally was able to coral the dog. I grabbed him, threw him outside, and locked the door. The cat slept peacefully on the rocker across the room from me.

Ah, sweet sleep.

But not for long. I had to use the bathroom. When I flushed, a gurgling sound emanated from behind the commode. I stooped to look and saw water gushing from a pipe. I ran into Joe and Gail's bedroom. "Joe, wake up, the pipe under the toilet's leaking and the bathroom's flooding!"

Joe jumped out of bed, grumbling and rubbing his eyes as he headed for the bathroom, with Gail right behind him. Halfway to the bathroom he realized he only had on his skivvies and began to head back toward the bedroom, while Gail yelled at him to come back: "If she hasn't seen it before, then she isn't missing anything." Joe stopped in his tracks, turned back and headed for the bathroom. "Well, thanks a lot!" he grumbled.

After sopping up all the water from the bathroom floor, Joe opened the back door to toss out the wet towels, and guess who ran in.

I passed the Grandfather clock on the way back to the sofa. I had only thirty minutes until I had to get up. I gave up. I stayed up.

But I still threw the dog outside.

17

Back Home To Plea Bargain

Our flight back to Tehran was uneventful. I always found myself alone on every flight as my kids thoughtlessly fell asleep. No one in my family had a problem falling asleep as soon as the jets fired up. Maybe the jet fuel had something in it that caused their neurological systems to quiet down. How I envied them.

And thinking of neurological systems brought back visions of my toxic apartment. I was not looking forward to the nausea and smell of petrol fumes. I knew I couldn't be pregnant, even though the signs were all there: morning sickness, nausea. But pregnancy was not an option and I'd made sure that would never happen again after I gave birth to my fourth child, Dennis the Menace.

My thoughts went back to the day I'd accompanied my husband to the surgeon's office for a vasectomy. I wanted to make sure *all* sperm were sent packing. *Dr. Gonad* * was an energetic, aging urologist, happily snipping away at his patients' vas' until retirement. He seemed eager to accommodate the exhausted-looking wife and mother, who normally was the one who made the appointment for her husband. But, of course, surgery only happened after the husband answered the requisite questions: How many children do you have? Are you sure you won't change your mind and want more children later on? These questions were put forth to make sure the patient wasn't undergoing this vasectomy out of threats from his wife, such as: You are cut off from now until you are *cut*! And, of course, the doctor added: Do you know your testicles will swell up to the size of bowling balls? Be very painful for weeks? And you must abstain from sex for four weeks. And, when you do have sex, you must wear a condom, as there might still be a few little guys who slipped under the radar, so to speak. Also, Doc *Gonad* was happy to tell a golf joke or two during the procedure. He said it helped his patients relax and forget what was going on below their waist. By the terrified expression on my husband's face, I doubted that.

On Earl's appointment day the doc was dressed in pink-stripped slacks, white Polo shirt, pink socks and white shoes. "Excuse the clothes," he said, "you're my last patient this morning and I'll be heading for the links as soon as I get your little guys on the run."

Earl grimaced.

He seemed like a pretty relaxed surgeon so I asked: "Any chance I can watch the procedure?"

A look of disbelief came over Earl's face. "What? No! I'm sure that's not allowed."

"No problem, be my guest, sit right here," he said as he pulled up a chair for me. "Everybody's gone home, so who's to care?"

"How about me?" Earl whined.

Dr. Gonad ignored Earl and went about his work. I watched closely as he prepped and draped the surgical site, injecting a small amount of anesthesia into the skin. I watched more closely as he made a small incision and pulled the *vas deferens* through the skin opening. I smiled as he snipped the little bugger, and wondered if it would be inappropriate to give the doctor a quick hug.

He turned to me and smiled. "How about that? Fast and easy, huh?"

"Absolutely!" I said, "…but doc, could you please make that a five-turn double cinch knot for good measure?"

Earl met our return flight in Tehran and accompanied us back to Esfahan. He looked so forlorn standing in the airport that I felt immediate remorse for being gone so long. But he'd insisted I take two weeks and enjoy myself. "It's too far and too expensive not to take more time. I'll be busy at work anyway." He asked about Chris, and I told him what had transpired. He looked dubious. "You know, we can't afford you going home every time he has a problem."

"I think he's in a good place now. But, you do know, if he needs me, I will go."

"Yeah, I know."

I shuddered as we approached our apartment. I didn't want to go in and smell those dreaded fumes. When I did enter, the fumes hit me immediately and the familiar waves of nausea swept over me. Even in the States, everything I ate tasted metallic, which I attributed to those terrible fumes. I had to believe they'd taken up residence in my throat.

Earl told me he'd been looking at rentals while we were gone, but found none that would fit our family. He said everyone was keeping an eye out for a place for us. Not to worry. My secret worry was: what if we do move and I still smell the fumes? I prayed to the God of Happy Homes to get us out of this place.

The kids' Christmas vacation was now over and time for my old routine. Because of a giant case of jetlag, I was down for the count. After I walked the kids to their bus stops, I'd limp home and fall on the sofa until it was time to go back and pick them up at 3:30. Trudy was kind enough to pick up any groceries I needed. I was still on the sofa when Earl returned from work. I felt cranky and nauseated. "This has got to stop," I told my bewildered husband. "I'm sick as a dog. Today was the worst day yet. We have got to find a place somewhere other than over a gas station."

"I've been working on it. You know I only have Fridays. Can't get much done in one day."

"But you don't have to work on it," I whined, "Can't you just go to the big boss and say you want to move your family to a place where they can breathe? Maybe, like Khaneh?"

"What? You know Khaneh is only for Supers. I'll just keep looking for something around here."

We'd had this talk many times. Khaneh was a private community out in the country, away from the horrific clamor and traffic of the city. As the weather had cooled, I'd played tennis with friends who lived there, and oh, how I envied them. Khaneh seemed worlds apart from the city, even from Iran. The place was comprised of expats and a few wealthy Iranian families. It seemed like the Garden of Eden. Evidently, it was built for the Shah's Air Force, with a section of it rented out to foreign company employees from all over the world. A lot of these companies had contracts to work in Iran for ten or more years.

I'd driven around the complex when visiting friends who lived there, and I knew it well. It was gated and manned by two grizzly-looking guards. A large field ran down the center, with houses on either side. Further down was a greenbelt that ran for three blocks with a park at the end where the kids played soccer and baseball. A great restaurant was further down with Italian and French cuisine. A few blocks further down, separated from the housing, was a nightclub with a disco and casino, with a footbridge that spanned a small creek, alive with Koi and a few ducks. The nightclub offered ethnic foods and a large gaming hall, rivaling something out of Monaco (not that I've ever seen Monaco). In good weather, the park hosted an outdoor movie, where everyone sat on the grass and watched old flicks on a huge screen. Two clay tennis courts and a large swimming pool completed the idyllic life style.

I didn't have to look any further. How could I *not* want to live there? My kids would have friends to run with, and I'd have no more worries about them being mowed over by crazy drivers with vendettas to settle. They even had a bus stop at the park to pick up the school children.

The good news was our company had leased out a number of homes in Khaneh. The bad news was they'd earmarked those for Superintendents. But I had a trump card I planned to use. I played tennis in Khaneh with Sara*, the wife of my husband's boss. When I'd told Sara about the gas station and my nausea, she suggested I go to the *big* boss, the Project Manager, and put my story out on the table. "Ask him to make an exception," she said. "Tell him you don't know how much longer you can take those fumes. Don't tell him I told you this, but I think my husband will be promoting Earl to Super soon, and I know there's a couple homes still empty. And..." she added with a sly tone, "I happen to know the project manager is a pushover for a sad story."

I liked her thinking but I wasn't sure Earl would. I didn't want to jeopardize his job by going over his boss's head, but, then again...

When Earl got home that night I followed him into the kitchen. "What if I talked to the PM about moving to Khaneh?"

"What? Are you nuts?" he said, as he opened a bottle of beer. He clearly didn't want to have this discussion when the sofa was calling his name. "And why would you even think about talking to him? There are certain channels you have to go through before you just walk in to the big boss."

"Because I'm desperate! Because I don't want to waste time going through all the housing channels! You know you'll make Super soon, so why not go right to the PM. He'd understand. He doesn't want the wives unhappy. I'll tell him I'm sick and would like to move to Khaneh where there's fresh air and a place for my kids to run. Otherwise, I'll tell him I'll have to go back to the states, and drag you with me."

"Yeah, right!" Earl settled on the sofa, putting his feet up on the precarious little coffee table. "He'll suggest you find another apartment away from the gas station. Or, maybe even say go ahead and leave, don't let the plane door hit you in the ass on your way out."

"Well, I'll also tell the boss how we've both been looking for another apartment, and there are none that fit our family. I'll also tell him about the death defying dance I do every morning when I walk my kids to the bus stop."

Earl's eyelids were descending.

"Well…?" I prodded.

"Okay, have at it. Just don't be surprised when he says no. And don't argue with him. His word is law."

Maybe I'd tell the PM one more little item: *you'll be making him a Super soon, anyway, so why wait?* How glorious that would be, I thought. I let the conversation drop, but I knew I was going for broke, and as quickly as possible.

Thursday evening was the start of the Iranian weekend. I knew the PM would be at the Clubhouse tossing down a few after work. I thought it best to get him while he was nice and mellow. Trudy drove me to the Clubhouse. I scanned the darkened bar, praying he'd be there. When my eyes adjusted to the dim light, I spotted him sitting alone with his head cocked toward the jukebox, which was blaring out a sad country song. One full bottle of beer and two empties sat on the table. Perfect, I thought. Mellow enough. "Hi!" I put on my best expaty-wife look. "Can I talk to you for a minute?"

"Sure can, darlin'." He pushed out a chair for me with the toe of his highly polished ostrich-skin boot. "What's up? Hubby beatin' ya?"

"Not yet. But I do have a problem."

"Shoot!"

I began to talk way too fast. I couldn't stop. I'd hoped to get all my rehearsed lines out before he could say "No!" "We're living in an apartment right over a gas station and you know they never shut their cars off, and one night I counted twenty cars with engines running and the kids are sick and I'm sick from the fumes and…

"Hold on, darlin'! Let's slow down and start all over."

I gulped in some air. *Slow down, dummy.* "Well, I…I just want you to know that I'm getting sicker and sicker from gasoline fumes, and I'm worried the kids will get sick and I don't know what to do."

He took a long swig of his beer, looked at the bottle as if it shouldn't be empty, then looked over at me. "So, what's stoppin' you from findin' another place? Why don't you check with Housing? That's their job."

Oh, crap, that's not what I wanted to hear. I had to move in for the kill: "It really isn't just the fumes. It's the traffic that scares me when I have to cross the kids to catch the school bus, it's the noise at all hours of the night, it's the dogs that look hungry enough to eat my kids, and we've looked for a place and can't find one and and I want to move to Khaneh where they'll be safe, otherwise I think I'll need to return to the States with them."

There, I'd done it. I held my breath.

He looked down again, looked thoughtful for maybe one minute, then said, "Well, we can't have you goin' home and leavin' your ole man alone, can we? What's his name?"

"Earl Cross, he's…"

"I know who he is. Good man. Call Ken in Housing and tell him I said to find you a house in Khaneh."

I nearly fainted. If I'd known it would be that easy, I'd have gone to him months earlier. But I also knew Earl had made a name for himself, and was liked by everyone on the jobsite. I'm sure they wanted to keep us happy. A happy wife has a happy husband!

"Really?"

"I said so, didn't I? Get goin' so you can get a house before they're gone."

New Year's Eve was spent with friends at the glorious Shah Abbas Hotel in town, named after the great Shah Abbas from the 15th Century.

The immense grounds and trees were decorated with colored lights. Inside were vaulted ceilings with lights reflected in the many enormous mirrors set throughout the vast lobby, giving the effect of a wonderland. Liquor flowed and everyone was in high spirits. We had a good life and we were thankful for it, but thoughts of home brought some tears.

Then came the surprise of surprises.

Our attention was called to a TV set above the bar where many of the expats had gathered. The scene was blurry, but we could definitely see what was going on: President Carter was in Iran! We'd heard rumors to that effect, but seeing our president here with the Shah seemed surreal. Things had to be okay, we all agreed. Why would Carter come to Iran if trouble were brewing? We all seemed to breathe a little easier.

Our two-week old newspaper arrived with this headline: *President Carter toasted the Shah at a state dinner in Tehran, calling him* "An island of stability in the troubled Middle East."

"An island of stability?" Does that mean everything's okay? By now we'd heard so many rumors we knew some had to be true. Were we really living on an "Island of stability"? We didn't think so. After Carter's visit to Iran, the *mullahs* were out in force again, preaching at the square and anywhere they could gather an audience.

1978 - Khaneh

18

Home In The Country

We moved to Khaneh the following weekend. It was heaven! Living in the country was glorious. Bird songs and cricket chirps now replaced horns, screeching tires and angry voices. Cut grass and earthy smells now replaced noxious fumes, rotting meat and urine odors. Smiling, friendly people now replaced angry scowls and unhappy faces. And, best of all, there wasn't a *mullah* to be found.

The streets were paved, sans holes or rocks. Many kids from Lauri and Denny's schools lived in Khaneh. After dinner they'd all get together, racing around outside, playing in the streets without the fear of being run down. Other than irritating the guards, my kids had the run of the place. After coming from the city nightmare, this was paradise—for them as well as me.

My new home consisted of approximately 2000 square feet of wood and stucco. The house had three bedrooms, two baths, a large formal dining room and large living room. The kitchen was small, but I wasn't too concerned with that. However it lacked the normal conveniences most women get cranky living without: dishwasher, garbage disposal, washer and dryer. Who cared? I was overjoyed and knew I could give up anything to have my kids in a safe environment and no more gasoline fumes.

I could even live with the furniture, which was put together with spit and promise. Most of the wood furnishings were made of plaster and covered with a wood-colored paint. It looked like wood, was painted to look like wood, but a chip showed plaster through-and-through. Our coffee table had to be replaced on a regular basis as it kept losing one or the other of its legs. We weren't rough on it, rather it was because the table was made like Paper Mache with paste. Any little bump or something heavier than a book placed on top could cause one of the legs to break. After a while it was rather funny. "Hey, don't set your coffee on the coffee table, set it on the floor."

I immediately joined the ladies softball team when I got to Khaneh—and immediately retired. Well, not really. Not until I was so injured I couldn't play anymore. Plus, I think the ladies appreciated me retiring. While trying to prove what a great athlete I was, I tripped over my shoestring while trying to catch a grounder, fell headlong into the second baseman, pushed her off her base and landed spread-eagle on my face. Trying to get up as nonchalantly as I could, I stepped on same shoestring and went down again. They all cheered for me. Next, I jumped for a high fly ball, but not high enough and the ball nicked the end of my fingernail, through the glove, and tore it in half. Well, being too mortified by my last solo, I decided not to scream and encored by catching a ball with my right hand (sans glove) and broke my index finger. Well, maybe not broke, but it felt like it, and it swelled to the size of a peach. So much for tennis, baseball practice or anything else that entailed using my hand. Earl had to fix dinner for a couple nights, help with lunches and help me shower, which he fought against like mad.

One of the downsides to living in a foreign country is missing your favorite foods. You crave the items that are nowhere to be found, or if they are, the prices are exorbitant. We did have a Mexican and pizza restaurant down the road from us, but sadly, the finished project bore a resemblance to a pancake with Ketchup on it.

Fortunately, our house was across a small field from the only store in Khaneh, which was named *Super 7-11. The store* carried many things that those in town did not. Unfortunately, anything imported was terribly expensive: Peanut butter was ten dollars for a very small jar; mayonnaise was thirteen dollars for yet a smaller jar. Cheerios was sometimes eight dollars, sometimes ten dollars, depending on how the merchant felt that day. Everything imported was in a dented can or torn box that looked like it had been packaged in the Neanderthal period. The idea of a "stock boy" or an "inventory person" was a non-starter. The packages were all randomly stacked (thrown) around the store. It was like going on a treasure hunt: Hey, whoopee! I just found a bag of powdered Oreos under a box of soap powder.

And, don't even get me started on the toilet paper. Nada! Zilch! However, you could purchase some from select stores in town that imported it. Most of the rolls looked like they'd been unrolled and rerolled by the family dog. Most merchants had the nerve to smirk when asked if they carried the dreaded item. I hated to ask for toilet paper because I knew I'd get the *tsk* with head thrown back, and then absolute silence: another of the Westerner's wicked wastes. I imagined they thought: Use your hand like we do, save the trees!

I decided to make, rather than buy, some of the foodstuffs that were so expensive. I started with pancakes. How hard could the process be? And why not make the syrup while I'm at it? I also decided to make my own peanut butter and mayonnaise. I figured nothing could be worse than the outdated stuff they sold at the store. At least it would be made fresh.

I purchased a torn bag of Pillsbury flour, one smashed, partly opened box of baking soda, with a few weevils thrown in at no additional cost, and a jar of maple flavoring with the label torn off—I sincerely hoped it was maple flavoring—and a torn, five pound bag of sugar, which I'm sure only weighed three pounds by the time I walked back to my house.

I could hardly wait to start making my own pancakes and syrup. First I sifted the flour searching for any unwanted protein source that might be taking up residence in the bag. Then there was the baking powder that yielded a farm crop of weevils. I added some nearly rancid oil and milk, one fresh egg—I'd hoped—and stirred. I poured the mixture onto a skillet and *viola!* There lay two of the saddest looking, concave pancakes in the history of homemaking. Martha Stewart would have slapped me up side the head.

But, that didn't deter me. I had to make some syrup for the pancakes, even if they looked and tasted like plaster casts. Sugar, boiled water and maple flavoring—I prayed—and heat over flame until sugar melts. All went well, however, until it was time to taste the stuff. It didn't taste exactly like maple syrup, more like molasses. I did notice my family walked a little slower after eating some of my homemade pancakes, sometimes holding their stomach with a pained look on their face. Oh well, hey, I was saving money, wasn't I?

Mayonnaise was another high-priced item. Okay, I thought, I can fix that. I got a recipe from a neighbor, made up a batch and proudly placed it on the table at lunchtime. My family thought I was amazing, that is until the oil began to separate from the egg yolks and the whole thing looked like a science project. Petri dish, anyone?

I next decided to tackle peanut butter. How could I do any worse than the pancakes? I couldn't find a recipe, but I figured it had to be pretty easy. What would you need other than peanuts, oil, and maybe a little salt. I'd found a sack of peanuts under some canned goods at the *Super* 7-11, and was on my way. I had some olive oil I felt could double for the peanut oil. How wrong I was! What I didn't know, but found out too late, is that peanuts need to be roasted *before* using to make peanut butter. They also should be *fresh*. Well, suffice it to say it would have held wallpaper for several centuries, had the consistency of alum, and if you didn't have water close by, you could very well choke to death.

A great benefit of living in Khaneh was the chance to meet other expats; women from other countries, other companies, and other parts of the States. I played tennis with some women who didn't even speak English, but somehow we all knew how to play the game without much talking. Instead of the normal green composition surface of our tennis courts in California, the courts were red clay. To reach the proper consistency for tennis the clay needed to be watered and tamped down every morning with a huge rolling machine. This was a time-consuming job if done properly, and could take nearly an hour. But the workers responsible for the courts would maybe work fifteen minutes tops, and then head off to another job. The consequence was the more you ran around on the red clay, the more it loosened and became air-borne, creeping into our shoes, socks, tennis shorts, panties and even a few millimeters higher. How the clay got that far north was an enigma. Once home, the undies had to be soaked in cold water for an hour or so, then hand-washed with very strong soap. Even after all that soaking and scrubbing the crotch was a definite shade of pink. I made sure to hang them to dry in the washroom, never outside on our clothesline for all the neighbors to wonder...

We still drove into town for many things, the bazaar, cleaners, hotels for dinner, but mainly we were content in our little city away from the craziness of Esfahan's roads. We were invited to Rallfe and Dori's home many times for her wonderful Iranian dishes. I saved all my questions about Iran for Rallfe, who always regaled us with stories: the strife Iran had been through over the centuries, the overthrow of great leaders. He and Dorri were full of historical facts of their country, and we never tired of listening and learning from them. For a time, Rallfe said, the

British occupied Iran and ran all the refineries, having no use for Iranians other than as laborers. They didn't think Iranians were bright enough to hold top positions in their company, even though most applying for lead jobs had engineering degrees. It seemed to me a travesty that educated people could not even hold jobs in their own country during the many occupations of Iran.

Our TV programs were helter-skelter, and left much to be desired. The station was fuzzy and hard to hear. We had no news from home or anywhere else for that matter. At least we did get a little laughter in the midst of our worries. One of the quirks we witnessed on the Government-run TV was the announcement of the National Iranian Time. Every night at 10 p.m., no matter what program was airing, the screen went blank, then a giant face of a clock filled the screen. Usually the hour hand was on the 10 and the minute hand was on the 12, at which time a booming baritone voice would declare: "IT IS 10 O'CLOCK, NATIONAL IRANIAN TIME." *BONG!* But one particular night when the clock appeared, the hour hand was on the 10, but the minute hand was on the 11, which showed it to be five minutes to ten. A second passed, then a massive, hairy hand appeared in front of the clock, pushed the minute hand to the 12, then announced in a booming voice: "IT IS NOW 10 O'CLOCK NATIONAL IRANIAN TIME." *BONG!*

A risk of living out in the country, we were to find, was the absence of any medical facilities. My daughter and I witnessed something that still makes me shudder when I think of it. We were about to leave for the *Super* 7-11 when I saw two workers leave our neighbor's yard and walk toward ours. Rain had inundated the surrounding countryside for four days in a row and our front yard was literally underwater. I wondered why these men were coming to work on a lawn two inches under water. I really shouldn't call it a lawn, as the yard was comprised of water, hay and mud. For some reason, no grass seeds were ever planted that

I could attest to. It seemed the hay was to take the place of grass, with no questions asked or answers provided. However, every day a worker or two would show up to water said hay, even if the hay was totally underwater as it was on this particular day.

One of the workers stopped at our gate while the other one walked into our yard. I said the usual *Salam* greeting and moved out of his way. He nodded. As the worker walked by me, I saw he carried a small board under his arm. I watched as he placed the board on the ground in front of the electric box, and watched as it disappeared under two inches of water when he knelt on it. He then opened the electric box and reached inside. I was aghast. Why would he put his hand into an electric box while he was kneeling in water? As I turned to leave I heard the worker begin to emit what I thought was singing (the singing from the mosques always sounded to me like someone in great distress). I looked into my yard to see where the noise came from and saw the worker shaking violently, with his hand still inside the electric box.

My daughter and I stood, stunned. The worker at the gate rushed past us into my yard. He shoved his foot into the kneeling man's side, knocking him away from the electrical box and the wire he'd been attached to. The injured man landed face down in the muddy water and hay. He didn't move. Voltage in Iran was 440, and I couldn't imagine anyone living with that much electricity coursing through their body. Nearby workers came running when they heard the yelling, all milling about speaking excitedly.

Lauri was shaking. "Mom, what should we do? Should we call an ambulance?"

Her cries brought me back from inertia. I had no idea where to call for an ambulance. I'd never even thought of needing one. I ran to my neighbor's. She had no idea how to get an ambulance. She called a friend who also had no idea. We stood on her porch as we watched several men grab the worker by his arms and legs and head for my porch. As they carried the inert body up the steps and into my house, I thought it best to return. I ran back to my yard and followed them into my living room, then watched with concern and amazement, as if I didn't live there. They placed the man face up on the floor, while hay, mud, and water oozed onto the carpet. Of course I didn't say anything, but it did run through my mind that they could have laid him on the front porch. *Shame on me*! But I knew it was too late for the poor soul. As they pulled off his sandals I could see the bottoms of his feet, which were the color of moss and his face the color of cement. I stepped aside as men working nearby ran into my house to see what had happened. Their hollering in Persian made me hopeful they were getting a plan together. Then, one by one they began to leave.

"Wait, you can't leave him here! What will I do with him?" I wailed. Of course no one understood me, so I began to wave my arms and holler right along with the rest of them. I ran outside not knowing what I would do if they all left, when I saw a van pulling up to my curb. Who had called them? It had been over an hour since the worker had been electrocuted, and I wondered why it took so long for help to arrive.

Two men stepped out of the van. One opened up the two rear doors while the other entered my house and gathered up the body. The onlookers helped the driver carry the worker outside, then began to stuff the body into the back of the small van. I could see they were going to have a problem when the two back doors wouldn't close. The dead man's feet seemed to be the cause, and I assumed that rigor mortis had begun to set in and that his body was stiffening up. The driver and his assistant began to push and shove the van doors against the protruding feet, hoping to get them to close. As Lauri and I watched in horror, the men stood around for some time, seemingly arguing about the problem. Then the two men got in the van and started the engine. Some of the onlookers seemed surprised and yelled after them, which they ignored, and drove off with the worker's feet and van doors flapping in the breeze.

I later learned the worker was DOA. Also I learned there was no ambulance service in Khaneh. No emergency personnel, only local workers who came running to help their fellow man. *Allah, help me!* After inquiring, I was given our company medic's phone number to call in case of a family emergency. Thankfully, I never had to use it.

However, friends of ours would, but this was after the fact.

Walt* and Ed*, Supervisors on Earl's job, had been driving at night on one of the infamous deadly roads when a massive truck broadsided their car. Ed told us later that he must have been knocked unconscious, as he thankfully had no memory of his trip to the hospital. Walt, however, had a terrifying memory of the trip. Walt was a six-foot-six, strapping guy who weighed at least 250 pounds. He said the two men jumped out of the truck and hefted both of them up and into the bed of their truck. Walt said he couldn't feel his legs or neck, and was terrified he might have a spinal-cord injury. The truck bed was hard and cold, he said, and he felt every bump and pothole in the road for what seemed like hours before they arrived at a hospital. Of course no neck or back brace was applied in case of spinal-cord injury, and no x-rays were ever taken at the hospital.

Ed was discharged the next day and told to go home and rest. When I heard that Walt would be there for a few days, I took a *Su-san* taxi to the hospital. As I walked into Walt's room I was instantly appalled. Dark and dank, with only one small window so dirty I couldn't see outside, and one small light bulb hung over the bed and one over the door. The walls were a prison-grey, the floor dingy. The bathroom was disgusting, with only a hole in the floor and a sink. I tried not to show my disgust, but I could see Walt was in too much pain to even notice his surroundings.

His eyes were closed as I walked up to his bed. A nurse walked in, smiled at me, then opened a small bedside table drawer and dropped in some pills—sans gloves. When she left the room, I tiptoed over to have a look. Surely she'd put those pills into a pill receptacle or something sterile. What I saw were multiple pills of multiple shapes lying scattered about the dirty drawer—along with a family of roaches skittering about.

"Oh, for God's sake," I yelped, "I can't believe this!"

Walt's eyes opened. "Whaaa?" he asked, weakly.

"Oh, Walt, I'm sorry. I didn't mean to wake you."

He closed his eyes again. "No, sokay, I been awake waitin' for someone to bring me somethin' for this pain."

I looked around the bed. No cord or call button existed to ring for a nurse. "Hasn't anyone given you pain pills yet?"

"No. I keep waitin', but they come in and out and no one stops to talk to me. I know they put somethin' in my drawer cuz I can hear em' but my back and neck hurt too much to move. I can't sit up to see what it is. Would you look?"

I used a Kleenex from my purse and lifted out a couple of pills from the drawer. I checked for any identification marks, a brand name that I might recognize for pain, but they were all blank. "I'll be right back."

I ran to the nurse's station. "*Aya shoma Engilisi*—do you speak English?" A couple nurses standing about smiled, but no one came forth. "*Dok-Tor?*" I said, with emphasis on the "Tor".

"*Baleh,*" said one of the nurses. *Bia*."

I followed the nurse down a hall lined with gurneys and occupied by very sick-looking people. She led me to a small office where she read a sign tacked on the door: "Doktor leaf."

"Do you know what pain pills are?"

She looked at me with a small smile. "*Baleh.*" She reached into her pocket and showed me three white pills. "Pain," she said.

I wasn't too sure about that. I returned to Walt's room and told him I'd be back with some real pain pills. I had the driver take me to the Club where I begged some pain pills from a woman who gulped them daily for back problems. She said she'd have her husband take more to Walt when he got home from work. As it turned out, our medic from the jobsite showed up that night and left Walt enough pain pills for a month. Walt's back was finally healed enough for his wife to get him into a wheelchair and take him home. He swore this would be his last hospital stay. Last I heard he was medi-vaced back to the states for surgery.

I made a mental note: *Don't do anything dumb to require a hospital stay.*

19

Bounced Checks & Murder

L ife in Khaneh was all I'd hoped for, but after a month I began to feel I should be doing something more than cards, tennis, and coffee klatches. I needed some mental stimuli. The kids were in school all day so I had no problem being gone all day. Also, I'd spent way too much money on treasures from the bazaar and gold shops, so I thought I should replace the money and ease my shopaholic conscience. A job! That's what I needed. I'd find a job. I called around to some of the American companies but found none were hiring.

One fateful day as I rode the bus into town for a much-needed haircut, I met a young Iranian girl, Farah*, who took a seat next to me. We began to chat and I was impressed with her command of the English language. She said she worked for BHI (Bell Helicopter International) at the Employee Relations office, located on Pepsi-Cola *Kuche*—street—in the heart of town. She said the main contingent of BHI employees worked at the Crown Prince Reza Pahlavi Army base (Havan-e-Ruz), about ten miles out of town. She said the government had awarded BHI a ten-year contract to train the Iranian Army how to fly and maintain the Huey helicopters. For this contract, BHI had sent their very best: Viet Nam vets who'd been chopper pilots and mechanics during the war. This sounded like a great opportunity for the Shah's Army and a windfall for these vets.

I hung on her every word as she related the benefits of working for a big company as a local hire; much more money than she would ever make if she worked for an Iranian company. I told her I was thinking of finding a job but none of the American companies I'd called were hiring.

"Oh, that's not true," she said, "BHI is hiring. They are looking for an assistant to the Security Chief."

That got my interest. She said the company had to hire someone unrelated to any BHI employee, as the job was a top-level security position. The applicant also had to be fluent in English, have a secretarial background, and pass a BHI security clearance. "Can you do these things?"

"No problem." As far as I could remember I'd done nothing illegal that would show up on anyone's blacklist. Maybe a jay-walk or two, but I was sure they didn't have any of those big-brother-is-watching-you cameras in our small town. This job opportunity sounded better by the minute. "Oh, that's perfect! My husband doesn't work for BHI, and I have an administrative background."

"Good," she said, "call soon so you can get the job."

By the time she left the bus I had the name and phone number of the personnel officer and directions to their office. As soon as I returned home I called and made an appointment for an interview. When I told Earl about the job possibility that night at dinner he was all for it. "Good," he said between mouthfuls of rice. "I'm happy for you. Now you can replace the money you've been donating to the bazaar, copper and gold shops."

My interview was at eleven o'clock the next morning. I hitched a ride with an Iranian neighbor who was going into town, but knew from then on I'd be risking my life on the Iranian bus system. I felt I looked very administrative as I arrived for my interview. I wore a modest black sheath dress and matching jacket; black hose and my only pair of black heels, which made my legs look wonderful, but my feet were screaming in protest. I arrived five minutes early as planned, and was given paperwork to fill out. On the sheet that asked me to list my experience with office machines, I checked everything listed, except shorthand and the mimeograph machine. *Did people still use that thing?*

Next I was given a fist-full of forms and sent to a desk to fill them out. These were questions pertaining to my country of birth; my employment history; why was I in Iran at this time; did I have a work visa; how long would I be living in-country; my husband's name and employer, rank, serial number and the size of my bra. Next came the typing test, that I clocked in at 105 words per minute. Last was a grade-school grammar quiz, and lastly a short I.Q. test that could have been answered by my children. I aced it!

The head of security, John Samuels*, who would be my boss, called me into his office. He asked me to take a seat while he scanned my paperwork, looking up now and then to smile at me. I glanced around his office. Very tidy! His desk held several framed family pictures. On the wall next to his desk was a large photo of John as a handsome officer, receiving some sort of decoration.

I studied the man who would be my boss. John looked to be about six feet tall, amazingly handsome, and probably in his early fifties. Startling azure blue eyes shone out of a rugged face. A lopsided smile belied his keen intellect and intense scrutiny. He had sandy-blonde hair, precision-cut in military style, and a football player's thick neck. He obviously took great care of his tanned and athletic-looking body—a habit he later told me was acquired as a thirty-year career man in the Marines. He was charming and disarming. On his desk was an in-box piled high with folders. A gold Cross ink pen rested in a holder. In a corner, a large pitcher of water and two crystal glasses sat on a file credenza. His desk and the room were orderly, the way a Virgo (that would be me) would have kept it. I knew I'd like to work for this man.

John gathered up all the paperwork, stacking them into a neat pile before him. "You didn't check off the shorthand box. I will be dictating all my correspondence, so that might be a problem."

"Actually, Mr. Samuels, I can type faster than I can take shorthand. You dictate and I type."

He smiled. "I think we're going to get along just fine, and you can call me John. Can you start tomorrow?"

Wow, that was quick. "Absolutely!" I had to assume my button-down appearance, wealth of knowledge in office procedures, plus my typing speed had made me the perfect candidate...well, that and not being related to anyone working for the company.

John then gave me a quick description of his job and what would be expected of me. He had his hands full, and I would need to be his right-hand man. His job entailed overseeing all problems of BHI employees and their dependents (in total about 5000), their welfare and that of their families, as well as dealing with any untoward behavior on their part while in-country. My job would be multifaceted: along with the enormous amount of transcription and correspondence, I would be required to take notes in meetings, and if necessary call the American Consulate daily for pertinent developments. Also, when he was out of the office, I would be required to process everything relating to employee-vs-merchants complaints, along with our office interpreter, and transcribe them for his files. He would go into further details at a briefing we would have when I started the job.

John signaled the interview was over as he stood, came around his desk and offered me his huge hand. I felt secure. As he held the door for me, he said, "Of course the job would be temporary, you understand, until your security clearance is completed."

"Of course," I said, as I searched my memory for any felony arrests that had slipped my mind.

Filled with excitement the next morning, I tore through my closet looking for something conservative. I could see I was going to have a problem with clothes for work. When I'd packed for the trip, I had no idea I would need anything other than slacks, jeans and blouses. I hadn't asked about a dress code, but I wanted to start with a good impression. I wore the only dress I'd packed, which was almost too formal; more for a funeral than the workplace. However, by the time I arrived at work I looked like I'd fallen out of a Whirlpool washer. February temperatures were normally in the 30s, but on my first day of work the temperature felt like it was close to zero. A light drizzle began as I waited for the bus, flattening my Hamill Wedge and sticking to my scalp. My conservative clothes did little to keep me warm. I did have a furry white ski parka that I'd put in my shipment, but how could I wear that over my dress? I'd look like a Polar bear in heels. I knew I was no different from most vain women who think of appearances before comfort. Also, my high heels that I hadn't worn in some time, were extremely tight and came to a severe point that held my toes in a vice-grip. I realized I should have worn my ugly boots as great gobs of mud and slush on the road layered my shoes. I looked like an escapee from a Siberian road camp—but my legs still looked great.

As the bus was my only option for transportation to work, I knew I'd be thumbing my nose at the Grim Reaper, but I still felt safer with more metal to protect me, as opposed to those little tin can taxi cars. Every day as I boarded the bus I prayed to *Allah* to watch over my children in case of my demise.

To catch the bus I had to cross a muddy field, then stand in front of the *Super 7-11* until the bus driver decided to get out of bed and do his job——he had a pretty loose schedule. Along the front of the store laborers from the fields gathered to warm their hands over trash barrels ablaze with black tires. Thick, black, noxious smoke floated wherever the wind took it, mostly in my face and hair. Getting away from the smoke and smell of burning tires and into a nice, warm enclosure was not an option, I assumed, as covered bus stops with benches were not part of the amenities planned when the infrastructure of Khaneh was drawn up.

The bus, when it finally arrived, would come roaring up the road and screech to a stop wherever the brakes happened to lock up. If I had to walk a half block to get on board, so be it. However, the driver always had a ready smile and nod for me when I dragged up to the door, dripping drizzle, smelling of burnt tires and splattered with mud.

Getting off the bus was another problem. Some days the driver might decide to alternate his stops and leave me four or five blocks from my destination. Other days the driver would drop me right at my corner, and I'd feel like giving him a big hug. I never asked why, I learned to go along with every change that came about. What else could I do? I highly doubted a corporate transit office existed where I could call to complain: *Hello, this is an irate commuter and I'd like to know why your bus driver changes his route every day?*

Alighting from the driver's arbitrary stop, I'd have to stand in the street and hail down a private taxi——if I was lucky enough to spot one——to my office and that could take another twenty minutes in traffic. Mostly, though, drivers would speed by, screech to a stop, rapidly back up, look at me, and then screech off. In hindsight I suppose I should have worn a headscarf, but I didn't want to mess my mist-soaked, smoke-filled coif. All things considered, I still felt the bus ride much safer than driving or taxiing.

That is until the day the driver lost his gearshift.

Because I was the last one to board the crowded bus after work, I usually had to take a seat next to the driver. One night as he rounded a curve, he gunned the engine while trying to ram the floor gearshift into another gear, when it broke free of its casing and came off in his hands. He stared at the gearshift as if it were a foreign object. He looked at the gaping hole in the floorboard then glanced my way with a shy grin. I imagine I looked terrified because he immediately tried to assuage my fears by jamming the gearshift back into the hole. The problem was, we were sailing along at about 80 kilometers per hour and his attention was focused on the hole in the floorboard while my eyes were fixed on the highway for signs of a collision. Every now and then he'd glance up, but most of his focus was on the floor.

"*Agha!*" I'd gasp as another huge bus came bearing down on us, taking his half out of our half of the road. Our driver looked up just in time to swerve onto the shoulder, while the bus fishtailed, listed to the left, then righted itself and jumped back on the highway.

"No problem, Ma-dam, ve are protected. *Inshallah*"—God willing.

I couldn't quite get into his comfort zone at that point, but hey, I'll take *Allah* anytime over a crash and burn. Eventually I learned to relax and trust *Allah*. I would open my book and travel on the wonderful vehicle of the written word while we soared helter-skelter through the Iranian countryside in *Allah*'s Mass Transit System.

My dress code soon fit in with the rest of the employees: slacks, blouse and sweater, and sensible flats. The Iranian women had various dress codes: Muslim women wore slacks, modest blouses that covered their necks, ankle socks, black flat shoes and a colorful scarf to cover their hair. My take was that the young Muslim girls probably covered up because their mothers demanded it. The non-Muslim Iranian girls wore whatever they felt like: short skirts, low blouses, long skirts, high blouses, and no one seemed bothered by it.

The Muslim girls were full of fun and chatter, seemingly no different than their non-Muslim sisters. I wondered if they envied the girls who let their long, shiny black hair flow freely, displaying their femininity without shame in their chic clothes. A few of the Iranian girls, Farah included, were born in Iran, of Armenian descent, and lived in an area called Julfa, populated mainly with Christian Armenians. These girls dressed as they pleased as well. The American girls, most married to BHI men working at the base, dressed in whatever the weather dictated.

Working as the assistant to the head of security was like reading someone's mail—a perfect fit for someone as nosy as me. Any correspondence our office received that didn't have to be kept in a locked cabinet—even interoffice notes or memos—had to be stored in a large metal container and burned at the close of the business day.

In the seven months I worked for John there was never a dull moment. Some of the Viet Nam vets were married to Thai girls, as Thailand was the R&R place for GIs during the war, and I'm sure the bargirls filled the lonely hours for those guys. After fighting in the fetid jungles, watching their buddies die right next to them, they needed some sort of diversion. And those Thai bar girls were there to give them a good time, and anything else they could afford.

The Thai women were notorious for gambling. Being away from their home in Thailand, and living in Iran—a country totally alien to them—gambling must have been a way to make the long days bearable. But in time their gambling got them into hot water. After hubby left for work, out came the dice and blank checks. The women would meet at one of the wives' homes and gamble until it was nearly time for hubby to return from work. When their money had been gambled away, the women would settle their debts via hubby's checkbook, not concerned about the beating that was sure to come once the checks bounced.

John would call me into his office: *Take a letter to Mr. Mashad*,* a local merchant, *ask him to please come to our office to discuss the "bounced check" problem.* Or: *Take a letter to employee number 12345* to report to my office immediately re the beating of his wife* (after a bounced check charge).

Often the Thai wives would show up at our office to demand that their husbands be reprimanded for beatings they'd received. "He beat me foh no reason," was the usual complaint. But more often it was the town merchants who lined up outside my office. Then the employee would be summoned to explain why the check had bounced and when the debt would be paid. Normally, the employee had to wait for his next payroll check to pay the merchant, but many times that next payroll check was gambled away before it even hit the employee's bank account.

Then there was the case of the woman who murdered her husband. The husband was a U.S. citizen, and a BHI employee. The wife was a Scandinavian* citizen, in country only as a dependent. That one was pretty sad. The report went something like this: *After a long night on the town, drinking and arguing, the couple ended up at home in their kitchen where the fight continued to escalate, with the wife's small dog yapping at their feet. The husband yelled at the yapping dog to shut up. The dog continued to yap while the wife continued to yell. The husband then kicked the dog across the room, offing the poor cur, which incited the wife to grab the nearest thing to her—a large butcher knife—and offed her husband.*

Sadly, the case was taken out of our hands. Because the wife held a Scandinavian passport, and was not a BHI employee, the company could not protect her. The Iranian police took the case and the last I heard the poor woman was ensconced in a cold, dirty jail cell. As far as I know she may still be there.

That should be a lesson to all quarrelsome men: Never fight in the kitchen.

I loved my job and was totally happy. The only thing I didn't like was coming home to a dirty house. Dust could accumulate in less than five minutes after you'd vacuumed. An expat neighbor, soon to leave the country, referred her housekeeper to me after I'd started working. I loved the idea of coming home to a clean house and was overjoyed. She said he was called a Houseboy in India. "He's a great worker," she said, "but…"

"But what?"

"Maybe give him some easy tasks when he first arrives, like washing the dishes or making the beds. Then before it's time for him to leave, have him mop the floor."

I must have looked confused as she followed with: "Well, when he gets to my house he's fine, but after about thirty minutes of hard work he begins to, oh, you know, have a rather strong odor about him."

"Stink?"

"Well, yes, quite a bit."

Malik* started the next week. He was a lovely boy, about twenty years old I'd guessed. I had a hard time conversing with Malik because he was so painfully shy. He had a terminal case of acne, which I assumed was the reason he looked down at his feet when I spoke to him. But, oh, my neighbor was so right! He emitted an overpowering smell; not only his body odor, but also something else unpleasant. I know that our diets give off different odors through our pores, so I'm sure Malik's diet, consisting of exotic Indian spices and cheeses, added to the mix. However, along with that odor was a whole lot of unchecked perspiration. When he really got going on his housework, the smell was unbearable.

Windows were pushed wide open before I left for work, but Malik's odor lived on through the day, the night and the next day. When the smell finally began to dissipate it was time for him to return. I swore the smell stuck to the walls and carpet. The kids would catch me sniffing around as I tried to find where that rank smell hung out, then ask me if I was looking for Malik.

Shortly after he began to work for us, another departing expat sold me her washer. A gift from the gods! Until then, I'd had to revert back to my sink-soak. I was ecstatic. I did my veggie-tumble while Malik was put in charge of the laundry duties. After doing the wash, he would then hang them to dry on our backyard clothesline, but this soon became a problem. Only four-foot high block walls separated the yards, and I didn't want the neighbors subjected to my dainties.

One Saturday, after a long and hot tennis match, and in a hurry to get to a luncheon date, I stepped out of my tennis garb, stepped into the shower, then exited, leaving the dirty clothes in a pile on the floor.

I'd done the unforgivable: I'd forgotten to "un-stain" my tennis panties. Unfortunately this happened to be Malik's washday. As was his job, he picked up all soiled clothes from the floor and hamper, tossed them into the washer—and then onto the clothesline.

When my friend dropped me at my house that afternoon I could see my tennis clothes blowing in the breeze, along with a startling pair of white tennis panties with a bright red crotch! I was embarrassed as hell, but I can't even imagine the horror Malik must have felt as he hung them to dry.

A plague of flies were among our houseguests in Khaneh. Our flyswatters were of no use against them. I think flies have a third eye on their back. Why else would they take flight before you even get the swatter above your head? But Malik found a way to rid us of the plague, although his method nearly killed us all. He came to work one day proudly showing me a spray can he'd purchased near his home. "No more fly, Ma-dam, I fix." When I returned from work that evening I found my family sitting on the back patio. As I stepped into the house I gasped. "What is that horrible smell?"

"Malik sprayed the whole house for flies," my husband yelled. "I think we need to get out of here for awhile."

The odor was downright lethal. I was sure whatever Malik used must have had a nuclear waste symbol on the front of the can, along with a skull and crossbones. We left to have dinner at the local nightclub, then sat outside and watched the stars until we felt safe enough to go inside. We left the windows open all night, even though the temperature was in the 40s; I was afraid they'd find us dead in our beds the next day. In the morning our windowsills looked like they'd been painted black. Dead flies were piled up three inches deep. I wasn't sure which was worse—the flies, the smell, or the sight of their carcasses on every windowsill.

After living through a few months of Malik's odor, as well as listening to my family's complaints about it, I knew I had to find a way to let him go—without hurting his feelings. I felt it would be easier to clean my own house and let the brass and copper turn black rather than inhaling those obnoxious odors. But as fate would have it, Malik gave us his notice first. He had taken a job closer to his home. I was relieved I didn't have to fire him...and he could save face.

Later, when I thought about Malik, I had to chuckle. I'm sure our Anglo food habits gave off a pungent odor as well. Our diets were so different from his, they had to affect our skin odor, and hence, him. I could hear him telling his friends: "I could not believe what odors those white people had!"

20

Now-Ruz & Field Trips

D ue to winter's heavy rains, the city of Esfahan began to sparkle as spring approached. The mosques' tiles caught rays of sunlight and gleamed with turquoise, topaz blues, while luminous gold domes dominated the skyline. The days were a delightful seventy degrees. Lilacs were in bloom and flowers tumbled over courtyard walls. Flower stalls were awash with color and intoxicating scents. The trees seemed to stretch their fuzzy branches while soft green grass covered the fields. It was truly a new beginning.

Iran has many more mourning days than happy days, but this holiday of *Now-Ruz*, which usually occurs on March 21ˢᵗ, the previous or following day, depending on where it is observed, is widely celebrated and is the happiest time of the year for the country. This is not a Muslim holiday, but strictly Iranian, and has been celebrated in spring for over five thousand years. Visits are made to neighbors' and relatives' homes and gifts exchanged. The long, wet and icy winter has taken its misery and moved on, and in its place new life has moved in.

This is the time when the Persians empty their house of any "old" dirt from the year past (our version of spring cleaning I would think) preparing for the celebration of *Now-Ruz*. Housewives sing as they wash floors, windows and sweep out their homes. Along the streets, at the river, and across bridges, women are busy washing their carpets. This was truly a sight to behold, and the first time I witnessed it I was shocked. Trudy and I were approaching the bridge in town when I spotted something in the road. "Look out!" I yelled, as she yanked the steering wheel to the left. "We almost ran over that carpet."

Cars behind us honked, then continued to drive straight ahead, right over the carpets without hesitation. *Chador*-clad women crossing the bridge on foot showed no sign of anything untoward going on. I began to look around at the landscape and saw many colorful carpets draped over the bridge railings, as well as in the street. I asked the Iranian girls I worked with, and they explained the theory of carpet cleaning "Iranian-style." First the carpet is spread across a busy intersection where cars would be sure to drive over them, loosening any dirt that might be trapped in the weave. Then the women remove the carpet and beat it with long sticks to remove any excess dust. After these two feats are accomplished, the women drag the carpets to the river, unroll them and beat them with rocks. After that the carpets are submerged in the river to scrub and rinse. When sufficiently scrubbed, the carpets are then set to dry over the bridge railings and in the fields, turning them occasionally for faster drying. Rug Doctor would die a thousand deaths....

I asked Dori if she'd ever washed her rug in the dirty river water. She responded: "Have you seen the carpets when they are finished?" She had me there. I made a point to look closer at the carpets on the bridge railings the next time we drove to town. I was amazed! They all looked colorful and vibrant, as if they were dry-cleaned. *Ladies, don't try this at home!*

Also in this beautiful month of March, Denny's school planned their annual field trip to the ancient cities of Shiraz and Persepolis. I was a bit nervous about my son being on the road, but how could I say no when the rest of the class were going. "Hey, I'm off work tomorrow, do they need any chaperones?"

"Mom! My whole school is going. I don't think there's room for mothers."

Well, that was succinct. "Okay, but I worry about you on those roads and…"

"Mom! If you went would that make the roads any safer?"

I hate it when kids are smarter than their parents.

"How long will you be gone?"

"As long as it takes to see the two cities. How do I know?"

I sat down feeling unwanted and unloved. I picked up the school flyer. Their first stop was Shiraz, which had been a regional trade center for more than a thousand years, and its history dated back to 200 B.C. Shiraz had once been the capital of Persia, and was considered the center of the arts and letters, housing scholars and artists of the time. Shiraz was also known as the city of poets, wine, and flowers, as well as the City of Gardens due to the abundance of fruit trees that grew there. Their crafts included mosaic artwork, pile carpet weaving from the villagers, and exquisite silver work.

Pictures of Persepolis shown in the flyer were also striking. The earliest remains of the city dated from around 515 BC. Its architecture was noted for the teakwood columns, resorting to stone only when the largest cedars of Lebanon or teak trees of India did not fulfill the required sizes. Persepolis or Parsa, which translates to "The City of Persians," was 70 km from Shiraz, and gave me more angst. They were to take quite a long road trip from one city to the other, and I had nothing to say about it. All I could do was put my son in the hands of

Allah and pray the trip went without problems. I felt my fears would be allayed by the enlightenment Denny would gain to realize that his country was only two hundred years old, whereas this civilization had been here for centuries.

I tried to keep busy. When I ran out of things to do at the house I took a *Su-san* taxi to the Club for some food and cards. I knew I'd be distracted listening to the wives' perceived slights by anyone they came in contact with, or a new case of diarrhea, inedible foods and wayward husbands; it was sure to keep my mind off the highways.

When Denny returned home late that night, I was never so happy to see this child in my life. *What pain in the arse? Not this kid!* He was the light of my life. Then he opened his mouth.

"Wow, what a waste of time!"

"What? What do you mean? Didn't you enjoy the beautiful sights?"

"Mom! If you've seen one dome you've seen them all."

So much for enlightenment!

"But the ride home was cool."

"Cool how?" I asked

"Our driver raced with another bus driver and he wouldn't even listen to the teacher when she screamed at him to slow down. But it was cool. Our driver won!"

Thank you, Allah!

One beautiful spring day after I'd returned from work and was recouping on the sofa, Lauri came in from school with news I didn't want to hear. She ran through the front room, dropped her books and yelled to me as she headed to her room, "Mom, I made the cut! I get to go to Cairo with the track team."

My gut tightened. "Oh, honey, how great. Are any of the mothers going as chaperones?" I waited, praying for an affirmative answer.

"Mom, NO! They only have so much room on the plane and…"

"Plane?"

"Mom, How else could we get there? They told us no mothers, just teachers as chaperones."

The idea of my daughter on a rickety plane going to another Middle Eastern country where they might have political problems, promised to give me diarrhea. I was silent as I thought of all the "What Ifs" that I'm so good at.

"Mom? Aren't you excited for me? I made the cut *and* I'll get to see the pyramids…"

"Of course I am, honey," I yelled back, while I headed for the bathroom. "Can we talk about it at dinner when Dad's home?"

"Don't worry about Dad," she yelled back. "I told him I might get a chance to go to Cairo if I made the team, and he said he knew I'd make it."

What could I say? My little girl so far away! Without me to protect her! Then I remembered what Denny had said: "Mom, if you went would it make it any safer?"

That night I tried to act excited for her, but her father was downright jubilant. "Just like the old man," he said. "I was fast as hell on my school's track team, but didn't get a chance to play in another country. Good for you, sweetheart."

I guess that sealed it. She was up from the table, running to phone her girlfriend, who'd also be going to Cairo. *Let go, Mom, she's growing up.*

The next day I called around to a few of her teammates' mothers. "No need to worry," a long-time expat mom told me, "They're staying in an American compound. They'll have chaperones around them at all times. Plus their van driver is one of the teachers at the American School in Cairo."

"Well, that's a relief, but…"

"Not to worry," one of the Brit mothers told me, "they'll be seeing the Nile and the Great Pyramids. That's a chance in a lifetime. Give it up, Mum."

I capitulated. She was going to experience something incredible. To see and touch the pyramids and relics in Egypt that her buddies in the States would only see in history books was pretty amazing. Hopefully she'd also learn something about another country and its culture.

It was the longest four days of my life. Thankfully, my job kept me busy, but at night I fretted while my husband extolled the advantages of our child's trip. "She'll remember this for the rest of her life."

When she was an hour late returning home from her trip I imagined everything that could possibly have happened, and even saw it in my mind. *Stop!* I said out loud. *Stop driving yourself bonkers. She'll be all right.* One hour later as I began to search our phone book for the State Department, she walked through the door. I grabbed her as if she'd been held hostage and gone for a lifetime. *Okay, pull yourself together.* I didn't want to transfer my neuroses to her. "Hi my darling," I said as she tried to escape my bear hug. "I'm so glad to see you. How was Egypt? And how did your school do in the relays?"

"Mom, you wouldn't believe that place. You think Iran has lots of beggars? Egypt has three times that many. Some are blind and crippled, with open sores. They walk around the streets and hold their hands out. It made me so sad."

"That should tell you how fortunate you are to live in the United States, in a country that takes care of its infirm people. Did you give the beggars any money?"

"I was going to but our chaperones told us to ignore them and not give them any money cuz they'd follow us around all day."

Well, so much for compassion and international relations.

But, still, she was impressed with the tours they took. She actually brought home some small pieces of a Pyramid. Or, she added, some rocks that were strewn around it—she wasn't sure. She had pictures of herself and her teammates on camels in front of the Pyramids, and pictures of them inside the plane. She loved the trip, she said, and best of all, her school had won the meet. However, she remained sad about the beggars and sick people. She asked again why no one took care of them. I wished I'd had an answer for her.

It was now gorgeous tennis weather. It pained me that I had to work during the week while my friends ran around the tennis courts. Fridays were family days so I scheduled my tennis matches for Saturdays. Between the job, the tennis courts, and the bazaar, I was in high spirits.

Earl came home from work one day all fired up. The company had asked him to stay on until November. They'd also offered him a week off for R&R. "How about taking a week in June to visit Spain?" Of course, the kids were excited. I was too, but only about the trip to Spain. Did I want to stay until November? I wasn't sure.

1978 - Spain

21

Ole' To El Toro

We were eager to leave Esfahan for a delightful week in Spain. We deserved it, Earl said. We'd all been such great sports to hang in there for so long. Living in Iran was not the easiest thing for foreigners, especially women. The kids didn't seem to have any problems though. They went about their merry way, only stopping to question a glitch in their idyllic life such as their weekly allowance being a day late or sandwiches not prepared and waiting to be devoured.

The airport was business as usual. Other than the usual noise and excitable passengers, nothing looked like a revolution might take place. The flight to Tehran was uneventful, a bit bumpy due to the wind, but we were airborne and that's all that mattered. After a five-hour layover in Tehran, we were on our way to Barcelona. "Ole!"

Shortly after our takeoff from Tehran, I began to eye the red handle on the emergency exit door. I brushed my hand over the bar as if to wipe away some bothersome dust. I could do it! The bar read: "PUSH DOWN, PULL UP" and I knew I could manage that quite easily. No one would blame me. I could feel my left elbow quiver as I rested it on the red bar. I could see the headlines now: WOMAN SUCKED FROM PLANE THROUGH AIRLINER'S EMERGENCY EXIT DOOR

It had been pure hell for two hours on this flight, and we had more ahead of us. As soon as I boarded the plane in Tehran I panicked. Everywhere I looked were children; infants in arms and toddlers with loud, outdoor voices. Did we pick a "Save the Children" convention week to go to Spain? Settle down, I thought. I can read and hopefully block out any unwanted noise.

But it didn't happen. Children's wails and whines came wafting up from the front and back of the plane, with no way to block out the noise of these little cherubs who obviously had no supervision from their parents. What's wrong with parents today? In my day... Well, who cares about my day? This was now and these brats could not be controlled.

Earl and Jim were fast asleep, and Lauri and Denny were playing a card game on their tray table. All I'd wanted to do was read a book and drink my coffee. Why did it have to be so hard? The little cherub in front of me was definitely on Speed. Up and down, over the mother and father, from one side of the aisle to the other. STOP! I'd had it. I put on my sweet face, tapped lightly on the mother's shoulder and asked: "I'm sorry, but would you mind settling your child down a bit. I'm trying to drink my coffee and her jumping has kept my tray table in constant motion. I can't even set down my coffee cup."

"*Scuze?*"

Oh-oh. *No entiendo!* Great! I gave a weak smile and sat back. I put on my blackout eye mask and tried to envision handsome *Flamenco* dancers with tight bums drinking *café con leche* on sidewalk cafes in Barcelona, then returning to our hotel room and falling into plump feather beds.

The infant across the aisle from me began screaming two chords above high C. I peeked under my mask to see the child push his bottle away, scream and turn bright red. The mother looked nonplussed as to what to do. I wanted to tell her the baby was probably suffering ear pain from the altitude and maybe a pacifier would help, but I was afraid I'd get another "*No entiendo*" look and didn't want to seem like a know-it-all.

I pulled down my mask again, put in my earplugs, leaned back and tried to block out the world. Just when I thought there might be a chance of peace, I felt something slam into the back of my seat. I ripped off my mask and there stood a little imp of a girl about five, with a whatayagonnadoaboutit grin on her face, obviously waiting for me to react.

"Hello," I said, hoping to sound somewhat pleasant. "Did you bump into my seat?"

Again, the "*No entiendo*" look. She gave my chair a swift kick and ran back to her seat. *Well, aren't you the Bad Seed.* She then ran up to another passenger repeating same. I looked for her mother. She was two rows back, across the aisle from me, and seemed to be watching her little girl with love and admiration, as if to say: Isn't she adorable? Then she picked up her book and began to read. The child then ran back and began yelling at her mother in what sounded like Arabic. When the mother shook her head no, the child began to scream, just opened her mouth and let it rip. I looked for a flight attendant to complain, but none were visible. The screaming continued as the child ran up and down the aisle.

Where was that damned flight attendant?

I finally spotted her in the galley, pushed the call button and she appeared. "Maybe you can't hear what's going on down here with that child, but she's been screaming for five minutes and it's driving me crazy. Could you please ask the mother to control her child?"

Her answer shocked as well as irritated me: "Ma-dam, I cannot say anything to the mother of the child as she has paid for a ticket, same as you, so maybe you should just ignore the noise."

That's when I began to admire the Emergency Exit Door next to me. For the child, the mother, *and* the flight attendant.

Whoever said Spain was cheap had to be a longhaired hippy that slept on the beach and ate sand crabs from the tide pools. Our first hint that we'd be spending *mucho dinero* was when the taxi driver refused to load us all in his cab. He told us he was not allowed to take more than four passengers at a time, but would come back for the rest of us. This was unimaginable to us after leaving a country that could pile in ten people—and still stop for more. By flailing his arms for ten minutes, Earl was able to hail down another taxi, but as we rode through town I noticed several taxis with five people crowded in. Oh, well, when in Rome…(or near there).

Our hotel was a grand old Spanish icon. A musty odor hung in the lobby and halls. The rooms were tiny, but the beds looked inviting. I flopped down on the feather bed, and it was heaven. After unpacking we left the hotel to check out the city. We'd arrived on a Thursday and had a fun-filled week ahead of us. Earl and Jim wanted to see the bullfights, but the taxi driver told us they were held only on Sundays. Now we had two full glorious days to explore Barcelona, then on to Costa Brava. We decided to walk the city as opposed to any more expensive taxis.

What a charming place is Barcelona. Flowers everywhere: decorated balconies, rooftops, and restaurants; on front doors and in pots around the doors. The whole city smelled of a sweet fragrance. Quaint sidewalk cafes were on every block, and dotting the landscape were Orange Julius stands and Wimpey's Burgers—where my kids took their repast. The people all seemed so happy and carefree. Barcelona is quite a multiethnic city. Its main tourist attraction was the *La Rambla,* or *Las Ramblas* as tourists call it. *La Rambla* is separated by a wide center divider filled with vibrant colored flowers and plants, and runs downhill to the port. Sitting at an outdoor café, the view was spectacular: flowers growing in bright profusion, mammoth cathedrals with spires that seemed to reach the sky, down to the azure blue of the ocean where a twenty-foot statue of Columbus faced out to sea from the port, along with a replica of his ship, the Santa Maria.

We were all hungry by 5 p.m., but our clocks were on a different time zone. As we walked along *La Rambla*, we stepped into restaurants only to be told they weren't serving dinner yet. Return after nine o'clock, *señor*. Barcelona springs to life after nine o'clock, we learned, at which time we'd be sound asleep. A decision was made. To become more cosmopolitan, tomorrow we'd take a mid-afternoon nap, then hopefully catch a Flamenco floorshow after dinner. However, we found out "dinner hour" could sometimes last three hours, so the entertainment never started before midnight.

The first night in bed was all that I'd hoped for. I didn't want to fall asleep in that soft, comfy bed, I wanted to lie there and soak in the comfort. But before I knew it, it was morning, and not a joint or bone ached. We decided to breakfast at the hotel before we set off on foot to explore the city. Unable to understand the Spanish-language menu, Earl ordered scrambled eggs and tortillas for the five of us.

"How many tortillas, *señor?*" the waiter asked.

"Oh, two apiece is fine," Earl answered.

The waiter looked befuddled, but being polite he didn't question Earl. We looked around for a bottle of hot sauce on the table, excited that we could have our much-missed California spicy food. No hot sauce? How could a restaurant in Spain not have any hot sauce? When the waiter returned with our *café con leche*, I asked him to bring some hot sauce when he had a minute. He returned with another bottle of Ketchup. "Oh, I meant hot sauce, like..." I scanned my memory for the words. I pointed to the bottle of Ketchup and said, "*mui caliente?*" He looked puzzled.

"What is very hot, *señora?*

Oh no, I said the wrong thing. "Um, do you have Salsa?"

"*Uno momento*," he said, then disappeared. When he returned he was carrying ten plates piled high with what looked like monster quiches—and another bottle of Ketchup.

"What are these?" Earl asked, surprised that the waiter had brought us Quiche when he'd clearly ordered scrambled eggs.

"Jou order tortillas, *señor*. Do jou not want them?"

It was then we learned that a "tortilla" in Spain is an egg-potato dish that looks for all the world like a giant quiche. We now understood his look of dismay when Earl had ordered ten of them. I also learned that "hot sauce" is very "un-Spanish." I guess I needed to go back to my school history books where I should have remembered that the Indians had introduced the hot, spicy food to the Spaniards, whose Mexican offspring carried on the love of all things hot.

We took a bus tour through the city and the surrounding hills, which were dotted with castles and courtyards filled with flowers. The cathedral we'd seen from the bus left such an impression we decided to visit it again on Sunday morning. At five o'clock we all munched on crackers and cheese to keep us alive until the nine o'clock dinner hour. Jim had met some guys at the beach that day and opted to party at a club with kids his age. Our hotel clerk recommended a great restaurant that also had a floorshow with Flamenco dancers. He also told us to try the *Paella*, which he said was Spain's favorite food. I had no idea what it contained, but when the waiter took our order, I said very continentally, "*Paella por favor.*" When it was set before me I tried to identify the contents: it was seafood of sorts. I did recognize a shrimp or two, but it also had some questionable looking things bobbing about. Being the parent I couldn't say "yuk" or anything disrespectful of my host country's favorite food, so I closed my eyes and took a forkful. Something very slithery made its way past my tongue and uvula, slid past my esophagus, and I thought I would upchuck. However, just a few dry gags escaped and it was on its way to my stomach. My watery eyes tipped off the kids. They would have nothing to do with it. Earl, of course, the man with the iron stomach, polished off his *paella,* and then mine. The kids first asked for tacos. The waiter raised a smooth, black eyebrow. Denny repeated his order: "A ta-co."

"*Pardon?* You would like it to go?"

"Never mind," I said, "just bring some *el pollo*. They'll eat that."

I had a feeling the waiter had a lot to tell his buddies when he got off work: "Jou won't believe the loco customers I had today."

The Flamenco dancers were amazing. The women were so incredibly nubile and beautiful I had to suggest to my husband that he might find the men's dancing quite enjoyable to watch as well. He was entranced. We had front-row seats with the wood stage about three feet higher than our table, and about two feet in front of us. The noise was deafening as they stomped and clicked their way around the stage.

"Mom?" Denny hissed. "When are they gonna be done?"

"Shhh! Try to watch and learn. This is Spain's cultural dance."

Before long, both kids were fast asleep, with their heads on our laps. *So much for culture.*

The next day was Sunday and we returned to the *Iglesia Grande* cathedral that we'd seen on the tour. We looked like small ants inside this immense edifice, and standing next to the enormous stone baptismal fount, brought to Spain by Christopher Columbus. The nave was so huge, from where we sat, the priest saying the mass looked like a small child. An enormous ancient organ piped ethereal music, as a young boys' choir filled the air with cherubic voices. At the end of the service, as everyone filed out, I noticed people, young and old, taking off their shoes. They all seemed to carry soft leather slippers in their bags, which they slipped on their feet once outside. While the country's folk music played from a boom box, the people joined hands, making a gigantic circle on the church landing. They began to dance round and round in circles, singing along with the music. It was a most moving sight. Old, wrinkled women were hand in hand with teenagers, young men in suits, with hippie-types in dungarees. I wanted so badly to get in the circle with them, but Earl held me back. "Just enjoy it," he said.

"Do they do this every Sunday?" asked Denny. "I sure wouldn't wanna dance in front of our church."

Then we headed for the bullfight arena. Lauri and I tried to beg off, but Earl was adamant. "It's an old custom of the country, and we shouldn't miss it while we're here."

Well, custom it may be, but it's a horrible thing to watch. I could not understand how anyone could call what we saw "entertainment." I felt it was brutality in its strictest sense. My only encounter with bullfights had been via a Hollywood extravaganza, wherein Tyrone Power did exquisite cape work and bull dodging for an hour to win the heart of Ava Gardner. But I was in for a rude awakening. In essence, a proud, fierce animal charges out into the arena. Everyone cheers as he charges at the first image he sees, El Matador, who then steps behind a backstop fence (the big baby), while the poor bull runs his head and horns into said fence. Then, out steps El Matador, to a thunderous applause again, as if he'd just accomplished an amazing feat of bravery. He then makes three, maybe four passes at the bull with his cape, then leads the dumb, unsuspecting beast towards the side of the arena. And, there, covered in protective armor, stands a noble horse. Perched upon this horse is El Picador (the monster). The Picador waits, ready to literally skewer the bull with his lance—which is easily about two inches in diameter— between the shoulder blades. In addition to this bludgeoning, the lance also severs the muscles in the neck of the brave bull, leaving him unable to lift his head, and therefore not able to zero in on the "Brave" (my arse) Matador for a good pass or an equal opportunity to show his prowess. After about ten minutes of this "brave" Matador sidestepping the wounded and confused bull, out comes the sword, which is about three feet long. The true test of a great Matador is to zero in on a small patch of fur about five inches in diameter, between the horns and behind the head, then drive the sword into the hilt and not get gored. HA! That's what el dumbo *gringo* thinks. What's really happening is that El Toro cannot lift his neck, which makes El Matador seem very bravo.

Well, enough! I nearly regurgitated. Lauri cried. Denny watched between his fingers and Earl and Jim drank Sangria and cheered, Ole!

Boo-Hiss! As Hemmingway said so succinctly: "Bullfighting is not a sport at all, it's a tragedy."

We rented a car for 900 *Pesetas* a day ($10.80) plus mileage, and motored up the coast to Costa Brava. What a splendid drive. It was reminiscent of the drive along Big Sur in Northern California. Gorgeous! I had no idea Spain was so green with so many huge pine trees and rugged cliffs of the reddest soil I'd ever seen. And, what a magnificent coastline! We stopped at the Del Mar resort along the beautiful Mediterranean. The sand was blindingly white. The air was sweet and salty. I kept inhaling deeply, hoping to fix it permanently in my mind. The kids headed right for the surf and we headed for the hotel.

Our room was sparse, but smelled of the ocean, which we welcomed. We spent very little time in the rooms as we ran from restaurant to restaurant trying to eat everything Spanish. We bought out the town in souvenirs. The kids had a great time by the pool, the ocean and beach front, going into every store. Jim checked out a few of the local Discos and did a lot of roaming around on his own. The three of them went horseback riding and swam together, but when Jim wanted to check out the girls, he told his siblings to get lost.

The next two days were overcast, so we decided to drive up the coast to France as long as we were so close. We drove the coast about seventy kilometers, and there sat France. Actually, if we hadn't been stopped at the border and observed huge signs posted along the way, we would have thought we were still in Spain. We stopped at a quaint little roadside café. After changing some *Pesetas* into *Francs,* we drank *cafe au lait*, which was not nearly as good as *cafe con leche*, but it worked. Poor Earl, being so polite, he always had to thank the servers and found his *khayli momnuns* and *muchas gracias* all coming out together. But we made it because somehow that kind of thing is universal.

When we returned to Barcelona at the end of our trip, I had to do the hardest thing I'd ever done in my life: we put our daughter on a plane to New York—by herself. I knew it was coming, but kept hoping she might change her mind at the last minute. I cried, her dad got teary-eyed, and I'm sure Denny was happy to see her go.

Before we'd left Iran, Lauri had learned that all her school friends would be leaving for the summer. She asked if she could fly home for the summer to stay with her grandmother and visit her friends. We talked about it. We agreed it would be a long and lonely summer for her. Earl, Jim and I would be working, Denny would be with his friends whose families were still in Esfahan, and she'd be lonely. She seemed so grown up at thirteen, we both felt she would be fine making the trip. We called and talked to her grandmother, who was delighted that she was coming. A few of my close friends offered to make sure Lauri was safely transferred back and forth to her girlfriend's and relatives. We purchased the tickets in Esfahan, and booked her travel from Barcelona to New York, then on to LAX. She'd return from LAX to Esfahan.

At the gate, the flight attendant assured us she'd be responsible for Lauri during the long trip to New York. She would escort Lauri to her next gate for the flight on to LAX. Family would be waiting for her when the plane landed. I was relieved, but still fretful.

Years later Lauri finally told me about her flight and how terrified she'd been. She said she didn't tell me because she thought she might not get another chance to fly somewhere alone again if I knew the truth. Evidently, the flight attendant did not tend to her on the plane, and did not accompany her to her next flight. Lauri said the flight attendant disappeared as soon as the plane landed. Instead, Lauri was left to fend for herself. Had I known she was alone, walking through the cavernous JFK airport all alone, I would have fainted.

Her flight back to Tehran from the States was okay, she said, because now she was a seasoned traveler and felt very grown up. Plus my sister told the airlines what had happened on her inbound flight, and they promised she would be supervised all the way home, and she was.

From Barcelona we flew to Rome, where we had a very short time as our R&R was nearly over. We caught a cab to town, found a hotel, then walked the streets of Rome. We walked to the Trevi Fountain, an amazing work of art carved from huge blocks of marble, about 15-20 feet high. Along the rim of the fountain were young boys, girls and adults, singing, selling their wares and having a happy time. We ate, shopped the tourist traps, and then were ready for bed.

The next morning we made a quick trip to the Coliseum and the Vatican. I couldn't imagine how anything could top the incredible sights in the Barcelona cathedrals, until we walked through St. Peter's Basilica and the Sistine Chapel. It is beyond my imagination how someone could carve from raw stone and granite, something so beautiful and breathtaking. We literally half-ran with our necks stretched, looking up at the beautiful paintings by Michelangelo. We weren't able to stop long enough to really enjoy the sights, as we had to get to the airport.

The Rome airport looked like a war zone. The place was awash with machine-gun toting soldiers, finger on the trigger and mind in Salerno. We learned later that Rome's beloved Prime Minister, Aldo Moro, had been kidnapped a few months earlier, tortured and slain. Signs were posted on buildings, and all over the airport, decrying his abduction. Although he'd since been found dead, they'd neglected to pull the signs down, which read: "VIVA MORO."

When we finally boarded, my run-away imagination ran amok as I walked down the aisle to my seat. After what I'd seen in the airport I felt that the bad guys might be sitting right here on *my* plane. Most of the seats were taken up by dark, Middle Eastern types with scowling faces, which all seemed to be turned in my direction. I'd seen those faces somewhere, possibly a year ago watching "Black Sunday," or your basic terrorist movies: black hair, black eyes, swarthy complexions, speaking with forked tongue—okay that part was my imagination.

I leaned back and tried to think pleasant thoughts. I was getting myself under control when the flight attendant came down the aisle handing out newspapers. Looming out at me from the front page made my stomach clench: "ISRALI RAID ON PALESTENIAN NAVAL BASE. What was going on in the world? Was Iran going to join in the fracas? What had happened since we'd been in Spain? Had the whole world turned radical? I looked over at Earl, my mentor and protector, who'd fallen sound asleep. I ordered a cocktail from the flight attendant, and decided I'd join him in slumber. After a few prayers and one more drink, I felt fortified.

That is until we began our ascent into Beirut.

My heart fibrillated when an announcement came over the speaker from our pilot: "Ladies and gentlemen, we will be landing in Beirut in a few minutes. Under no circumstances are you to leave your seats, the plane, take pictures, look out the window or do anything suspect." My heart was now hammering in my ears. I was sure everyone near me could hear it. "Please now pull down your window shades and relax. We will be airborne shortly."

"What now?" I asked my half-awake husband.

"Just relax, do what the pilot says and we'll be fine."

As the plane touched down, I turned to lower my shade and to take a quick peek outside. I laid my head back against the headrest and rolled my eyes as far right as I could roll them. Dumb thing to do! The tarmac was alive with soldiers armed with machine guns, tear gas canisters and bayonets.

And then we stopped. And waited! The air on the plane soon became quite gamy, with over two hundred hot, ticked-off travelers. Grumbling could be heard coming from all parts of the plane. Children ran up and down the aisles, even though we'd been warned not to leave our seats. Grab the little rug rats, I thought, that would teach them a lesson. Okay, don't get crazy, I told myself. I began to breathe deeply and tried to get myself into a Zen state. My husband and kids now were sleeping comfortably. Two hours later we were airborne. I sighed with relief that no one had commandeered the plane—yet.

Shortly after our return to Esfahan, Jim's job came to an end. His part of the site was completed and he was eager to leave. A kid from the States, a local hire who worked for his father, had asked Jim if he wanted to fly back to the States via Europe. It worked out perfectly; both of their jobs ended within a week of each other, and off they went, Europe-bound. His postcards were full of the fun and experiences the two of them had. I was glad my son had that chance before he had to return home and find a job.

1978 – Esfahan

22

Rumors, Ramazan & Martial Law

The month of July was fraught with high winds, hot temperatures, and cranky natives awaiting the start of Ramazan. When Earl and I drove to the bazaar one Saturday morning I noticed many more *mullahs* on the streets and brought it to his attention. "I think you're getting paranoid again," he said. "You're listening to rumors again, right? If you weren't working at that job you wouldn't hear all this stuff. No one I talk to seems worried."

He was right, I was hearing these rumors at work, but the difference was, it came from Iranians who had relatives in Tehran. They spoke of mass murders in outlying villages by SAVAK, who were ordered to kill demonstrators. Also, rumor had it that the oil workers were about to go on strike. When I mentioned this to my husband he laughed: "Hey, if anyone should know that, it would be me. We're not having any problems on the jobsite, and we would've heard if the oil workers were going to strike." His advice was to keep a deaf ear when the Iranians talked. "Everyone likes to be the bearer of bad news."

But things had changed at work. It was palpable. John would not discuss rumors with me, which frustrated me more: "A dangerous thing, those rumors," he said, "best to just ignore them. If and when I get any information you should know, I'll pass it on. As of now, everything is A-OK."

Later that day he called me into his office. He had a new assignment for me: I was to phone the U.S. Consulate in Tehran every morning for a status update. Why would I have to do that if everything was A-OK? Something was brewing. I decided to forgo any trips to the bazaar for a while. When I did call for a status update, the attaché's reply was always the same: "No new updates."

Was this place collapsing underfoot and were we the last to know? Earl seemed so calm about the situation. "Aren't you at all worried about the rumors? Do you think it's safe to stay until November?"

"Listen, I've told you this before. If trouble was brewing the company wouldn't ask people to stay on, they'd be sending us home. Until that time, I'm not gonna' worry about it."

But it was obvious that the Iranian employees knew something. They scrambled away like pheasants from buckshot when anyone mentioned the Shah. I could see I would get no answers, so I walked over to Marci's* desk. "Okay, what's going on?"

She said she'd heard some of the local hires were missing from the base. They hadn't shown up for work, and the general feeling was it had to do with SAVAK.

"Maybe it's only a coincidence. How long have they been missing?" Just as I was about to get the news, John walked in. "Dodie, could I see you in my office?"

He smiled as I took a chair. "I think it would be best if you didn't ask or discuss anything about the country while you're working for me."

I told John I would never discuss anything to do with my job.

"Fine," he said, "but best to keep to yourself for awhile. Lots going on."

I asked John if he could share that information with me. "Not now," was his terse reply.

Work continued to be exciting, with wives and merchants filling the halls with their complaints. For a couple of weeks I was so busy I didn't have time to be paranoid. John came and went several times during the day, which gave me time to take a breather. While he was out of the office one morning, I took the opportunity to check out any new rumors. I moseyed over to some of the Iranian girls' desks. "So, what's going on? Anything we foreigners should know about?"

For the first time I noticed a reluctance on their part to talk. Even Farah looked away. They'd always loved to gossip, but today were closed lipped. "Anything new?" I asked again. Marci, one of the gals from the States, spoke up. "Don't bother asking. No one knows what's happening."

"No," one of the girls answered. "It's because ve are not supposed to talk about Shah." And that was the end of it. No one was willing to talk. I'd hoped that meant there was nothing to talk about.

Toward the end of July we were invited to visit friends in Tehran. Ron and Helen*, a couple we'd met in Esfahan who worked for the company. They lived in an upscale section of the city, and told us all was peaceful in their neck of the woods. I asked John if he felt it was safe enough for us to go to Tehran. "Go," he said, "just keep a low profile."

We caught a short hop from Esfahan and enjoyed two busy days with them. They lived in a grandiose villa they'd rented from the owner while he was on an extended holiday in Europe. An eight-foot block wall encircled the villa. The grounds were covered in gardens of exotic plants, chrysanthemums, zinnias and many more exquisite flowers I could not name. The interior of the home was enormous. Plush Persian carpets covered the tile floors, while the walls glistened with gleaming tile, enormous mirrors, and artwork. The tiny kitchen was outside the house, along with a wood-burning stove; quite a paradox from the spectacular house. He told us that wealthy Iranians do not like the smells from the kitchen to permeate the house, hence the outdoor kitchen.

I couldn't help but be envious. I could see myself giving garden parties here, maybe even inviting the Shah and Farah. That, of course, would only be if he were still in good standing with the US. No one quite knew for sure. After questioning our hosts over cocktails, they assured us that things were fine in Tehran. No problems, no demonstrations. "I did hear something about trouble in the outlying villages, Ron said, "but that's a long way from here. Just relax and enjoy. We'll know when it's time to leave."

I decided I wouldn't worry about it while we were with our hosts. Rumors, be damned, we were here to see and enjoy the wonderful sights of Tehran. The first night our friends took us to the *Kuroush,* a fashionable hotel with exquisite food, flowing liquor and dancing. The grounds were meticulous, by order of the Shah, and many state dinners with foreign dignitaries had taken place there. The huge poplar trees and floral gardens were spectacular, thanks to many gardeners and caretakers. After a wonderful evening, we sat outside in their beautiful gardens. They regaled us with stories of trips they'd taken while working oversees. "Be sure to visit Bangkok on your way home," Ron said. Then take the Pacific route home. You can stop at Singapore, Tahiti, Bali, and Australia if you make the right plane connections."

Earl and I talked about it later that night and agreed it was a wonderful plan. I'd make the reservations from work. All we needed was a departure date. The next night the four of us drove around the north side of Tehran for a glimpse of the Shah's wealth. A complex of eighteen palaces and residences of the two Pahlavi Shahs were set in a landscaped three hundred acre park. Although somewhat austere on the outside, the palaces on the inside were said to be ornate and bejeweled. Ron said there was quite a paradox here: the Shah surrounded by such wealth, while in other parts of Tehran adults and children with birth defects roamed the streets begging for money and food. Blind, crippled, bodies warped and bent, leprosy-like sores on feet and legs, toes missing, sometimes both feet, sometimes legs or arms. We all wondered aloud: How could a country let this happen? Why did the Shah have his minions looking for spies against his regime instead of building rehab homes for these poor people?

For dinner our friends took us to an upscale Persian restaurant near their villa. The food was outstanding, and we gave our compliments to the chef. After eating we walked down to the basement for the floorshow. Several exotic-looking women were belly dancing to the delight of all the men present. The things they could do with their belly fat! The fat on my stomach just seemed to lie there without any personality. I thought I could learn by watching the dancers' different muscle groups as they released and tightened, but with so much fat on their bellies, the muscles were not delineated. It didn't seem gross, rather quite amazing. We stayed for a few drinks, watched the dancing for an hour or so, then drove back to their home. The next morning we flew back to Esfahan.

At work a couple days later, I was eager to share the fun I'd had on my trip. "Great food," one Iranian said. "You pick the right place for good belly dance," another said. Then Davood*, one of our Security translators who'd been listening to my story, asked me if I'd like to see the morning newspaper.

Davood spoke excellent English. I would call on him throughout the day for my translation problems. His job every morning was to scan the Iranian newspapers for any security issues that John would need to know regarding Americans. Normally, I never bothered with the paper as it was printed in Farsi. But this morning Davood shoved the paper in front of me. He pointed to a picture on the front page: "Meezes Dotie, is this the restaurant you speak of?"

I looked at the picture. "What's this?"

"It is the restaurant you visited in Tehran, No?"

My mouth dropped open as I came face to face with terror. There, on the front page, was a burnt shell of a building. It was the same Tehran restaurant we'd dined at two days earlier. The picture showed the basement dance hall, charred and burned beyond recognition. Ash heaps on the floor had replaced the tables, chairs and decorations. There was no first floor.

Davood explained that the article blamed the Islamic revolutionaries who had firebombed the hotel to be rid of the evil alcohol and decedent dancing. He said the paper did not say how many people were present at the time, or how many had been burned to death.

I felt sick. How terrible for those poor people. Celebrating one minute, and burning alive the next. And how lucky we'd been to escape that carnage. Davood tried to soothe my terror by saying this was an isolated incident. The Shah would take care of these fanatics. Not to worry. However, I wasn't the only one worried. The American women who worked with me were very concerned about the rumors floating through the company. You could see the worry in their faces as they talked at breaks and in lunchrooms. Most of the Iranian men in the office seemed to take this as a big scare tactic, and were not about to enter into female gossip.

Chantel* confided her worries to me. We were at lunch, sitting off by ourselves in the break room. "At least *you* can get out if you have to," she said. "We can't."

"What? Why not? If things get bad, then we all have to go."

"No, you don't understand. You hold your own passports, right?"

"Of course."

"Well, then you're very lucky." She wiped her eyes. "BHI told all employees that our passports had to be turned over to the Iranian Government as a condition of the job. It was stupid for the company to agree with this, but it was a good, cushy job, and a long one. No one could have imagined that some day we might need to have those passports to get out of the country. No one ever mentioned the word "trouble."

"How long will they keep your passports?"

"Our company signed a ten-year contract with the Government, with the proviso that they would hold our passports until the end of the contract. I guess if we have to be evacuated, then they'll find a way to get us our passport. But I sure don't like the idea of waiting that long."

Ramazan was officially on, and for three days the pious were supposed to fast and visit the mosques to pray. But during this time, the streets were alive with parades of men beating themselves with chains for their sins. Only this time I was told it was way beyond religious; it was bordering on anger.

When I arrived at work the next day, the girls were ready and waiting for me. They told me that street gangs had taken advantage of the hype going on in the parades, and decided to join in the madness. They'd vandalized some of the bazaars, and also bombed the incredible Shah Abbas hotel. They said men and women were on their rooftops yelling and cheering them on, while watching young militant gangs run the streets, looting and causing mayhem. I was dumfounded. Living in Khaneh, I was blissfully unaware of all this. It was like living in another world from the city of Esfahan. I could not imagine such violence. Why? What was this all about?

The Iranian girls, young, chic and modern dressers, didn't seem as concerned: "Shah will strike down demonstrators," to which they all agreed. Many of them felt the majority of people loved the Shah and were steadfast in believing he had it all under control. The Muslim girls had nothing to say, but looked fearful every time the subject of the Shah came up. I wanted to believe the non-Muslim girls, so I felt relieved— for a while. But after work, as the bus slowly made its way through the unusually crowded streets, I noticed pictures of the Shah had been torn from windows, lying in gutters and flying through the air on gusts of hot wind. What is going on? If they get rid of the Shah, will they be after us?

I called Rallfe that night, hoping he would tell us it wasn't true. We looked forward to our talks with Rallfe. He had relatives in Tehran, and we felt they had a finger on the pulse of the country. As Earl and I sat around the table throwing one question after the other at him, I wondered what would happen to him if the Americans pulled out. The refinery would surely close down as the engineers responsible to build it and keep it running were mainly Americans, some German, some Koreans and some Japanese. No refinery—no job. If it was true what I'd heard at work, then no foreigner was welcome.

Rallfe told us he heard there were demonstrations going on all over Iran. He'd also heard that people were shot at, and some even killed the night before in Esfahan.

"Shootings in Esfahan? We'd heard nothing about that."

"Who's to blame for all the demonstrations?" Earl asked. "The guys that work for me seem ok. I've haven't seen any problems on the jobsite."

Rallfe explained what little he knew: "The men on the job would never discuss the Shah with anyone, they never know who might be SAVAK, because they infiltrated everywhere. But we think it's the *mullahs* and some of the so-called fundamentalist college kids students that are getting things stirred up. Their mantra is: 'Down with the Shah. Out with the Americans.'" Rallfe said that he and many of his friends felt that a subversive group had infiltrated the college as students, and they were promoting the revolt and getting the people riled up. He said most of the demonstrations and noise in the streets were started by these same students and street gangs that have been hired to get the country into this upheaval."

John had been doing a lot of closed-door meetings lately, which I was not privy to. I assumed he was being briefed on conditions in Iran. But when I tried to get some information from him, he'd always tell me we'd talk later, and off he'd go. Because John's goal was to keep his employees safe, and not cause hysteria, he had a lot more on his mind than to quell my fears. His company was there to train the Shah's army. I wondered what would happen to those BHI employees if the Shah were to be run out of Iran?

AUGUST 8, 1978: Monstrous tanks rumbled down the main streets of Esfahan this day. The American paper we received two weeks later in our care package read: *The Shah has instituted Martial Law in Esfahan and three other provinces in the country after demonstrators marched against his rulings and demanded his removal.*

It happened so suddenly: One minute life was carefree, the next minute *mullahs* were everywhere and we were under Martial Law. I did hear about minor disturbances in town, but living so far from the city, I hadn't a clue how far it had escalated.

That is until I saw the tanks!

I couldn't believe my eyes. What the hell was going on? I stormed into John's office and sat without being asked. "Okay, please tell me why those tanks and soldiers are in town. Should we be getting out?"

"Nothing will come of it," he said as he leaned back in his chair and stretched. "It's just the Shah's way of showing power. It'll be over soon and the tanks will roll away. If anything, you should feel a little safer with those soldiers in town."

As security chief, I'm sure John knew full well about the upheaval. He'd dictated several memos to that effect, but nothing about Martial Law. He said later he'd expected it with all the problems going on in most of the small towns and villages, and especially after the Ramazan parade and bombings here in town. There would be no more of that with the military around, he said. "But don't be too worried about the Martial Law thing. It's just a show of force that's only going to last until things calm down. So far the Shah has control of things."

So far?

After work, as our bus moved through the city, Marshal police could be seen everywhere. Hopefully they weren't going to allow any demonstrations on their watch. I felt a little relief knowing that they would quell any uprising in my path. I wanted to believe John, but it terrified me to see those huge tanks. And next to the tanks stood stern-looking soldiers, AK-47s at the ready.

Did I feel safer?

The next morning on the slow ride into work, I took a closer look at the soldiers. As our bus pulled alongside one of the tanks I was shocked to see such young boys in uniform *and* wielding huge rifles. Those boys couldn't have been much older than sixteen; most pimply-faced with a dusting of black hair under their nose. Yet here they were, taking responsibility for possibly killing someone who didn't obey their orders. Unconscionable! I was told that Iranian boys were inducted into the army at sixteen years of age, served two years far from home, and then sent out, quite unprepared and undisciplined, for battle. I felt sorry for those kids. They should have been out playing soccer instead of dressed in hot fatigues standing in the brutal August heat. As the bus crept by the tanks, the boys would put on their war faces, aim their rifles at the bus windows, then look away as if to say we weren't that important.

Gradually I got used to seeing the tanks and soldiers, and forgot the feeling of eminent danger. What would my friends at home think about all this? I doubted they would believe me. I had to record this invasion for posterity. A few days later I packed my small camera with a fresh roll of film, stuck it in my purse and set off for work. As our bus moved slowly through snarled traffic, I spotted a huge tank parked in an intersection on my side of the bus. Leaning against the tank were two adolescent-looking boys in army fatigues, AK47s swinging loosely by their sides while they checked out a gaggle of perky young schoolgirls.

What I didn't see was the officer standing just behind them.

I grabbed my camera, aimed and clicked just as the officer stepped forward—and looked directly at me. I froze! I heard someone in the bus hiss: "No, Ma-dam, you must not take picture, you vill be arrested." Oh boy!

The officer ran towards the bus yelling *Ist, Ist*—stop—blowing his whistle in rapid sequence. The driver tried to find a place to pull over but the traffic would not yield. I took that opportunity to remove the roll of film from the camera, tuck it under my butt, placing the open camera on my lap to show the officer that it was empty. My heart nearly stopped as he boarded the bus. Well over six feet, he had to stoop as he stormed down the aisle toward me. He sported an oversized handlebar mustache that seemed to be growing out of his nose as well as his mouth. His unruly jet-black hair stood up as in surrender all over his head, bringing to mind an Iranian Don King. He had rows of decorations on his uniform that suggested he was a power to be reckoned with.

And he was in a foul mood!

The Iranian passengers sat quietly and stared intently at the floor. The officer walked directly to my seat and held out his hand. "You! Gif me cam-ra!"

I was terrified. My mouth was so dry I couldn't get my tongue off my teeth to speak. "Oh, thorry *Agha*, *bebakthid*," I whined. "There ith no film in thith camera. I wath playing—*baazi*." The two words I did not want to hear from this mammoth was: "*Bia inja*"—come here! I tried to look contrite as I handed him the open camera. "Thee? *Baazi*. Only playing."

His giant, hairy hand swooped down and grabbed the camera from me. "*Buro, buro!*"—hurry—he yelled at the driver as he stormed off the bus. The frightened driver hit the gas pedal as our heads whiplashed, and a collective sigh of relief could be heard from the passengers. I took a peek around me after we'd gone a few blocks. Evil eyes stared out at me from the men, but I could swear I saw one of the *chador*-clad women wink at me.

During the next week John was on the phone, out the door, or off to meetings. He had a tight look about him that worried me. That night, Rallfe and Dori were again invited to dinner. It was like rewarding a stoolie for their inside information. "It's not good," he told us. The general feeling of the revolutionists was that the evil imperialists from the West (that would be us) were here to overtake their country, demonizing Islam and westernizing the country. The Shah was now deemed the Western man's devil, and was the cause of the nation's decline from the Islamic teachings and way of life.

"Not good" was a misnomer. I asked Rallfe if he thought this would blow over, as most expats seemed to think. He didn't know. "Only time will tell. Maybe the Shah will listen to the people, if it isn't too late."

Confusion ran amok. Many expats felt the Shah would quell the protestors. If not, we certainly thought that those in the know at the big white house on Pennsylvania Avenue would say: "Come home, y'all." Until that happened, the men on my husband's job were content to stay and work. It made we wonder if Americans had any idea what their government was doing; at home or abroad. This whole thing was a shock to me. I thought everyone loved the Shah, and the US as well, so why did the Iranians want him out? Along with us? If every window in town had held his picture, was it there by force? Did the people really hate him? I had much to learn.

A curfew was immediately imposed by order of the Shah, and signs went up all over town and were very explicit—in Farsi as well as English—THREE OR MORE PEOPLE TOGETHER ON THE STREET AFTER DARK WILL BE SHOT.

This was a big imposition to our tennis group. We ladies met at the Khaneh tennis courts in the evening when the sun was down and much cooler. Even though we were in a complex with gates and guards, we were told the curfew was to be followed everywhere. This didn't leave us much room to negotiate. We discussed our problems at length. We decided that if we walked to the courts, one at a time, we wouldn't be noticed or shot. We made sure we were never in a twosome as we strolled along. The court had massive lights encircling the area, so we felt it was obvious we weren't up to any subversive activity. We did manage a couple nights of tennis before our husbands put a stop to it. I guess they decided it would be inconvenient for them if we were arrested or shot. Who would do the shopping and cooking?

Things seemed to quiet down after Martial Law was imposed and the rumors seemed to be dwindling. We continued with our expat lives: movies and cards at the Club, but we had to have a company van drive us back to Khaneh before curfew. The bazaars were closed because of the riots, so shopping was out of the question. I continued to go to work every day, and slowly began to think maybe John was right; the Shah had things under control.

Then we heard about the oil strike in Abadan, about 200 miles from us, which led to huge demonstrations. Rallfe told us he'd heard the Shah's army was brought in to disburse the mobs and many demonstrators were wounded, along with many deaths. As the deaths were mourned in huge marches of grief, as well as demonstrations against the Shah for the murder of innocent people, the army was then called to move in and control the demonstrators—or kill them if necessary. Even innocent mourners were targets if they were gathered near the demonstrators, he said. Then came the horrific news of a cinema fire in Abadan where hundreds of men, women and children were burned alive. The word spread that it was the work of SAVAK, but later investigation showed it was a man who'd been hired by the *Tudeh,* the Iranian Communist Party. Supposedly he confessed, saying he was paid by the revolutionaries. He said he barred the doors from the outside. The people didn't have a chance.

Next the Korean restaurant in town was fire-bombed, we assumed it was because they had pork on their menu, which is a no-no to Muslims. We'd never eaten there; Earl said he was afraid he'd be eating a *joub* dog in the shape of a pork chop.

There were times when John went to Security meetings at the Consulate and I was not invited. Rumors raced through the company. "It's no big deal," someone would offer. No news came to us from the government-controlled television or radio, so we relied on many of the

Iranians in the company who had friends or relatives in the cities being attacked. Not much work was done during those days. You could see the office staff—Americans and Iranians—huddled around the coffee machines, whispering, looking worried, and every now and then you'd hear someone exclaim: "No! That didn't happen." The rumors were growing exponentially, as the coffee pots were drained.

Next we heard that the Shah was in deep trouble. He was said to be guilty of hundreds of murders by SAVAK. Some Iranians began to speak up against the Shah, which had never happened before, and which almost certainly cost them their lives. Now as I called the Consulate in Tehran every morning to get an update, the response was: "Keep a low profile." There was that phrase again. What did that mean? Bend over when you walk? Why weren't they telling the American companies anything?

1978 – Esfahan

23

"Go Home!"

I decided against going into town, other than for work. Things seemed to quiet down again at work. The usual gathering and whispers around the water cooler and coffee machine continued, but nothing new. In our small complex of Khaneh, no one seemed too worried. My husband echoed what John had told me: "Things will settle down, just a few radicals causing problems."

Then I received an invitation to leave.

Because I loved how Farid did my Hamill wedge, I wasn't about to discontinue my visits to him once a week, *mullahs* or no *mullahs* On hair days I'd leave work a little earlier and hail down a car-taxi to his shop. But the appointment on this particular afternoon lasted longer than usual and it was dark when I exited the salon. The street was uncommonly quiet, only a few cars and busses scurried about. I was standing in front of the salon, hoping to flag down a taxi, when I heard steps behind me and turned to see a *chador*-clad woman approaching. She leaned in next to my ear: "Vat are you doink here?"

I was surprised! "What?" I wasn't sure I'd heard her correctly.

"You should not be here. Go home!"

Did she mean Khaneh? Or America? "*Bebakshied?*"

"I say you should not be here. Leaf!"

I stared at her in disbelief. Was she *ordering* me? With my sense of righteousness I was not going to go down without a few questions. "Why? Am I in danger?"

"*Baleh.*"

Something about the look in her eyes told me I had better listen. I turned and ran down to the corner, turned left and crossed the street. I waved down a car-taxi, and was shocked to see I would be the only passenger. I leaned back to catch my breath and breathe a sigh of thanks. I paid him to drive me to Khaneh, which he was happy to do, visualizing a nice tip.

When I got home Earl didn't seem perturbed by my story as he flipped through a two-week old newspaper from home. "Really," I said, "Do you believe that? It scared me at first, but then she might have just been a xenophobe."

"Don't be out after dark," my husband said without looking up from his paper. "I don't want you in the city after dark. Get your hair done on Saturdays. You don't need any more stimulation." Earl did not want to hear anything about an uprising, ousting, or anything to do with scare tactics to drive us out. He had a job to do, and loved it! Again he emphasized: "As I've told you countless times, if there were any danger to Americans, the President would call us home. "

Right!

The next morning at work everyone was abuzz about something. "You're not going to believe what happened to me last night," I began, "when I was…"

"Never mind that," one of the Iranian girls interrupted, "did you hear about the German man who was killed last night?"

"Huh?" They told me what they knew, which wasn't much, just hearsay around the streets, they said. One story was that a German expat was trying to enter a bank after it had closed, and someone shot him. Others argued that they'd heard he was going to hold a secret meeting and didn't want SAVAK to hear about it. "Where?" I asked, hoping it had been somewhere other than where I'd been.

"The bank in town," one of the girls offered, "across the street from your beauty salon."

I sat down. When I could breathe again, I told them my story. Again, I heard the familiar "…just a bunch of radicals trying to scare people." But the story of the secret meeting made sense to me when I thought of the woman who'd told me to "Go Home!"

Heading to work a week later, I was surprised to see a line forming in front of one of the Government buildings. As we drove nearer, I was shocked to see Iranians, three and four deep, lined up around the block waiting to get in. What were they lined up for? When John returned to the office I told him what I'd seen. He said the majority of those people were hoping to get a Visa to leave the country, but because no new Visas were being issued by order of the Shah, they were still waiting, hoping he would change his mind. "The Shah probably knows that most of them are wealthy Iranians trying to get out of Iran with their money. If a revolution does come down, I'm sure those Iranians know their American dollars would be confiscated, or worthless with a new regime."

This didn't make sense to me. Why were the Iranians trying to get out now? Maybe we should be leaving, too. John disagreed. "Let's wait until we hear something from the Consulate. People panic. We'll be the first to know if there's a problem. Trust me."

Note to self: *Don't trust anyone who says:"Trust Me."*

I still called the American Consulate in Tehran every day for updates, with the same answer that day as the other days: "Keep a low profile." But surely they had the inside track on what was happening. So why didn't they tell us to prepare to leave, or at least tell us it was a possibility? If Earl was right, they would do so at the appropriate time. I tried to keep that in mind as I went about my duties. But I still couldn't help but wonder about those people who were trying to leave their own country. Were they leaving parents behind, children, and relatives? Or friends they'd grown up with and hoped to grow old with. If a revolution did happen, would they ever be able to get back to see their loved ones. It was too painful to even imagine that happening.

I again reminded my husband that it might be time to go. I felt I had an inside track to what was going on because of where I worked. But when he pressed me for more specifics, I had none. All I could say was if the Iranians were trying to get out of their own country, didn't that tell us something?

"Listen," my husband said, "I work with these people every day. They aren't concerned. So why should we be? The Iranians running to get out probably made their money illegally and don't want to be jailed. Stop driving yourself nuts. I'll let you know when it's time to go. You know I wouldn't stay here if there was any danger to my family."

Famous last words!

Then the picture hit my desk.

Opening the mail every morning was my first duty. Anything marked as personal, I put on John's desk. Everything else I opened. Most were from the head office in Texas. But this particular morning I saw an envelope marked: "AMRIKINS" in very wobbly handwriting. When I opened the envelope a Polaroid picture dropped to my desk. I picked it up and froze. The picture was of a scorched bus, lying on its side with blood-red paint scrawled across the picture: "Death to Amrikins" and "Yanke go home."

My heart skipped a beat as I recognized that particular style of bus. The Shah had designated those Government of Iran buses to transport the expat children to school—and my children rode those buses every day. I ran into John's office with the picture. "This can't be real, please say it's not."

He took the picture from my shaking hand. "I'm afraid it is. I've already been briefed. This is an isolated incident. I hope you don't think this is common. The GOI bus was targeted by extremists to scare us, but don't worry, they now have armed guards on every GOI bus."

Was that supposed to make me feel better?

That's all I needed to hear. My kids would never ride those buses again. I told John I would be leaving the country as soon as we could get our stuff packed up and get our tickets home. He said he was sorry to hear that, and added that he felt I was acting irrational. It fell on deaf ears. If my kids were in danger, *adios!* John asked if I'd stay a little longer until he could find someone to replace me. I said I would stay until Earl got our tickets home. I would take the kids out of school immediately.

I had a message for my husband as he walked in the door from work that night. "Tell the personnel office we want the money for our trip home."

Earl looked at me as if I was nuts. "What are you talking about? You know I have to stay until November. What happened today? Listening to those rumor mongers at work again?"

I told him about the Polaroid picture.

I could see he was shocked, but he wouldn't admit it: "What makes you think that happened here in Esfahan?"

"The picture was addressed to BHI, to the Security Department. Who would send it to our office if it happened in another city?"

"Listen to what you're saying. These fanatics want the Shah out, right?" They want to scare the hell out of everyone so the foreign companies will leave. Those are the Shah's buses, you're an American company, so what better way to scare the hell out of the expats?"

We hashed it out long into the night. When he found he couldn't sway me, he said it was probably best for us to go if I was that worried. Go and take the kids, he said, but he would stay and finish his contract.

I didn't want to have my husband sent back to the States in a body bag. I ranted on it for another hour. "Think of the kids. Are you being fair to them?"

"Dodie, you know I wouldn't stay if I thought I was in danger. This job means big advancements for us. Please give me enough credit that I'd know when it was time to go. I'll make the arrangements for your travel at work. Go ahead and take the kids out of school."

I phoned the schools and asked them to mail the kids' transcripts to our post office box in the States. I told them we had an emergency at home, would be leaving as soon as possible, and would not be returning. I hung up the phone and felt immediate relief. Later that week I heard that the schools were closed. So, it wasn't just my paranoia; someone up higher had made that decision.

Later that week the office was ablaze with news when I arrived. Davood, our Security translator read from the Iranian newspaper: It reported that people in Jaleh Square in Tehran were shot while protesting against the Shah. The number of people dead was not known. Supposedly it was a peaceful march, Davood read, yet they were attacked by the military. Now Tehran was under Martial Law as we were.

I wasn't surprised anymore. I told Davood that I'd be leaving soon, that I was worried about my kids, and Earl was staying. He was shocked. "Don't believe what you hear. The Shah will end all this. Then you'll see. His people love him. All you hear about is bad things. He is a good man. He cares about our people. It's the college students who are riling up the people. Don't worry, you stay, I promise it will all go away."

Now he sounded like my husband.

John was gone when I got to work. His message said: "I'll be back." I certainly hoped so.

1978 – Esfahan

24

"It'll Blow Over"

The next night, one of the Supers on Earl job hosted a BBQ for the employees. I secretly felt that it was a Rah! Rah! meeting to alleviate any employee's fears about what happened in Tehran, but held my tongue. The talk began again about "...things blowing over." The women were silent. I listened as I heard the unanimous agreement of the company men: "I'm sure we all agree that the company would immediately call us home if there was a problem. They've got a finger on the pulse of what's going on here. I'd trust them before I'd trust the flaky fanatics who're trying to scare everyone. And...surely the company's in touch with the American Embassy in Tehran. They'd know if things were unsafe in Esfahan..." Blah..blah..blah!

I listened. I didn't interrupt, but when they were through with their grandstanding, I spoke up. When I tried to explain my fears about all the Iranians wanting to leave the country, and the firebombed bus, they pooh-poohed me saying I was a rabble-rouser. I gave up. They were not going to budge, not with a ten-thousand dollar bonus calling their names.

On the way home from the BBQ, Earl told me what his boss said to him before we left: "If you leave the job before your contract is up, you'll not only forfeit the end-of-job bonus of $10,000, but also lose all hope of having a career with this company."

"What? That's emotional blackmail. How could he say you'd lose your career with the company? In other words, he'd put a black mark on your personnel records?"

"That's what happens when you leave a contract job before it's finished."

I had one more ace up my sleeve. I knew Earl would feel guilty if he let his kids down, and I would use every trick in the book to get him to leave with us. "If you stay and we go, what happens to our plans about stopping in Bangkok and all the other places where I made reservations? We were going to take a month to get home. What do we do about that? The kids are really excited about it, but I won't do it alone."

Earl was silent for a long time. "Let me get a feel for what's going on at work. I'll ask around to some of the Iranian engineers on the jobsite, maybe they know more than Rallfe is telling us. In the meantime, just start packing up things you want to take home and get rid of the stuff you don't want."

It was now time to plan a garage sale. When expats leave the country to head home, big garage sales are advertised and attended by all newbies. Furniture and household goods are sold at a minimal price, thus the newcomers do not have to do much shopping to set up housekeeping. I felt I could get rid of most things because of the numerous companies from other countries. Possibly the non-Americans that worked for them felt safe here and were not planning on leaving. I began to empty the house of things I could live without. I dragged all my bric-a-brac to work and sold it. I took orders on my furniture, collected the money, and gave them a "paid" ticket to pick up the stuff after we'd excited the country. I didn't yet have a date, but they trusted me. I'd be prepared when it was time to go.

A few days later John called me into his office. He'd finally got the word from the American Consulate that we were to coordinate an evacuation meeting with all supervisors on the job. He said it was just a precaution, and didn't mean it was about to happen. I wondered how they would go about evacuating personnel who didn't hold their own passports. I would not worry about that right now. I had other things to take care of. I told John I'd start the process, but would only work until we were to leave. He'd have to put the rest of the plan together. I think he knew he wouldn't need anyone to replace me.

The office had a going-away party for me, with food and gifts. I could see the worry in the American girls' faces as we hugged goodbye. I wondered how long it would take to get any of them out of Iran. John gave me a huge bear hug, then stepped back and shook my hand. "Good luck on your trip home. We'll miss you, you know. I'm sure we'll be working here for a long time. It's just a matter of all these rumors that we have to look into and clear up, but I'm pretty sure it'll all blow over."

We all hugged goodbye at the office and hoped we'd meet again.

It was finally time to prepare our exit from the country. Earl called HR and the wheels were set in motion. While waiting for our exit date, I decided to have some friends over for a farewell dinner, an early Thanksgiving we called it. We bowed our heads as each one asked a blessing from their own deity. We prayed for our safety as well as the innocent people of Iran. As the day wore on we all struggled to maintain a normal Thanksgiving gaiety but couldn't avoid a somber resolve. Conversations would start and then trail off. We tried to take solace in the hope that our government would get us out safely. At the end of the day, we embraced our friends a little longer, a little harder, not knowing if we'd meet again.

After the kids were asleep, I turned on the television, hoping to hear what was going on in Tehran. We wanted to see if the "new" rumors we'd heard were true. Had the radicals commandeered the television stations? Had the violence escalated any further? Was there any hope of a compromise between the radicals and the U.S. government? Was Carter going to step in or stay out?

The streets of Tehran flowed into our living room filled with hundreds of screaming radicals. Some held burning American flags; others held effigies of Jimmy Carter hanging from a noose, as well as "Death to Amrikins" signs. I turned off the TV after five minutes of pure disbelief.

Earl finally admitted his feelings: "I never thought it would go this far. What the hell is our company doing? Why haven't they told us all to return home?" These were questions everyone was asking now. I tried to think only positive thoughts to help me sleep that night. We'd be gone soon, and this nightmare would be over for us. I conjured up the beautiful places we would visit on our way home.

When we finally got the date of departure from the company, I called the agent and changed our dates to Bangkok. The travel agent had assured me the tickets I'd purchased could easily be changed once we got to the ticket counter at the Esfahan airport. I didn't want to argue with her, but she was in Bangkok with smiling faces and dancing girls; I was in Iran with scowling faces and rumors of killing Americans. Somehow that made me a tad nervous. Also, we heard that other expats who'd already left the country a few weeks earlier had waited in the airport on benches for days trying to get a flight out of the country. I didn't want to sit in the Esfahan airport with guards everywhere and wonder if we'd ever get on a plane.

I called the travel agent again. No problem, she assured me. Four other clients had just flown out that morning to Bangkok without any problems. Evidently Bangkok was not a destination that the military was worried about. Flights were departing on schedule.

The next day I packed everything we'd need for our trip. Thankfully, Earl had packed most of our things for shipment, and a company van would see that they were delivered to the port at Kharq Island, where they would (hopefully) be shipped home. I prayed our possessions would be on a ship headed to the States. We got a call a few days before we were to leave. The good news was our shipment had reached the port. The bad news was all employee freight would be held up due to a workers' strike at the port. We had no idea if we'd ever see our belongings again. But, they were just possessions, I told myself. We had our lives and were headed out of Dodge.

I made a mental note: *Remember, Persian silk carpets are just things!*

In the capital city of Tehran, radicals were firebombing establishments that Americans visited. Any place that served liquor and provided dancing were targeted as against the Holy Book. Living in Esfahan, only 300 miles from Tehran, was way too close for me.

For the most part we'd lived a quiet, comfortable life. We had many Iranian friends and neighbors who looked out for us if we needed anything. Men from my husband's job shared dinners and great stories of their culture with us (which Rallfe translated). There was a mutual respect among us. However, as the revolution began to take shape, our Iranian friends no longer came for dinner. They warned us of dangers to Americans, and told us the students were planning demonstrations that could get ugly. They told us to stay away from the city.

As most Americans, we took our freedom for granted. We assumed because we were U.S. citizens, everything would go smoothly for us. And it did—while the Shah was in his palace. Now we heard that he would be forcefully ejected from the country. We heard that radical college students were running the streets of Tehran with the sole intent of purging "The evil American imperialists" out of their country.

An unmarked company van picked us up at our house two days later. The night was bitingly cold, the sky moonless and jet-black. Wind pushed our van from side to side, while the driver drove at his normal break-neck speed. I couldn't stop the shakes that overtook me. Earl seemed calm. I was sure he tried to stay that way for us, his terrified family. "Just remember, we're on our way to a tropical paradise. No problems. We'll get our tickets, board the plane and it'll all be over."

I still have flashes of our perilous trip that night as the driver stomped on the gas pedal, then the brake, then the gas pedal, over and over as we made our way to the airport. Earl felt the Iranian driver might want to listen to our conversation so he put his finger to his lips. Both of us were at a point of not trusting anyone, even an Iranian company employee.

The traffic was the normal crazy pattern, even this late at night, but I noticed that most of the traffic was going the same direction we were, and the oncoming lane was sluggish. When we arrived at the Esfahan airport, I understood why. The airport was pandemonium. Hundreds of frantic-looking people, most of them Iranian, were trying to get out of the country at the same time, and it seemed on any plane that had room. Everywhere I looked were little bands of the militia, armed with AK-47 rifles. My God, would we get shot before we got out of this maddening crowd?

Earl pushed his way through the mob holding Denny's hand, while I followed holding tight to my daughter's. "Keep your eyes on me," he yelled. "Don't let anyone push in front of you." I nodded, while trying to quell the lump in my throat and tears from starting. I reached out and hooked my index finger through a belt loop in Earl's jeans: Just try and get through, my expression said, and you're dead. As we approached the ticket counter, I heard Earl yell at a man who'd tried to push ahead of him: "Wait your God-damn turn!" Two other men came from behind, pushing Lauri and me to the side, then heading for Earl. "Back of the line, *Agha*," he yelled, as he pushed them out of our way and approached the ticket agent. The men fell back, cursing and waving their arms at him, but none seemed to want to press it any further.

I prayed to whichever God was listening at the time: Please don't let my husband get in a fight. I was sure a foreigner would be the first to be shot. Everywhere I looked were soldiers, loaded down with rifles and ammo belts slung loosely around their waists. All I needed was for the soldiers to find a reason to drag us out of the airport. No one seemed to listen as people were pushing, yelling, and screaming. It was obvious that the Iranians wanted to get on a plane, any plane, as much as we did.

The agent took the tickets from Earl. I prayed silently that she'd forego the dates on them and let us go through. I think she was as thrashed as we were, as she took the tickets, pointed to the gate, and called on the next person in line. We headed for our gate. Now the crowd was more aggressive. Even the women were screaming at each other, and at the men. I was amazed to hear this as I'd never heard an Iranian woman open her mouth to protest a man's decision. Getting through the jet-way was another struggle, with Earl pushing his way past people who tried to break in line, while I still held tight to his belt-loop. By now both the kids were terrified. I heard Lauri yell at someone who wanted to push ahead of her and was glad she had the chutzpah like her father. After twenty minutes of pushing and struggling to get a foothold, we finally boarded and found our seats.

The terror of what we'd been through stayed with me, even though we were now in our seats. I could hear the jet engines roaring but the plane sat motionless for over three hours. My heart felt as though it was in full fibrillation. Then I felt a slight tremor under my feet. Was it my imagination? Were we really moving? I held my breath as I felt the plane inch forward.

We *are* moving!

The airport buildings slid slowly past my window. As the plane's tires lifted off the tarmac I was finally able to let go of the panic. Mentally I pulled back on the yoke as the plane began to gain speed, then altitude. I exhaled, slowly. Tentatively. We *are* finally leaving this terrifying place.

My cheek became numb from the freezing glass of the window as I strained to watch the fires and ropes of smoke below; a city burning, growing smaller as we ascended to our cruising altitude. I struggled to shake the fear that held me so rigid in my seat. I closed my eyes and tried to slip into a zone of REM, but acrid fumes invaded my dreams. Memories seared through my mind. Screams assaulted my ears. I saw the charred human remains caught in a flash fire of pipe bombs in the Polaroid that had landed on my desk at work: DEATH TO AMRIKINS—YANKEE GO HOME.

They were chasing me, trying to stone me as I ran for my life.

A foreign voice startled me awake. The pilot announced that we could now remove our seat belts. I shook my head to be rid of my recurring nightmare. Next to me my husband and two little ones were asleep, leaning against each other in peace.

I smiled for the first time in days.

It was over.

###

2012, USA

Epilogue

More than thirty years have passed since those terrifying days in Iran. History recorded the terrible results of the revolution: the hostage crisis; the loss of life; the Shah's flight to Egypt; his cancer and his entry into America; his death, and the horrible facts that surrounded the takeover by Khomeini.

The *Imam*, Ayatollah Khomeini, who'd been exiled by the Shah, had been busy making plans to return to his country in grand style. From his home in Paris he was recording his messages on cassette tapes while ranting about the devil Shah, the evil American imperialists, and the return to Islamic law. The cassettes were being smuggled into the country and dispersed by the *mullahs* who were called to action by this faraway voice. As history shows, the plans for the overthrow of the Shah had been going on underground for a long time, possibly as long as two years.

The Iranian people were told by Khomeini to throw down the gauntlet, strike out and run the filthy infidels out of the country, dethrone the Shah, and take him to trial as a traitor to Iran and Islam.

The feelings were that the Shah and upper classes got greedy; the poor people felt like they were left out in the cold and so were susceptible to the fundamentalist *mullahs*; a revolution sounds like a good thing when you feel you have nothing to lose.

Many anti-Shah Iranians, frenzied to take back their country and return to the Islamic way of life, were excited by what they heard on those tapes. Now the *mullahs* had a *cause celeb*. A leader! A fire within! They began to act with unobstructed power now that the Ayatollah's new regime was sure to take over.

Many stories have been told about that time in history; some fact, some fiction. But who can really know. It was believed by many that it was the *Tudeh,* the Iranian Communist Party, who were responsible for killing people and blaming it on SAVAK. Did they bring in the street gangs to rile up the people to demonstrate in the streets? Riots were started, urged on by the anti-Shah revolutionists, where innocent people were killed, trampled, and all was blamed on the SAVAK, ergo the Shah. Many Iranians believe that once the Shah realized his country was falling apart, he made a decision to leave, hoping that peace might somehow be restored if he were gone. His plan was to return once the people realized who was behind the revolution.

At that time I wondered, as the revolution became a reality, how could one man, thousands of miles away, influence a whole country? Wasn't the Shah untouchable? Didn't he have the almighty power of the U.S. behind him? While I worried and fretted, most of my expat friends preferred to sweep it under their Persian carpets.

We'd heard it all. We'd heard that the Shah was a despot; heard the grizzly stories about SAVAK. But we also heard about the good he'd done for his country; the literacy he wanted for his people; the agragarian programs he'd started for the poor country people. He was the Shah, and he had invited our countrymen to come here and build oil refineries. We didn't want to believe the bad stories.

Epilogue

As unrest began to escalate, those who loved the Shah now loved him quietly. Our pro-Shah Iranian friends were terrified about this takeover. They feared the Islamic revolution would give the power-hungry *mullahs* a newfound status (and as it turned out, they were right). They worried about the Shah being thrown out, possibly murdered, and how it would change their country. These were educated Iranians. Many owned businesses in town and worried that the new Islamic state would put an end to their freedom and lifestyle. These were artists, poets, and intellectuals. Some worked for the Shah in high positions, lived comfortable lives and were content in their status. Now it would surely end if the Shah were deposed.

Those who hated the Shah for many reasons wanted to blame him for everything: banning the *chador*, modernizing their country and bringing in thousands of foreigners to make this happen. We heard words such as *Tudeh, Mujhadin, Fedayeen*, but no one seemed to know who the good guys were and who was the boogeyman. It would be years before we learned what horrible things were taking place while we went on about our lives.

None of us knew it at the time, but learned many years later through President Carter's memoirs, that he was concerned if he backed the Shah with U.S. intervention, harm could come to the many Americans still living and working in Iran. He also struggled with what might be the correct response to another sovereign nation's internal difficulties. He did not want to go to war, and knew Americans would not be behind him if he had, having so recently gotten out of Vietnam.

Time has a way of revealing historical results with a jeweler's loupe, and its impact on the world. As we know today, Iran is still under a brutal leader—minus a turban—while the government answers to the *mullahs*, and possibly the *Tudeh*. But the country and its people are still fighting for freedom—to live, dress and pray as they chose; to have the freedom to watch, read, to write anything they chose.

Many books have been published about the revolution, and I've read many of them. I can also understand some of the Iranian peoples' hope in Khomeini: He promised them their country back; he promised them their Islamic religion back; he promised them a pure and honest government. However, what they got was a tyrant who told them how to live; killed those who opposed him; closed bookstores that carried any intellectual materials that were not to his liking, and they soon realized the mistake they'd made in welcoming back the *Imam*.

The sad thing about the revolution is summed up in an interview with Farah, the Shah's widow, as to the misplaced hope of the young Iranians who overthrew her husband: "They thought Khomeini would open the door to paradise." Instead, they got more of the same.

As to why the greedy American corporations left their people to fend for themselves, I have no answer and give them no excuses. They most assuredly knew what was coming down, but the almighty dollar was more important than the safety of their employees.

Three months after we'd returned to the States, I received a letter from a friend who worked with me at BHI, but was not yet out of the country. It was February, cold and blustery in Esfahan, and she wrote of their problems: they had run out of heating oil and were so cold they could hardly move around the apartment. She said her Iranian landlady would sneak a few things into their apartment, always warning them if she was caught aiding them she could be imprisoned.

She also told of changes in the city after we'd left: liquor stores were demolished and burned by order of the *mullahs*; alcohol was strictly forbidden. Anything the Shah had allowed was struck down. From her second story apartment she could see fires in town, and hear the constant sound of gunfire. They were terrified. She wrote that my boss, John, had been the target of the mob running the streets: He'd heard a noise in the courtyard below his bedroom window and saw some men around his car. When he ran outside to check on the noise, he found that the soft top of his car was on fire. He ran into the house, grabbed some towels and ran back outside, barefoot and in his boxer shorts, to impede the fire. What he didn't notice was that someone had poured benzene on the ground around his car. As he beat at the flames with towels, they snapped up the benzene at his feet, which ignited, sending flames upward, engulfing his body. She didn't know much else, other than that he had been medivac'd back to the States.

I never heard from her again, and I pray John made it out okay and that he lived through that awful night. Whether or not my friend made it home, I don't know. Maybe after this book is published, she may pick it up and find me!

Many years later we heard that some of our acquaintances from the job, who'd vowed to stay on until the job was finished, had to be evacuated, and had to leave all their possessions behind. They were smuggled out via a bus to an airfield, and then out of the country. I never got the whole story, but I hope they made it home safely.

We left many Iranian friends behind, and I pray that someday they will have the freedom they have fought so hard for. As their population is now standing up and yelling in the streets to have their rights back, I'm sure it is just a matter of time for that to happen…

and I say, *INSHALLAH!*

LIFE CHANGES

What I took away from the experience in Iran is this: "There's no place like home," as Dorothy so succinctly put it. I had to learn patience, control, respect for other cultures, and above all, that no matter where you travel you can't help but come back a little different. I was fortunate to have Iranian friends to help me through the quagmire of their customs and their views on what was transpiring at that time, and because of them I was able to see both sides of the story.

We drove by our old neighborhood when we returned from Iran. It had not turned into a ghetto. Our neighbors were the same wonderful people. The lawns were still neatly manicured. Our house looked the same. Nothing had changed, except... it was not ours anymore.

Jim now has his own Stateside job to run as a Superintendent, is married to a fantastic woman, and has two beautiful children; one of whom I'm sure you'll see on the PGA Tour in a couple years. Lauri is my tennis geek, and married to an incredible man. She has three wonderful sons, the oldest works for Uncle Sam in the Navy. Denny is now a Battalion Chief with the fire department. He is married to a lovely, *patient* wife, and has three amazing daughters, one of whom turned out just like him—frenetic!

My husband, Earl, was diagnosed with leukemia a month after we returned from Iran, and died in 1985 at age 51. My son, Chris, died in 2001. We're not sure if it was murder (which all the facts pointed to) or of his own doing, but I chose not to pursue it. He is out of pain and I try to remember that.

I now live in a beautiful part of the world with the love of my life, a little MaltiPoo named Beau Britches, and I'm happily writing my memoirs and anything else that comes to mind.

My first book: *A Broad Abroad in Thailand* covers the incredible year I spent in that beautiful country, and is available through Amazon.com and my website: www:abroad-abroad.com. You can also order my books at any bookstore.

Please feel free to give me a review on Amazon.com. You can send your comments about this book, or anything that comes to mind to: http://www.abroad-abroad.com

ABOUT THE AUTHOR

Dodie Cross is an award-winning author who has traveled the world writing about her life in foreign countries. Read about her Thailand travails in her Award-Winning book: ***A Broad Abroad in Thailand: An Expat's Misadventures in the Land Smiles***

Dodie and the love-of-her-life, a little Maltipoo named Beau, live in Palm Desert during the beautiful winters and travel during the summer to cooler climes.

If you would like to give a review of this book, please go to my Amazon page under "Reviews." Interested in a book club talk or just want to contact me about bad expat experiences, go to my website at: http://dodiecross.com

Made in the USA
San Bernardino, CA
03 November 2014